Steffensen

Moments of Glory
South Carolina's Greatest
Sports Heroes

★

Moments of Glory

South Carolina's Greatest Sports Heroes

1913-1977

by John Chandler Griffin

Summerhouse Press
Columbia, South Carolina

The greatest thing in the world is to compete and win.
The second greatest is to compete and lose.

----Bobby Riggs

Contents

Introduction

How It All Began

Cause and effect—how one darned thing just leads to another, is a funny thing. And I'm sure the poor general who lost that cursed horseshoe nail never dreamed he'd eventually lose the war because of it, otherwise he'd have hustled around and found a spare nail somewhere. But such is the nature of cause and effect.

From my own personal experience, I never dreamed some eight years ago that those weekly sports features I was grinding out for various newspapers around the state would one day result in this nice little volume you're holding in your hands at this very moment. But again such is the nature of cause and effect.

I remember the moment it all began as though it were yesterday. It was a blistery hot afternoon in early August of 1989, and I remember strolling into the office of the sports editor of the largest daily newspaper in South Carolina. I'd never heard of him, and he didn't know me. I literally just walked in off the street, in other words. I introduced myself to the somewhat startled sports editor and told him that I had a great idea for a weekly sports feature.

"I'm listening," he said (unconvincingly). He was warily looking me up and down and probably wondering how I'd slipped past security.

"It'll be sort of a nostalgia piece, all about some former athlete from this state, what he did to distinguish himself in college, and an account of what he's been doing since we last heard of him. I plan to call it "Where Are They Now?" or "Whatever Happened To?" or some other appropriate title. I'm going to do all the interviews and write it up myself, and now all I need is a major newspaper to publish it. And that's where you come in."

He leaned back in his chair and stared at the ceiling for long moments. "Well, I'll agree it's not a bad idea," he said finally, measuring each word carefully. "But I don't know you from Adam's house cat. How do I know you can write? Did you bring any samples of your work?"

Actually there were no samples of my work, since I had written nothing at the time. So I avoided the question.

"Look, why don't I do a couple of articles and send them in. You can take a look at 'em, and if you don't like 'em I'll back off. Fair enough?"

He nodded reluctantly. "Fair enough. But what kind of money are we talking about?"

"You tell me, Boss." I thought it might be a little early to call him 'Chief', the way they did back in those old 1940s newspaper movies.

He laughed and threw out a figure, one which truly surprised me in its generosity. (At that point, it had not even occurred to me that I might get paid for doing these articles!)

"Fine," I said, and we shook hands. Feeling like Red Barber, I turned to leave his office. As I was going out the door, he called me back:

"What'd you say your name was?"

"John Griffin."

And thus began my career as a free lance sports writer.

I can honestly say that the public response to these articles was very gratifying, and soon several other newspapers around the state were also carrying them.

So, for the next three years I conducted at least one interview per week with some well known athlete from the past. (I believe the first two interviews I conducted were with Doc Blanchard and Allen Morris). From these came the experience and confidence I needed to tackle my first sports book, *The Centennial History of USC Football* (1992). Since then I've published three other books (including, oddly enough, a biography of Thomas Wolfe which the North Carolina Society of Historians judged the Best History Book on North Carolina of 1996), and I now have a couple of others placed with publishers.

Which just goes to prove that cause and effect, how one darned thing just leads to another, is still alive and well in the world of us mere mortals.

Wild Stories

And I can honestly say that I thoroughly enjoyed every interview I ever conducted. There's something captivating about former great athletes.

They have an easy, laid back manner, a certain charisma, that accompanies their deeply ingrained feelings of self confidence. And truly, after five minutes of conversation with one of these fellows, I felt I'd known him all my life.

Their anecdotes of life off the field were as enchanting as their stories of life on the field, maybe more so at times. W. R. Wilburn (USC football, 1963-65), for example, who was voted *South Carolina's Most Outstanding Athlete* in '65, cracked me up with stories concerning him and his best buddy, All-American quarterback Dan Reeves, and their many misadventures at a beer joint down in Five Points, feeding all their money into pinball machines. Yep, in addition to being Saturday heroes, they were also just typical teenagers.

Indeed, if there was an award for *Most Misadventures*, I can think of nobody whose life has had as many twists and turns, ups and downs, as that of Art Baker (now Special Consultant to Coach Brad Scott). But Art is an incredible guy whose rich sense of humor (and self confidence) has seen him through many a tough time. Yep, if there were a *Most Misadventures Award*, Art Baker would win hands down.

I'll admit that I especially enjoyed talking with the older fellows, those who came along during the Depression days of the late-thirties and early-forties. It was always most gratifying to hear their stories of hardship and how they labored to overcome those hardships. The late George Floyd (Clemson football, 1939-40), for example, laughed uproariously when I asked him if he drove himself up to Clemson. "Listen," he said, gasping for air, "back then there were about three cars on campus. Heck, we were lucky just to have a pair of shoes to wear."

And Bill Gilmore (USC football, 1931-34) said that upon his graduation in 1935 he took a job selling tobacco products in Charleston. Every day, he remembered, he would trod the hard sidewalks from one end of Charleston to the other lugging a heavy sample case. "Talk about hot," he said, "Charleston is the hottest place in the world during the summer. But it was a job, and during the Depression you were lucky to have a job. But after two years the company finally gave me a car to drive. My right shoulder is still lower than my left from carrying that sample case around for so long."

It was also Gilmore who told me a story about his celebrated teammate, the late Earl Clary (known nationally as the Gaffney Ghost), one of the finest running backs in the history of USC football and famous for his zany behavior both on and off the field. "We were playing Villanova up in Philadelphia, and we held a 7-6 lead with only about a minute left in the game. We were on the verge of pulling off a huge upset, but the Wildcats had a fourth down on our two-yard line and we were digging in to stop 'em. I was playing linebacker and Earl Clary was a defensive back.

Well, Villanova broke their huddle and were walking up to line up over the ball, and I could feel my adrenaline really starting to pump. I mean it was really a grim situation. Well, at that moment I felt somebody tap me on the shoulder. I whirled around, and there stood Earl Clary with a little grin on his face. He nodded towards the grandstands and said, 'You know, Bill, I believe there are more folks sitting up there in those bleachers today than live in the whole town of Gaffney.' I said, 'Get away from me, Earl, I got work to do.'"

Inspirational Stories

Or if you're into inspirational stories, tales of poor boys who used sports to pull themselves up by their own bootstraps, I have enough of those to outfit a small Salvation Army. But of them all, I believe that our *Inspirational Story Award* would have to go to good old Tom Wham (Furman football, 1946-48), a poor boy whose mother was forced to place him and his two younger brothers in Thornwell Orphanage following the death of his father in 1942. But thanks to his ambition in the classroom and his prowess on the football field, he won a scholarship to Furman University. There he became an All-Southern end and was drafted by the pro football Chicago Cardinals. With the money coming in now, Tom immediately brought his little brothers home from the orphanage, and made sure his mother had enough money to live well.

Possibly tied for First Place with Tom Wham would be Lou Brissie, a young baseball pitcher whose blazing fastball won him a place in the Textile Leagues of South Carolina when he was only fourteen years old. But then disaster struck, and young Lou was forced to undergo 21 major surgeries to repair his left leg which was shattered by an enemy artillery round in Italy during World War II. Doctors told him he'd never walk again. But then in '46 came a letter offering him a minor league try-out. Incredibly, Lou tossed away his crutches, went out and set a new Sally League record when he recorded 23 wins for Savannah. The next year he was brought up to pitch for the Philadelphia A's, and the rest is history. Still, throughout his long and fabled Major League career, he was always forced to wear a heavy metal brace on his left leg. Pain was his constant companion. Yet, because of his grim determination to realize his lifelong ambition to pitch in the Majors, he overcame all obstacles and today is remembered as one of the greatest pitchers of all time.

And then there's Buck George (Clemson football, 1951-54), a poor Catawba Indian lad who was raised on a poverty-stricken mill village in Rock Hill. He thought that everybody ate cornbread and buttermilk for dinner every night, he said, until he sat down at the chow hall at Clemson in '51. But his senior year at Rock Hill High he was named to the All-State team at tailback in football. Frank Howard wasted no time in recruiting Buck for Clemson, and sure enough Buck George became an all-time great wingback for the Tigers and played in the Blue-Gray game his senior year. Today, thanks to his athletic ability, he holds a supervisory position in a large corporation in Rock Hill. As for his own family, one daughter's an attorney, the other, a dentist.

And the list goes on and on.

Most Modest

Thinking back now over the 150 or so interviews I conducted over a three year period, I would have to say that Clemson's All-American tailback, the great Bobby Gage, earned the distinction of being the toughest subject to interview. Earned it hands down, in fact. Not because he was horsey or uncooperative (actually he was one of the very nicest fellows I ever talked to), but because of his apparently innate sense of modesty and humility.

It was Gage, in case you've forgotten, who played tailback on that unforgettable Clemson team of 1948, leading them to wins over ten opponents during the regular season and then to a 24-23 upset win over Missouri in the Gator Bowl. And if you look at those games, take them individually, you'll find that it was Gage's heroics that sparked the Tigers to wins in contest after contest.

It has been said that it was this '48 Tiger team that saved Frank Howard's job and kept the Gator Bowl from going bankrupt. It was also this team that brought Clemson national recognition, changing their image from that of a bunch of country boys playing cow pasture football to that of a national power. From now on they would be regarded as a finely tuned Gridiron Power to be reckoned with by the Big Boys from coast to coast.

Should you take a look at the Clemson record book, you'll find that after almost half a century Bobby Gage still holds numerous offensive records with the Tigers. Or, if he isn't number-one, his name

will be included among the top-five in almost every offensive category. (On defense he intercepted ten passes during his career, placing him among the top-five defensive backs in the history of Clemson football.)

But as great as he was, as many games as he won for the Tigers, he is still the very picture of modesty. For example, I asked him: "Bobby, versus NC State in '48, the score was tied 0-0 with only moments left in the game, and it looked like Clemson would end the afternoon with a tie to mar their record. But then you took a punt at your own ten-yard line and ran it back 90 yards for a touchdown to give Clemson a 6-0 win. Would you comment on that? How did winning it with such a sensational run make you feel?"

Gage smiled and shook his head as though dismissing such foolish praise. "John, you must remember that I had all those big fellows like Ray Clanton, Frank Gillespie and Phil Prince out in front of me leading the blocking. All I had to do was follow 'em. Anybody could have done what I did. All the credit in the world must go to my great teammates."

And that's pretty much the way the entire interview went. I would remind him of one heroic play after another where Gage had saved the day for the Tigers in the final moments, and get about the same response to them all—"All the credit in the world must go to my great teammates."

Now humility is a wonderful trait, and I can think of quite a few modern day athletes who could use a shot or two of it, but those possessed of this trait are not good subjects for interviews. To the contrary, what the writer truly wants is a flamboyant subject who isn't above just a little boasting, a fellow who will tell you just how great he was and then furnish numerous examples to prove his point. It's this sort of fellow who will literally write your article for you.

(A close runnerup to Gage in the category of *Most Modest* would have to be the fellow who's considered the finest football player ever to don a pair of cleats for the Clemson Tigers—the great Banks McFadden (1937-39).

Most Humorous

As for the *Most Humorous* subject of an interview, that distinction goes hands down to Frank Howard whose recent death saddened sports fans throughout the nation.

To my surprise, I found Howard to be very courteous, erudite and highly intelligent (he actually attended the University of Alabama on an academic scholarship). In fact, a few minutes into our meeting I accused him of being courteous, erudite and highly intelligent, a charge which prompted a look of indignation to cross his face. But then he admitted that his image as the prototypical tough talking, tobacco chewing, country bumpkin was a PR ploy suggested by an early Clemson sports publicist. If Clemson was the college of our rural population, then Frank Howard, in order to win and keep the support of that rural population, should become a caricature of the good ol' country boy. It was a role he played to the hilt.

So, after enjoying a very pleasant conversation with Howard, I hit the button on the tape recorder and suggested that we begin the interview. At that point, he jammed a wad of tobacco in his cheek, eyed me like I was some goldbrick halfback he'd just caught goofing off at practice, and growled, "Les git it, Buddy!" And, truly, from that point on, he became COACH Howard, the tough guy I'd heard about for so many years. The transformation was amazing, like watching a professional actor walk out on stage.

At any rate, for the next hour then I sat back and laughed my head off as Howard reeled off one hilarious anecdote after another.

He will truly be missed.

A close Runnerup in this category would have to be Art Baker. Art played football for PC back during the late-forties, and after a career that includes head coaching stints at Furman, The Citadel and East Carolina, plus a successful interval as Chairman of the Gamecock Club, he is now Special Consultant to USC's Coach Brad Scott. But Art has done it all, and he had me rolling in the aisles as he recounted both his adventures and misadventures in the world of athletics.

Another close Runnerup in this category would have to be the late Rhoten Shetley, Furman's great All-Southern fullback of the late-thirties. During an illustrious career than spanned half a century, Shetley was an outstanding athlete, coach and attorney. For over two hours on a very pleasant evening recently he told hilarious stories from all three phases of his life.

Who Was South Carolina's Greatest Athlete of All Time?

But the question I'm most frequently asked is, "Who is our most outstanding athlete of all time in South Carolina?" Which is like asking Who was our greatest teacher of all time? Or the greatest cook, or greatest automobile mechanic. But there are just too many unknowns, too many intangibles, too many apples and oranges floating around in the mixture to even take a stab at answering such a question.

But it doesn't hurt to speculate.

As far as weight lifters are concerned, there's the late Paul Anderson, a Georgia native who played football for Furman during the late-forties. He went on from there to win gold medals in the '56 Olympics in Melborne, Australia. No one else, to my knowledge, associated with South Carolina, has ever enjoyed such an illustrious career in weight lifting as Paul Anderson.

As for tennis, there is Allen Morris, another Georgia native, who was an All-American at Presbyterian College in the early-fifties. Allen then went on to win at Wimbledon and become one of the most feared players in the world. Later he would become Men's Tennis Coach at UNC. Thus I would agree that Allen Morris is probably the finest tennis player ever affiliated with the great state of South Carolina.

Which leaves us with football, basketball and baseball. And here's where things get really sticky.

In football, for example, there's McColl native, Doc Blanchard. Doc played football at Army during the glory years of Academy football, 1944-46. (Some sports historians call the Army team of '44 perhaps the greatest college football team ever assemble.) Doc's running mate was Glenn Davis. Together they were known as Mr. Inside and Mr. Outside, the most famous running duo in the history of college football.

How good were they? Well, both were named All-American for three consecutive years. Blanchard won the Heisman Trophy in '45, Davis in '46. But at 6-3 and 220 pounds, Doc ran with the speed of a gazelle. He was truly a phenomenal football player during his era and remains the only native South Carolinian ever to win the Heisman Trophy.

And there's George Rogers, a native of Georgia, who won the Heisman Trophy while playing for USC during the late-seventies. Certainly Rogers would have to be considered in any discussion (or argument, or knock-down-drag-out fight) of just who's our all-time outstanding athlete.

Another prominent candidate would be Clemson's all-time great tailback, Banks McFadden (1937-39). In '39, after leading the Tigers to an outstanding 8-1 regular season record (they lost by one point to national power Tulane), McFadden then sparked this little cow pasture team to a big 6-3 upset win over mighty Boston College in the Cotton Bowl. Incredibly enough, he was named All-American in both football and basketball and set several national records in track his senior year. The Associated Press thus named him America's Most Versatile Athlete for 1940. Obviously then, McFadden's credentials are impeccable.

And there are others in the realm of football.

Take Frank Gillespie, for example, who was named All-Southern in football, basketball and baseball during his career at Clemson (1946-48). He was also a straight-A student in a tough electrical engineering course and served as President of the student body. (In time he would say goodbye to the big money of pro football and the engineering profession to become a Baptist minister.) Thus, in my opinion, Frank Gillespie must be considered a valid candidate for *Most Outstanding*.

And there's Seneca native, Jimmy Orr. Orr was named to the All-SEC team as a Georgia receiver, but was considered too small and too slow to make it in pro ball. But with Baltimore he teamed with Johnny Unitas to form one of the most feared passing duos in the history of professional football. Today he still holds Colt and NFL reception records and is a member of the Colts All-Time Football Team.

But so far we've been talking mainly about great offensive players when offense is only half the game. The other half is defense, and I don't know of anybody who excelled in this area more than Whitmire native Donny Shell. A small, skinny kid, Shell received only one college football scholarship his senior year, and that was to South Carolina State. But by his senior year at State, he had beefed up considerably and was named to the all-conference team as a defensive back. But again, when it came to pro ball, he was just too small to be taken by anybody in the draft. Thus he tried out with the Steelers. Surprisingly, he made the team. Not only did he make it, but over the next fourteen years he became a fixture as a defensive back and set all-time Steeler and NFL records that still stand today.

But that's football. What about basketball?

Well, again we're comparing cars and boats, but any discussion of South Carolina's all-time greatest athlete would have to take into consideration a guy from Corbin, Kentucky named Frank Selvy.

During his three years of varsity competition at Furman (1952-54) Selvy was twice named to the All-American Team and in '54 was named America's Player of the Year. That was the year he led the nation in scoring with an incredible 41.7 points per contest average (this record has been broken only once in the past forty-three years). He also set another all-time NCAA scoring record, one that has never been broken, when he hit for 100 points versus Newberry College. So what can I say about Frank Selvy? His performances speak for themselves.

And there's USC's all-time great, John Roche. A three-time All-American (1969-71) and twice ACC Player of the Year, Roche led USC to the ACC championship in 1970. He would then go on to a great ten-year pro career.

And there are others.

As for baseball, what can I say? There are just too many candidates for *Most Outstanding* in this sport, some living, some long deceased, to even make a wild guess. For example, there's Lou Brissie, whom I've already mentioned. And also Marty Marion, born in Richburg, S.C., who became an all-time great with the St. Louis Cardinals (at 6-4, he was the tallest Major League shortstop ever to play the game). And what of Sumter's Bobby Richardson? He was an all-star second baseman for the New York Yankees back when the Yankees were the YANKEES and still holds more Major League records than you could shake a Dodger at.

But there are also such great old timers as Pudden Head Wilson, Van Lingle Mungo, and Bobo Newsome. They, too, had their day in the sun and were as great during their era as the young fellows of today are in theirs.

So, Sports Fans, you'll just have to reach your own conclusions about who's the greatest this or that in any field of athletic endeavor. Again, there are just too many aspects of each game to be considered, so many that my computer just blew a fuse.

Suffice it to say that every young man included in this book was great in his own way and went out day after day and gave it all he had. Which is all you can ask of any man.

Moments of Glory

*South Carolina's Greatest
Sports Heroes*

1913 - 1939

Jake Jacobs and His Famous Jacobs Blocking Trophy

One of Football's Most Prestigeous Awards Had Its Beginning Right Here In South Carolina

William P. "Jake" Jacobs, II, started and quarterbacked Presbyterian College's first football team in 1913. Among his many other exploits, he is also the father of the famous Jacobs Blocking Trophy.

There's no question about it, one of the most prestigious awards any Southern football player can earn is the Jacobs Blocking Trophy. Yet few realize that this award originated right here in South Carolina or that its guardianship has now been passed down through three generations of the Jacobs family.

It all began with William P. Jacobs, II, who entered Presbyterian College in 1912. His father, by the way, was the Rev. William P. Jacobs, who founded Presbyterian College in 1880. As it turned out, young Bill Jacobs, or "Jake" as he was called, was a chip off the old block, who quickly established himself at Presbyterian as a young man of tremendous drive, determination, and creativity.

Among his other achievements, in 1913 he helped organize PC's first football team, serving as both quarterback and manager of that memorable eleven.

It was then that it first occurred to Jake Jacobs that the fellows who actually made the team go, those hulking linemen who opened the holes for all those glorified Tinker Bells to go tippy-toeing through for long gains, rarely received any recognition whatsoever. They were the real heroes, he decided, silent and unsung though they were.

Jacobs decided to remedy that situation, and there was no stopping him once he made up his mind. Thus in 1928, while coaching at Thornwell Orphanage (founded by his father in 1875), he designed a large silver cup. Engraved upon it are five linemen leading interference on an end sweep.

Originally the cup was called the Jacobs Interference Trophy and it was awarded annually to a lineman selected by the S. C. Sports Writers Association. The first recipient, in 1928, was Clemson's O.D. Padgett.

In 1933 Jacobs fashioned another trophy, this one to be presented to the best blocker in the newly formed Southern Conference, which at that time included all the teams that now comprise both the SEC and the ACC and stretched from Maryland to Mississippi. The first recipient for the Southern Conference was George M. Smith of Virginia Tech.

In 1935 the Southeastern Conference was formed, necessitating still another trophy. The first recipient for the SEC was Riley Smith of Alabama.

That same year, with the nation now in the depths of the Great Depression, Jake Jacobs was named President of Presbyterian College. Considering his successful background in business, the trustees were hoping he could put debt-plagued PC back on its financial feet. This he accomplished, and today many say it's largely due to his leadership that Presbyterian survived the Great Depression.

But Jacobs assumed the office of President, and, armed with his ambitious and creative nature, he immediately began searching for some means to put tiny PC on the national map. Certainly they lacked the resources to become a powerhouse in football, bas-

This pompadoured specimen of Clinton produce is the only original Jake in captivity. Jake, really, is in a class of his own. He entered college in 1907, and, after groping along in the dim dominions of the Prep. department for a season, became alienated from the ties of his native environment and transferred his rapidly diminishing ignorance to another institution. However, he soon repented the error of his ways and blew back into the fold—where he's been blowing ever since. It is rumored that he is in love, and that he is an ardent advocate of woman suffrage. Jake is a paragon with the artist's pen and brush, as attested by the pages of the "Pac-SaC". As an athlete he baffles description, and as a singer he is constantly inspiring us to—profanity. When it comes to having a pull with the Faculty, this chap occupies a whole pedestal to himself. And he enjoys the unique and enviable distinction of reducing "cramming" to an art. What it takes to grab off A's without undergoing the trying ordeal of brain exertion, he has it. Jake's a good egg, rhetorically speaking, and has a double prospect of "going some" in life, having chosen the traveling profession, you see. S'long, old pal, and luck be to you!

Jake Jacobs received a good spoofing in the 1913 PC Yearbook, the Pac Sac.

ketball, or baseball. But what about tennis? Jacobs now had a new goal to pursue.

Thus he began laying the foundations for what would soon become one of the top tennis programs in America. He began by organizing tennis clinics at PC that attracted high school tennis players from throughout the nation. To conduct these clinics he hired the finest pro players the country had to offer, fellows like Don Budge and Bill Tilden.

Then PC began granting tennis scholarships and soon became one of the top tennis teams in the nation. Indeed, by the 1950s, still pursuing the course laid down by Jacobs years earlier, PC was recognized as one of the top tennis teams in America. In 1957, for example, led by All-American Allen Morris, PC defeated the University of Miami, the number-one team in the country, snapping the Hurricane 72-game winning streak in the bargain. As for Allen Morris, he went on to win the national championship and represent the U. S. at Wimbledon. Later Morris' teammate George Amayn would duplicate this feat.

But PC's tennis program was just typical of how Jacobs pursued any endeavor with force, imagination, and intelligence. He would later serve as president of the U S Lawn Tennis Association, and was inducted into the Southern Tennis Hall of Fame.

Following Jacobs' death in 1948, the trophy tradition was carried on by his two sons, William Jacobs III and Hugh Jacobs.

At a banquet held at Presbyterian College in 1937, William P. Jacobs presents the SEC Jacobs Blocking Trophy to Leroy Monsky of the University of Alabama. Seated directly behind Jacobs and Monsky is the South Carolina All-State team for that year.

The formation of the ACC in 1953 required that they begin presenting a fourth trophy each year. The first recipient from the ACC was Bill Wohrman of USC, who won it both his junior and senior seasons.

It was at this point that the Jacobs changed their method for choosing a recipient for the award. Heretofore, sports writers had selected the winners, but then one evening at a presentation banquet, Hugh Jacobs asked the young winner to describe his most exciting game of the year. The young man replied, "Well, it would have to be the first game, Mr. Jacobs. Because I broke my leg in that game and didn't get to play again the rest of the year."

"As a result of that unsettling revelation," Hugh Jacobs chuckles, "we decided we'd best let the coaches themselves start selecting the recipients. At least the coaches would know whether a boy had even played or not."

Today the awards are presented by the third generation of the Jacobs family, William Jacobs IV, an engineer with Monsanto in Greenwood, and Hugh Jacobs, Jr., art director at WIS-TV in Columbia.

So after 70 years, players and coaches alike agree that the Jacobs Blocking Trophy has become an integral part of the great football tradition that exists throughout the South, one that should be perpetuated for generations yet to come.

★

Jake Henry and Dode Phillips

At The Age Of Ninty-Nine Jake Henry Remembered Dode Phillips And The Golden Age of Erskine Football

Today Jake Henry spends much of his free time trimming the grass and pruning the rose bushes in the backyard of his comfortable Columbia home. Which doesn't sound too unusual and wouldn't be—except for the fact that Jake was born in 1897 and once was the doughty teammate of Erskine College's legendary runningback, Dode Phillips. Together, Henry and Phillips formed one of the most feared running duos in the South.

Both were from Chester and were the best of high school friends. In fact, in 1916, with a squad of only thirteen players, led by Henry and Phillips, Chester won the state championship in football. College coaches from throughout the South pleaded for their services. But Dode Phillips was the son of an Associate Reformed Presbyterian minister, and so both he and Henry were determined to enroll at Erskine College, an ARP institution. And they paid their own way.

"No, Erskine didn't offer us scholarships," recalls Henry. "We didn't play for money but simply for the love of the game."

And play they did. From 1917 until 1921 (the 1918 season was canceled because of the flu epidemic), Henry and Phillips played 60 minutes of 35 consecutive games. In fact, in 1921, despite a rugged 9-game schedule, the Seceders (they would not become the Flying Fleet until later) made only three substitutions all season. These were truly the Iron Men of gridiron legend.

Erskine fielded their first football team in 1915. But by 1917, with players like Phillips at fullback and Henry at quarterback, the Seceders were beginning to assert themselves as a state power.

Henry remembers, by the way, that another outstanding member of their 1917 squad was famed novelist Erskine Caldwell, author of the sensational novel *Tobacco Road,* who was listed as the "snapperback" or, in today's terminology, the center.

Henry recalls that the highlight of the 1917 season came at the expense of a highly favored South Carolina squad. Erskine was trailing 13-7 late in that contest when Phillips hit Jake Todd, a 5-4 speedster,

Jake Henry was an outstanding athlete at Erskine College, then went on to an outstanding coaching career. The playing field at Dreher High School in Columbia is today named in his honor.

with a 60-yard bomb for a touchdown. Erskine thus beat USC in an upset 14-13.

But Dode Phillips' big year came in 1921. At 5-10 and weighing 190 pounds, he was bigger than most linemen of his day and had great speed. Against Newberry that year, trailing by 3 points late in the game, Erskine began a drive on their own 7-yard line. Over the next five minutes Phillips carried the ball on 22 consecutive plays, going over for the winning touchdown on his final carry.

Dode Phillips, a star halfback at Erskine, in 1931 was voted South Carolina's All-Time Most Outstanding Football Player. Pictured here (L-R): Manager Miller, Dode Phillips, and Football Coach Parrish.

Against The Citadel that same year, Phillips ran the opening kickoff back 95 yards for a touchdown, then later scored on a 30-yard pass interception, and it was another win for the Seceders.

But his finest moments came in the final game of the '21 season against the powerful Tigers of Clemson College. In that contest he scored both of Erskine's touchdowns to lead them to an impressive 13-0 upset win.

By season's end, Erskine had scored a total of 172 points. Phillips was credited with 122 of those, making him one of the top scorers in the nation. He was also named to the All-Southern team that year,

pretty heady company for a country boy from tiny Erskine College, then with an enrollment of only ninety-eight students.

In baseball, Phillips slammed twenty-one home runs in 1921, and both he and Jake Henry were named to the All-State baseball team.

Phillips then went on to play AAA ball in the International League. But he refused to play on Sunday, which sorely limited his options as a pro player.

In 1924 he was named head coach at Erskine, a position he would hold for many years. Jake Henry says that at the age of forty-five Phillips, dressed in his street clothes, would sometimes punish his varsity defense by running the ball himself and forcing them to try and tackle him.

In 1931 Phillips became a charter member of the S. C. Athletic Hall of Fame. A newspaper poll conducted that same year among state sports writers named him the most outstanding football player ever produced in South Carolina.

Later he would hold various administrative positions at Erskine and was serving as admissions director there upon his death in 1965.

As for the very modest Jake Henry, in 1948 he became Dreher High School's first football coach. Today many remember his Blue Devil teams of the 1950s as the terrors of the state. He would later serve as athletic director for the Richland County School District.

To honor his many years of service, the football field at Dreher High School is known as the Jake Henry Athletic Field.

So how long ago was 1897? It was nine years before the Wright brothers flew their first motor-powered glider at Kitty Hawk and seventeen years before World War I. But, as Jake Henry says, "I'll be a hundred next year, then I'm planning to start on my second century. I'm looking forward to it. It should be fun."

We sincerely regret the recent death of Jake Henry.

★

Tatum Gressette

At Ninety-Seven He Was Still Going Strong

At the age of ninety-seven, Tatum Wannamaker Gressette enjoyed the distinction of being the oldest living man on earth ever to have served as captain of the Carolina Gamecocks. But age didn't slow him down in the least. I met with Gressette recently and he was complaining of a pain in his hip. I assumed that, like many elderly people, perhaps Gressette had pulled a muscle getting out of the shower. I asked him if that were the case.

"No," he replied, "I played a round of golf yesterday and this fellow showed me a new swing. I foolishly tried it, and time I did, I knew I'd twisted the wrong way. Felt something pull in my hip."

"Oh."

Gressette was a friendly, out-going sort of fellow and would speak to anyone at the drop of a hat.

Born in St. Matthews in 1900, he distinguished himself in athletics at an early age. Then, in 1918, while World War I raged in Europe, he entered Furman University. He enrolled there, he says, for only one reason: to play football for the Purple Hurricanes.

Soon he was billed as a triple-threat tailback who could run, pass, and kick with the best of them. He had also developed the rare knack for drop-kicking a football. He could drop-kick sixty yards, and he could kick it with great accuracy. He easily made Furman's starting lineup as a freshman.

He did so well, in fact, that Richmond University persuaded him in the summer of 1919 to depart Furman and try his hand (or foot) with the Spiders. So he enrolled at Richmond. But then, two days after his arrival at that grand old institution, he received a letter from the football coach at The Citadel offering him a still better deal. So, being a man of vision, Gressette caught the next train bound for Charleston and enrolled at The Citadel.

He'd hardly had time to have his head shaved, he says, when who should knock on his door but several prominent USC alumni, including Tom Stoney, the mayor of Charleston. They told Gressette that they were tired of watching Clemson College trample USC and were out raiding colleges across the South in hopes of putting together a team that would put a

Tatum Wannamaker Gressette at the age of ninety-seven was the oldest living captain of a USC football team. In 1919 he enrolled at three different colleges before finally becoming a Gamecock. It was his 25-yard field goal that gave USC a 3-0 win over Clemson in 1920.

Carolina's starting eleven of 1920. Gressette is lined up directly behind the center, at the tailback position.

stop to it.

Gressette was impressed with the dedication of these USC alumni, and he wanted badly to become a part of such an all-star team. Thus, the next day he arrived in Columbia, bag and baggage, ready to don the garnet and black of the Carolina Gamecocks.

Because he had enrolled at four different colleges in two weeks, the University, after some deliberation, decided that they'd have no choice but to list him as a transfer student (after all, fair's fair!), which meant that he'd have to sit out the 1919 season. And, sure enough, with Gressette on the bench the Gamecocks again went down before the Tigers (for the seventh consecutive time).

It was then that Carolina, aware of their new secret weapon, coined their famous slogan: Just Wait Till Next Year! It has become a slogan, unfortunately, with which Gamecock fans have become all too familiar.

Then came 1920, and USC hired a new head coach, Sol Metzger, who had produced big winners at Penn, and optimism was running high that he'd do the same at Carolina. Yet, despite their high hopes, the Gamecocks were 2-2 going into the Clemson game, with wins over PC and Wofford and losses to Georgia and UNC.

Clemson, on the other hand, had wins over Erskine, Newberry, and Wofford, a tie with PC and losses to Auburn and Tennessee.

Big Thursday rolled around on October 28th that year, an unseasonably hot day, with a record crowd of some 7,000 perspiring fans crammed into the old wooden bleachers at the Fair Grounds.

"Clemson had beaten us seven years in a row," recalled Gressette. "Of course, Mr. Stoney and those fellows had recruited me for only one reason—to beat Clemson. And I was determined to give it everything I had.

"I'd spent the past year getting right. I don't mean to sound like I'm bragging, but I tried to put a spirit into that 1920 team. I told 'em that we could win if we thought we could win. We had to get right mentally.

"We weren't an outstanding team, but we finally got that old Gamecock spirit. For two weeks prior to that game, we met every night, and we kept talking it, talking it, beat Clemson, so that by the time Big Thursday rolled around, we were convinced.

"I'd never heard of brainwashing at that time, but that's what it was."

The big game finally opened, and on the second play from scrimmage Gressette caught Clemson napping and completed a 40-yard bomb to end Dave Robinson, down to the Tiger 40. But then the Tigers held.

Now facing fourth-and-ten, the Gamecocks huddled. Gressette called the play.

"I told the boys on the line to hold 'em out for just two seconds, and I'd get us a field goal. Just give me two seconds."

And that's how it went. Gressette took the snap from center, took two paces back, then calmly unleashed a booming drop-kick that cleared the uprights some 25 yards away. And the 'Cocks took a 3-0 lead.

It was a bitterly fought defensive struggle from that point on. Then, fifty-nine minutes later, jubilant Carolina fans and players swarmed onto the field to celebrate their 3-0 win over the Tigers. It was the first time they'd beaten Clemson since 1912.

For the rest of the year Gressette was known throughout the state as "The Golden Toe". He became the toast of the University, and it's said that Columbia merchants refused to let him pay for anything.

In 1921 he was elected team captain, and under his leadership the Gamecocks enjoyed one of their best seasons ever, defeating Erskine, Newberry, PC, and The Citadel, while tying Florida and UNC, and losing only to Furman.

More importantly, they again beat Clemson, blanking the Tigers 21-0, the first time in history that USC had defeated Clemson two straight years.

Following his graduation in 1922, Gressette coached for a couple of years in LaGrange, Ga. He then went on to become head coach at one of the most powerful high school teams in the nation, Augusta's Richmond Academy.

"We had championship teams and played schools all over America. I remember we signed a two-year contract in 1928 with Gaffney High. That was back when Earl Clary was playing for 'em. Clary would go on to become one of the great runningbacks in the history of USC football and was known all over the South as the Gaffney Ghost.

"But they were the best in the state that year. Still, we beat 'em 58-0. They cancelled the second game."

Then for the next eleven years, from 1929-39, Gressette served as head coach at The Citadel. "But we just never had the material to compete on an equal basis with the teams on our schedule," he says. "But we did beat Clemson in 1929, my first year down there."

In 1940 Governor Jimmy Byrnes appointed Gressette Director of the South Carolina Retirement System, a position he held until his retirement in 1972. But still he wouldn't let go of football.

He founded the BAM Club (Buck A Month) at USC in 1940, the forerunner of the Gamecock Club. That same year he became a football referee. Over the next thirty years he would work some of the biggest games in the country.

The real highlight of his career, he says, came in 1926, when he met a young school teacher from Spartanburg named Elaine Carson. They were married that same year.

Some seventy years later, they were still married. Gressette, by way of explanation, said: "It's simple. I love her, and she loves me. And believe me, I'm certainly not in the market for a later model."

They have three children, five grandchildren, and three great-grandchildren.

Gressette is a former president of the S.C. Golf Association and a member of the S.C. Golf Hall of Fame. He is also a member of the S.C. Athletic Hall of Fame.

We sincerely regret the recent death of Tatum Gressette.

★

Bill Gilmore

He Served as the First Co-Captain of a Carolina Football Team

Speaking of sports highlights in the great state of South Carolina, here's another first for you. Back in 1932 the University of South Carolina football team decided to go with co-captains, instead of the mere captains they had used for the first forty years of their existence.

By that time the Gamecocks had enough quality players that they could substitute on occasion. By having co-captains, they could feel pretty sure that they'd have a captain on the field at all times. Their very first two co-captains were gentlemen by the names of Harry Freeman and Bill Gilmore.

Freeman, a Georgia native, is now deceased, but we recently had the pleasure of speaking with Bill Gilmore, and he gave us the following story.

It seems that young Bill was born and raised right there in Columbia. His home was on Marion Street, which he assures us stood practically in the shadows of the State House.

"I was born in 1908 and spent my growing up years on Marion Street, which runs almost exactly between the University and Columbia High School."

Gilmore has good reason to remember both institutions. He was a student at Columbia High from 1925-29, where he excelled as an athlete, and remembers that the Capitals were then coached by former Gamecock great, Harry Lightsey. In 1929 the Caps defeated Gaffney for the state championship. Gilmore served as captain of that team.

Indeed, Gilmore was considered one of the top high school athletes in the state in '29, and Duke University camped on his doorsteps hoping to entice him to play for the mighty Blue Devils. But Gilmore's old teammates from Columbia High, Bru Boineau and Monk Shand, had cast their lot with the Gamecocks, and thus Gilmore decided that he too would don the garnet and black.

By 1930, Gilmore had become the starting center at Carolina. The legendary Billy Laval was head coach at that time (1928-34), and Gilmore remembers that Laval was noted for his imagination.

"Coach Laval came up with those star-burst

Bill Gilmore in 1932 would serve as the first co-captain of the Carolina Gamecocks.

jerseys we wore back then—in hopes of better hiding the football, you know. Then, as though those were not enough, he had pieces of leather, cut out in the shape of a football, sewn to our jerseys. Made it real

The late Harry Freeman, the other "first" co-captain of the Gamecocks, and noted for his rugged line play at right guard.

tough for the defense to figure out who had the ball."

Not only was Laval creative, but he was also a total perfectionist. "Everything had to be just so," says Gilmore, laughing and shaking his head. "He used to take me on recruiting trips with him as the driver. He had a '27 Ford, and one day we were riding along and Coach Laval kept staring at our radiator cap. Back then, you know, the radiator cap sat on top of the hood where you could see it. Well, out of the blue he says, 'Stop the durn car.' So I pulled over and Coach Laval got out of the car, sort of mumbling under his breath. Then I saw the problem—the cap

wasn't lined up exactly straight with the hood. So Coach Laval tried to twist it straight, but it was too tight to turn. So then he just stood there bumping it with the heel of his hand till he got it perfectly straight. I guess he bumped that cap for five minutes. Of course it wasn't doing any harm the way it was. It was just that Coach Laval felt it should be perfectly aligned with the hood. That's the way he was with everything."

Gilmore says that Coach Laval had another odd habit. He always started his second team in every game. "I'm still not sure what his philosophy was in doing that, but we first stringers would sit on the bench for the first five minutes of every game. Maybe it was intended to give us time to get over our jitters."

Gilmore lived in Maxcy dorm, and like the rest of the team took his meals at a private home just off campus called the Levers' house. "It was a family home, but they maintained a training table for the football team. I think that's how they made a living during the Depression."

But where did the students park their cars?

"Cars!" gasps Gilmore. "You remember the Great Depression hit in '29, and nobody had a penny. Cars? We were lucky just to have a pair of shoes. Why I remember back in those days you'd see lawyers out making a buck by pumping gas for somebody and

In 1932 the Gamecocks upset a great Villanova team 7-6. Gilmore is in the center of this photo, still in his center's stance as Grayson Wolfe gets off a booming punt.

were glad to get it. But I was luckier than most, I guess. I got a job working as a grounds keeper at the Pacific Mills playground. Paid ten cents an hour."

During Gilmore's three years as a starter at USC, the team went 16-12-3, including big wins over such powerhouses as Duke, LSU, Sewanee, Villanova, and a tie with Auburn.

He still remembers Carolina's win over LSU in Baton Rouge in 1930, a trip that would prove a financial disaster. "Back then we packed our uniforms in duffel bags. And after that game we went back to our hotel and Coach Laval stored our duffel bags in a big closet until we got ready to go. Well, it wasn't until we'd arrived back in Columbia that we discovered that someone at the hotel had stolen our uniforms and filled those duffel bags with old dirty sheets. Uniforms cost a lot of money, so that theft just about put the Gamecocks out of business."

He also has fond memories of his celebrated teammate and best friend, Earl Clary, called the Gaffney Ghost by opponents everywhere, and still considered one of the best running backs in the history of USC football. "Well, Earl was a real easy going sort of boy, not the type to get real excited about anything. I hate to say it, but I guess he and I both were sort of majoring in football at the University. But I remember we were playing Villanova in Philadelphia in '32, and we were leading 7-6 with about two minutes left in the game. Villanova had the ball down on our five yard line, facing fourth and one.

"Of course if they made that first down, we were in big trouble. So you can imagine the pressure we were under. I played linebacker on defense, and we were lined up waiting for Villanova to break out their huddle.

"Well, about that time Earl Clary tapped me on my shoulder pads, and I turned to see what important tip he had for me to stop the Wildcats. But he just grinned and said, 'Say, Bill, you know what?' I says, 'What, Earl?' He says, 'You know, I believe there are more people sitting up there in those stands today than live in the whole town of Gaffney.' I says, 'Get away from me, Earl. I got work to do.'"

Gilmore also remembers the Clemson game of '32—and for good reason. His sponsor for that contest was a beautiful Columbia girl named Harriet Kirkland. Gilmore would marry her in 1934. They recently celebrated their 64nd wedding anniversary!

Following his graduation in 1933, he became employed by the R. J. Reynolds Tobacco Company in Charleston for the princely sum of $17.50 per week.

Then it was on to the Brown and Williamston Tobacco Company. Not only was he paid a better salary, he was even given a company car. He retired from that company in 1970.

Today he and Harriet have two children and four grandchildren, and maintain two homes, one in Hendersonville, N.C. during the summer months, and one in Ft. Lauderdale, Fla. during the winter months.

But Gilmore has come a long way and served faithfully in every capacity. We wish him many happy returns!

★

Frank James Howard

"Whatever Clemson is today, Frank Howard made it happen!"---Banks McFadden

The following article is culled from a series of interviews I conducted with former Clemson football coach Frank Howard in his office at Clemson's Jervey Athletic Center in the fall of 1989.

The reader should note that despite what we've heard about Howard being raised in Barlow Bend, Al., and "walking barefooted down a barbed-wahr fence with a wildcat under each arm," he was in fact raised in Mobile, Al., attended the University of Alabama on an academic scholarship, and then helped support his widowed mother by working as an academic advisor at the University of Alabama. Hardly the bumpkin we've all come to expect.

He is an inveterate Southern story-teller in the tradition of Mark Twain and Will Rogers. It should be noted that in many of Howard's stories, he, like Twain and Rogers, emerges as a man of great rural wisdom, who delights in poking fun at the high and mighty. In other stories, again like Twain and Rogers, Howard emerges as a man of rural naivete, the butt of his own jokes.

Here now, to tell his own story in his own immortal words, is the venerable Frank Howard.

I owe everything I am today to Coach Jess Neely (Clemson head football coach, 1930-39). After I finished college I'd planned to take a high school job up in Hopkinsville, Kentucky, at $2,400 a year, and I was going up on Saturday to sign up for the job. But on Friday I got a letter from Coach Neely saying he'd give me a job here at Clemson as line coach at $2,200 a year, provided I could coach track as well.

In the first place, I'd never even seen a track meet. Plus I was gonna have to take a $200 cut in salary. But I came anyway.

In 1931 the athletic department at Clemson consisted of me, Coach Neely and Bob Jones. That was it. Plus, I was also the trainer. Back then the trainer didn't have anything to work with but hot towels. So when the water was hot, I was the trainer. When the water wasn't hot, I wasn't the trainer.

Times were hard back then. I remember I had an ol' boy come in one day, boy named Charlie Moss (fullback, 1931). Charlie said he was having trouble

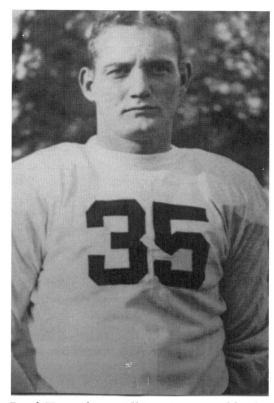

Frank Howard as an All American guard for the University of Alabama (1928-30).

with his shoulder. Asked me to rub it with some Absorbine, Jr. Said they sold it down at the drugstore.

So I went down and paid a dime for a bottle of Absorbine, Jr. Then I came back and pulled the stopper outta that bottle and waved it under Charlie's nose, let him smell it real good, you know, so he'd be sure it was Absorbine, Jr. Then I soaked my hands in some real hot water and started rubbing Charlie's shoulder. When I'd finished, ol' Charlie said, "Good gracious, Coach, my shoulder feels better already. There's nothing like that good ol' Absorbine, Jr."

Well, I put the stopper back in that bottle, went down to the drugstore and got my dime back. Things were real tough back then.

It was also my job to keep the grass cut on the playing field, and every day from noon til one I ran the cash register at the student shop. Plus on Saturday mornings I'd stand on the street and try to sell football tickets for a quarter to anybody passing by. I'd let Boy Scouts in free.

Today Clemson's got about a hundred coaches and a dozen athletic directors. As I came through the office this morning I said, "Good morning, A. D." Well, about ten people jumped up and said, "How you doing, Coach?"

But things were very informal back in those days, especially the way we had to recruit. I remember one time Coach Neely sent me up to scout these two boys who played for Abbeville. Well, I drove up to Walhalla where they was playing, and when I got there they told me that one of the referees hadn't shown up. So I volunteered to help referee. Thought I could watch these two boys better if I was down on the field, you know.

On the first play of the game this boy from Walhalla hauled off and threw one of those bullet passes, but instead of watching the ball I was watching those two boys from Abbeville. Well, just as I looked up that darned pass caught me right between the eyes, knocked me winding. So I spent the rest of the game stretched out on the sideline.

When I got back to Clemson I was scared to tell Coach Neely that I hadn't really got a chance to watch those ol' boys play, so I just said, "Ah, coach, I didn't think too much of those boys. I don't believe I'd waste a scholarship on 'em."

But those boys came on to Clemson anyway. I'm talking about Bob Sharpe and Charlie Timmons. By the time they'd graduated both of 'em had been named to everybody's all-everything teams, you know, and so I told some 'em, I says, "When you can take two ol' boys as sorry as they were four years ago and turn 'em into all-everythings, well, that's what you call real coaching." *(Note: Both Sharpe and Timmons have been inducted into the Clemson Athletic Hall of Fame. It was Timmons who scored the only touchdown in Clemson's great 6-3 upset win over Boston College in the 1939 Cotton Bowl.)*

I remember another time this fellow up in Virginia called me and said he knew this great big boy I oughtta go talk to, said the boy weighed almost 160 pounds. This fellow went on to say that this boy's great-great-granddaddy had come over on the Mayflower, and his uncle had been a Supreme Court

Howard in 1959. He coached Clemson to two Southern Conference titles and six ACC titles.

justice, and his granddaddy had once been governor of the state, and so on.

So I told him, I says, "Sir, right now I'm looking for somebody to play fullback. But I'll sure give your boy a call if I ever need anybody for breeding purposes."

Then I got another letter from this fellow down in Charleston, said there was this great big boy down there I oughtta go look at. Well, back then it took about ten hours just to drive to Charleston. The roads were just red clay, and my car wasn't air-conditioned, and of course I had to stop along the way and fix a flat tire. So by the time I got to Charleston I looked pretty bad.

But I went up and knocked on this boy's door, just knowing I'd soon be signing up this big 300-pound tackle. Well, the door opened and this little bitty boy about as tall as my belt buckle comes out and I says, "Excuse me, is John Jones at home?" He give me this big grin and said he was John Jones. My heart sank. I really didn't know what to say, so I took a deep breath and says, "Well, Mr. Jones, I was just wondering if you'd like to subscribe to *The Saturday Evening Post?*" Then I got back in my car and drove another ten hours back to Clemson. But that's how it was back in those days.

As most people know, I'm originally from Barlow Bend, Alabama. All of us was from Alabama. My mother was a McCarl, and she was from Peachtree. My daddy was Augustus T. Howard, and he was from Laurensboro. But my granddaddy owned a plantation in Barlow Bend, and that's where we all lived when I was born. I had three older sisters and one younger sister. Except for one sister, they're all dead now. I guess that makes me the last of the Mohicans.

Daddy hired a little black boy to live with us and keep me out of trouble. His name was Little Arthur, and he was the only playmate I had until I started to school in Mobile. And I had a pony named Little Bill. I remember me and Little Arthur standing in the barn feeding Little Bill peanuts. That's the last thing I remember about Barlow Bend. I felt sad to leave.

Mobile is about three wagon greasings from Barlow Bend, and I started to school there when I was six. I claim I grew up in Mobile, others claim I never did grow up. When I was about nine I went to work on a bread truck delivering bread all over town. I did that from 3:30 in the morning until 7:30 when I went home to go school. When I got older I worked inside the bakery making pies. It's called Smith's Bakery and it's still in business.

I went to Murphy High School in Mobile and played all three sports. And I was president of the junior and senior classes. When I graduated they gave out six medals. One of 'em had to go to a girl, of course. I didn't win but five of the others.

But I got to the University of Alabama more through baseball than through football. I was the catcher on our high school baseball team, and the University sent this scout, Russ Cohen, down to take a look at another boy. But I really got after it that day and Coach Cohen went back and told 'em they oughtta sign me up, which they did. Actually, I got the *Birmingham News* Scholarship, which is an academic scholarship.

To tell the truth, I had wanted to be a chicken farmer and had thought about going to Auburn. But Auburn had just lost 26 games in a row while Alabama had just been to the Rose Bowl. So that's how I wound up at Alabama.

By the way, when I became head coach at Clemson in 1940, Russ Cohen was the first person I hired. The fellow who got me my scholarship in 1927 became my line coach in 1940.

Of course I had to work when I got to Alabama, 'cause I had to send money home to Mama every month. One of my jobs was tutoring the dumb football players. Well, I remember this ol' boy came over to my room in Garland Hall one day and said he'd got hold of our professor's final examination. So he got out a bluebook, and I started telling him the answers to all ten of the questions. Pretty soon he had his bluebook all filled out and ready to be turned in.

But evidently that professor had gotten wind of somebody having a copy of his exam. So when we got to class the next day we found there was only five questions on the exam instead of the ten we'd answered the day before back in my room. That ol' boy looked at me like 'what in the dickens am I supposed to do now'? I just shook my head and went ahead and answered mine. I think I was the first one through. But it was all on the up and up as far as I was concerned.

Then I went to work as a bouncer at the university dance hall. They had a dance for students every Saturday night, and it was my job to keep out drunks and troublemakers. The job paid $75 a month, which wasn't bad back then. I'd keep $25 and send the rest home to Mama.

But everybody picked on the boy who had the job before me. They picked on him and made fun of him, and he wouldn't do anything about it. So the very first night I was there this big ol' boy came in and he'd been drinking. I says, "Hey, Buddy, you can't come in here like that. Now you just get on outta here."

See, this was one of the boys who picked on the boy who had the job before I did. Well, he frowned up and says, "You won't get away with putting me outta here. When you get off tonight I'll be waiting for you, and I'm gonna make it hot for you."

I says, "I'm sorry, but I've already got plans for when I get off tonight. So the thing for me and you to do is to go out and settle this thing right now."

Well, I turned that boy every way but loose. Blackened both his eyes, busted his nose and knocked out two of his teeth. By Monday morning it was all over school—"Don't mess with that new boy. Ol' Frank don't take no guff." After that I didn't have a bit of trouble with anybody.

Now me and ol' Bear Bryant played together at Alabama, you know. They brought Bear in my junior year down there. They had to tutor him two years to get him in, and they never did get him out. But

FRANK HOWARD
1989 Hall of Fame Inductee
Clemson Head Coach 1940-69

In 1989 Coach Howard was inducted into the National Football Hall of Fame. Here he stands beside Howard's Rock at Clemson's Memorial Stadium.

freshman class—for three years in a row.

I remember one time when I first got to be head coach at Clemson, ol' Bear called me up and says, "Frank, how about giving me a job up there?"

I says, "No way, Buddy."

He says, "How come, Frank? Something bothering you?"

I says, "If I hired you, Frank, inside of six months you'd have cut my throat, drunk my blood, have my job, and have Clemson on permanent probation."

Ol' Bear was quiet a minute, then he says, "Yeah, but is there anything *major* bothering you?"

But I'm glad I didn't hire ol' Bear. We always had too much fun coaching against each other. I remember another time we were speaking at a coaches convention up in New York. Me and Bear was sitting up there on the stage, you know, looking out at about 300 coaches gathered in the audience, and ol' Bear looked at me and says, "How many great coaches do you think are here tonight, Frank? I mean really great coaches?"

I says, "I don't know, Bear. But I'll tell you one thing—there's one less than what you're thinking."

As for my personal life, I got married back in 1933 to Anna Tribble from Anderson. And I got two receipts to prove it—a girl named Alice and a boy named Jimmy.

I guess one of the things my family and I are most happy about happened back on December 5, 1989, when we all went up to New York so I could be inducted into the National Football Hall of Fame. That's the highest award they can give you in football, you know.

Well, we all went, my family and me. The banquet was at the Waldorf-Astoria and that's where we all stayed. Rooms were $260 a night. But this was a once-in-a-lifetime deal, so I reckon it was worth it.

A bunch of us was inducted that night, so Archie Manning spoke in behalf of all of us. I could tell the 800 folks out in the audience was disappointed that I didn't get to make my two-hour acceptance speech, but they had to settle for Archie.

Now I'll tell you, after a week in New York, it was mighty good to get back to South Carolina. You don't know how good a tree looks until you've been in New York City for a week.

I'm just sorry that ol' Bear Bryant didn't live to see it. He'd be giving me a fit about it right now if he'd been there.

In conclusion, I have a motto I'd like to leave with you. It's one I made up and have tried to live by. It's this: The man can who thinks he can.

You see, by rights I oughtta still be down in Mobile making pies for Smith's Bakery. But I honestly believed I could do something better in life and I was crazy enough to give it a try. Others can do the same—if they'll only believe.

We sincerely regret the recent death of Coach Frank Howard.

★
Harvey Kirkland

For Fifty-eight Years He Was An Integral Part of the Sporting Scene in South Carolina

Retired Newberry College football coach Harvey Kirkland said there is no game in the world that compares with football. "It's life in a nutshell," he said. "The cynics laugh about us telling the boys that football is just like real life. But it's true. There are so many parallels."

Kirkland, by the way, devoted most of his eighty-three years to athletics, so he was speaking from personal experience.

"Sometimes in football you work real hard and it pays off. Other times you work your head off but get beat—just like in real life. But win or lose, you've got to have the heart to come back and try again. You never quit—not in football."

Born in Batesburg in 1913, Kirkland attended Bateburg-Leesville High before entering Newberry College on a football scholarship in 1933.

He remembered the Depression was in full swing during his college years, and the enrollment at Newberry was down to about 300 students. Needless to say, students had no problem finding parking spaces back then.

"Parking spaces?" He laughed in disbelief. "Listen, during the Depression, our daddies didn't even own cars. If I wanted to go some place, I just trotted out to the highway and stuck my thumb out. Besides, I didn't have a nickel for a gallon of gas, anyway."

The athletic department at Newberry back then consisted of head coach Fred "Dutch" McLain and a line coach.

"I played tailback in the single-wing formation. In those days everybody ran the single-wing, and everybody ran the same basic defense. But Coach McLain really taught us the fundamentals of the game. I can't tell you how much I admire that man."

Following his graduation in 1937 Kirkland coached for four years at Bamberg High, then spent a year at Carlisle Military Academy. Then came the war and he would spend the next four years with the U.S. Navy.

In 1946 he became head coach at Summerville High, where he began a football dynasty that continues to this day. During his six years there he won two state championships and tied for another.

Kirkland began his coaching career at Newberry in 1952. He retired in '67 with a .720 winning percentage, an impressive performance when its remembered that Newberry College is the smallest institution in America that grants football scholarships.

Then in '52 he was named head coach and athletic director at Newberry College. "I wouldn't have left Summerville for any other job in America," he says, "but it's such an honor to return to your alma mater that I couldn't turn it down."

It was a position he would hold for the next fifteen years, longer by far than any other Newberry coach in history. During that period he coached 110 games, winning 72 losing 28 and tying 10.

Which is a pretty impressive record when it's recalled that Newberry is the smallest college in America to offer athletic scholarships.

He coached many outstanding players during those years, but he refused to single out any for special recognition. "In fact, I requested that I never be asked to sit on the committee that selects players for the Newberry Hall of Fame. There were just so many boys who never received any special recognition, but were really outstanding in their value to the team. They were all Hall of Fame guys as far as I'm concerned."

Kirkland retired as coach in '67, then taught in the physical education department for another twelve years, until 1979. From then until '81, unable to resist the offer, he served as equipment manager for his old friend Art Baker down at The Citadel.

But then he decided it was time to hang it up.

He and his family continued to make their home in Newberry, where Kirkland spent his leisure time hunting, fishing, gardening and keeping up with the Indians' football program.

He is a member of the Newberry Athletic Hall of Fame and was proud to point out that his son, Harvey, Jr., served as the starting quarterback for the Indians from 1964-66.

Newberry may be the smallest kid on the block, but they've got heart and they always hold their own with the big guys. A lot like Harvey Kirkland.

Harvey Kirkland as the starting halfback for Newberry College in 1935.

We sincerely regret the recent death of Coach Harvey Kirkland.

★
Benny Tompkins

He Was The Main Cog In The Winningest Gamecock Basketball Team Ever

Question: The Carolina Gamecocks once ran off a string of 32 consecutive basketball victories over a two-year period. This record-setting performance occurred:

A. 1933-34, with the Gamecocks led by Bennie and Freddie Tompkins.
B. 1969-70, with the Gamecocks led by John Roche and Tom Owens.
C. I'm a loyal Clemson fan, and I could care less whether USC ever won a game in the past or ever will in the future.

If you answered B, you're totally wrong. In fact, Roche and Owens had not even been born when the Gamecocks, led by brothers Bennie and Freddie Tompkins, stood the college basketball world on its lanky ear by winning 32 consecutive games.

It all began in 1933 when four young men (Bennie and Freddie Tompkins, John Rowland, and Dana Henderson) from Athens, Texas, made their first appearance in Gamecock uniforms. The Tompkins brothers, by the way, had been named to the High School All-American team in 1930 and played in the national high school All-American Game in Chicago, with Bennie serving as Captain of that team.

So how did these four Texas lads wind up in Columbia? Bennie Tompkins, who served as Captain of the Gamecocks in both '33 and '34, explained:

"Well, Dana Henderson and I finished high school a year earlier than Freddie and John Rowland. So we spent a year at Terrell Prep School in Dallas waiting for Freddie and John to catch up with us. See, our high school coach sent a bunch of football players to USC, and he was supposed to be hired as a coach himself up there for doing that. So he sent us four on up, too. See, back in those days there were no basketball players in South Carolina. That's because there were no high school basketball coaches in South Carolina. Back then South Carolina considered basketball to be a minor sport, something that just occurred between football and baseball seasons. The coach was usually some teacher who'd never even seen a basketball game. But see, that teacher had his choice,

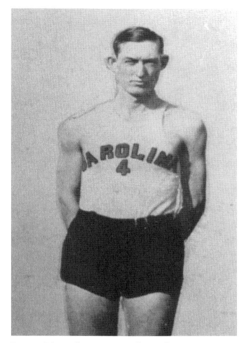

Benny Tompkins, twice elected team captain, led the Gamecocks to their most successful seasons ever, as they went 35-3 during the 1933-34 campaign.

either he could coach basketball or he could have early morning bus duty for the next six months. That being the case, the colleges had to go out of state to find the talent they needed."

Oddly enough, the 1933 Gamecocks were coached by Billy Laval, head football coach, who was quoted at the beginning of the season as saying, "I really don't know very much about basketball." For reasons that remain something of a mystery, Laval was filling in for Coach A. W. Norman who decided to spend the year coaching the freshman team. Norman would return to coaching the varsity in '34.

But as irony would have it, Laval's '33 Gamecock team would go 17-2 on the season, giving Laval, who didn't "know very much about basketball," one of the highest career winning percentage (.895) of any coach in the history of Carolina's basketball.

Tompkins remembered that the team began the

Freddy Thompkins, Benny's little brother and also an All-Southern selection. He is today a member of the South Carolina Athletic Hall of Fame.

year minus the services of several key players and thus suffered defeats at the hands of both Vanderbilt and Kentucky. Once those players returned and the team was healthy, they were unstoppable. Following their two initial losses, they ran off a string of fifteen wins (including a return match with Kentucky). They also knocked off UNC, Maryland, and NC State along the way to winning the Southern Conference Championship.

A big part of their success, said Tompkins, was the height of their backcourt men. "Back then guards were supposed to be like five-eight or five-nine. They were fast, shifty little guys. But I was six-three and Freddie was six-five. We simply overpowered those little guys everywhere we played and proved the value of having tall guys in the backcourt."

As for 1934, it was just like 1933—only better. Norman returned as head coach and the Gamecocks ran off eighteen consecutive, lopsided victories, including an 84-9 route of PC, and two wins over Clemson by 41-15 and 42-17 scores. They were number-one in the Southern Conference and, with 32 consecutive wins under their belts, considered the team to beat in the conference tournament.

But that, unfortunately, is when disaster struck. Freddie Tompkins and Dana Henderson were sidelined with, of all things, the mumps. And sure enough, NC State eliminated the Gamecocks in the first round of the tournament.

Tompkins shook his head when thinking of that loss. "We'd beat State every time we'd ever played 'em. But I just couldn't get the team going

that night. Every time we called time out, all the boys could talk about was Dana and Freddie and how much we missed 'em. But we could have won anyway if the boys had played together. But I just couldn't get 'em together that night. It was all psychological."

But still the team finished with an 18-1 record, the most successful season ever for the Carolina Gamecocks.

Over this two-year period they stood at 35-3, a .921 winning percentage, still another all-time Carolina record.

Bennie and Freddie were both elected unanimously to the All-Southern Team, and Freddie would later be inducted into the USC Hall of Fame.

Reminiscing about those bygone days, Bennie explained some of the differences in the game as it was played then as compared with today:

"The scores were lower back then because the clock never stopped running. Not for anything. If the game started at eight o'clock, assuming you had a fifteen minute half-time, then the game would end at nine-fifteen. If we wanted to kill a little time off the clock we'd just simply roll the ball very slowly down the court to the ref. Or we'd just fool around at the free throw line. That'd take time off the clock.

"Also our classes were tough back then because we traveled by bus. Say we played Duke, State and UNC on Thursday, Friday and Saturday nights. That meant we had to leave Columbia on Wednesday morning, so we'd miss four class days that week. But they didn't have any special academic programs for athletes. We had to study and pass like everyone else. Believe it or not, all the boys on the team graduated and went on to do well."

Did Bennie still keep up with Carolina basketball? "Shucks! Listen here, man, those 'Cocks don't put a foot down on the floor that I'm not there to see 'em do it. If it's in your blood, you gotta stick with it. I haven't missed a home game now, in either football or basketball, in over twenty years."

On the personal side, Bennie was active in operating his business, Security Cleaners. "Man, yeah! I had a call from my nephew in Tyler, Texas recently wishing me a happy New Year, and he asked me when I was going to retire. I told him I'm not but eighty-four now, but soon's I get old enough, I'll be glad to hang it up. If it wasn't for running my business, I'd have to be home right now helping my wife do housework, and if there's anything I hate to do, it's housework. That's one of the great advantages in owning your own business. But that's just between you and me."

We sincerely regret the recent death of Benny Tompkins.

★
Banks McFadden

He Remains Clemson's All-Time Mr. All-American

Over the past half century now, with sports fans throughout the state, the name Banks McFadden has become synonymous with all that is good and great about Clemson athletics.

In 1940, for example, McFadden was named to the AP All-American football team. That same year he was also named to the AP All-American basketball team. And in his spare time, so to speak, he captured twenty-eight first place finishes and set three state records in track.

Not a bad year by anyone's standards. Which is probably the reason the Associated Press named him America's Most Versatile Athlete for 1940. (This award becomes even more impressive when it's remembered that there were quite a few versatile athletes in America in 1940!)

It might also be noted that since the beginning of time Clemson University has retired the jerseys of only three athletes: Steve Fuller in football, Tree Rollins in basketball, and Banks McFadden in both football AND basketball.

Just name your sport and McFadden could do it—and do it better than anyone else. He was truly an incredible athlete.

Born in 1917, Banks spent much of his youth working as a delivery boy in his father's mercantile store in Great Falls, S. C. His father was very good to him, McFadden says, and would always give him time off to play in local sandlot baseball games. Unfortunately, young Banks would frequently be met at the door by his elder half-brother, Tom Wallace, who would order him back to work. "When I was a kid I thought Tom was mean as a snake," McFadden laughs.

But then Banks entered high school and things began to happen. His coach, by the way, turned out to be, of all people, mean Tom Wallace.

"He did one heck of a job at Great Falls," McFadden remembers. "When I was a little water boy running around with the team we went up to Rock Hill, and they beat us 80-0. But by my senior year we went out and beat Rock Hill, Winthrop Training School, and Camden, which were about the biggest schools in the state. Tom had as much to do with the

McFadden was the first Clemson athlete ever inducted into the College Football Hall of Fame.

success of Great Falls athletics as anyone who's ever been there."

As Banks well knew, brother Tom was a stern disciplinarian. "He told you what to do, and he meant it. It wasn't until I got to college that I really appreciated what Tom had taught me in high school. But I never had a single problem with any of the coaches at Clemson."

In 1936 Banks was offered numerous college scholarships. Tom Wallace urged him to enter Duke. But Banks' mother had the final say, as is often the case, and she wanted him to attend Clemson College. In other words, the score wound up 1-1 in favor of the Tigers.

At that time Banks was a real beanpole of a kid, standing 6-3 and weighing all of 165 pounds. Frank Howard, then an assistant under Coach Jess Neely, remembers the first time he ever laid eyes on McFadden:

"We were out on the old practice field, and McFadden came strolling over. I looked at him, and he looked like a crane, a tall, skinny boy. I said to

Named to the All-American football team in 1939, Banks McFadden remains one of only three athletes in the history of Clemson University to have his jersey retired. In the College All Star Game in 1940 he scored the college boys' only touchdown in their contest against the NFL champion Green Bay Packers.

A mainstay at center for the Tigers, McFadden was also named All-American in basketball in 1939. He was also a record-setting track star and was named America's Most Versatile Athlete by the Associated Press.

myself, 'Good gracious alive, I wonder why Coach Neely ever gave this boy a scholarship?' But as time went on he improved considerably."

Indeed he did. A three-year starter as a single-wing tailback, McFadden could run, pass and punt with the nation's best, and in 1939 was named to everybody's All-American team. That was the year he led the Tigers to a 9-1 season (they lost only to national power Tulane, 7-6), including a shocking 6-3 upset win over Boston College in the Cotton Bowl.

Fans remember that game as a classic defensive struggle, which the Tigers won thanks largely to the punting efforts of Banks McFadden (he punted 11 times that afternoon, averaging a phenomenal 45 yards per kick). At game's end he was presented the Cotton Bowl MVP Award.

But football was only a part of the McFadden story. Playing center in basketball, he led the team in scoring for three consecutive seasons and was named All-Southern each of those years (it should be remembered that this was during the era when the Southern Conference included all those teams that now comprise the ACC). His senior year he was named to the AP All-American team, thus becoming the only athlete in the history of Clemson University to be named All-American in both football and basketball.

Today he very modestly brushes aside talk of post-season honors. "I had great teammates. I just happened to be the guy in the glory spots—center in basketball, tailback in football. But it was teammates who made the honors come my way."

In 1940 he was named the starting tailback for the College All-Star team and again distinguished himself by scoring the Stars' only touchdown as they went down 19-7 to the NFL champions Green Bay Packers at Soldiers Field in Chicago.

It was immediately following this game that McFadden was involved in a near-fatal auto accident near Liberty, S.C. which caused him to lose his hearing in his left ear. Still, he was the Brooklyn Dodgers' first draft pick that year.

"Dan Topping was the owner of the Dodgers and, he offered me ten thousand dollars to sign a contract," explains McFadden. "Heck, growing up during the Depression as I did, just one dollar was a lot of money. So of course I signed."

He recalls that Jock Sutherland, head coach of the Dodgers in '41, selected him as the starting tailback following the first game of the season. Beside him in the backfield there was his old friend, the late Rhoten Shetley, an All-Southern fullback from Furman University, plus Duke's all-time great, Ace Parker. By season's end McFadden led the NFL in both rushing

Banks McFadden in action against Tulane in 1939, a game the Tigers lost by a score of 7-6. This would be the only blemish on their record before they went on to upset Boston College 6-3 in the Cotton Bowl.

yardage and average yards per carry. NOt bad for a rookie.

Then came World War II and McFadden volunteered for the Air Corps. His ambition had been to become a pilot, but the deafness in his left ear disqualified him. So after four years of working as a communications officer in both North Africa and Italy, he was discharged in 1945 as Colonel Banks McFadden. No matter what the situation, he always rose to the occasion.

Once again a civilian, he married Aggie Rigsby of Manning, then returned to Clemson to join the coaching staff of Frank Howard, of whom he maintains the fondest memories.

"Frank Howard," he says, "was always an enthusiast, a sort of booster club type. He was always right on top of every player at every practice, and was always either a morale builder or a critic, depending on what the boy needed at the moment. He was the finest coach and athletic director in the South, and everything you see at Clemson today was begun by Frank Howard."

And Banks McFadden was right there to help Frank Howard make it all happen. Truly, with only a couple of brief timeouts, McFadden has had his finger on the pulse of Clemson athletics now since 1936! He retired in 1985.

Among his many other honors, McFadden has also been inducted into both the Clemson Athletic Hall of Fame and the National Football Hall of Fame.

He and Aggie continue to make their home in Clemson, and on June 13 will celebrate 52 years of marriage.

Looking back over his life now, McFadden says, "I wouldn't change a minute of it, not for a million dollars."

★

Rhoten Shetley

This All-Southern Fullback Became A Fine Lawyer

For almost half a century now, until his retirement just a few years ago, Rhoten Shetley was considered one of the finest attorneys in Greenville County. And for good reason. He was a big hearty fellow with a quick, deep laugh. Just the sort of fellow you'd want on your side if you're ever hauled into court.

When we explained our purpose in being there and asked him if he'd sit still long enough for an interview, he replied jokingly, "Well, I don't know. When folks hear that I got my name in a book, they'll all be saying, 'Ah, Lord, wonder what they've caught him at now?' But go ahead and ask your questions. I reckon I can stand it if you can."

But there was nothing funny or charming about Rhoten Shetley back when he was playing fullback for Furman University (1936-39) and blasting enemy lines for big yardage in almost every game. The Southern Conference back then, remember, stretched from Maryland to Georgia, and Furman played (and frequently beat) the best the conference had to offer.

During Shetley's freshman year, for example, Furman went 7-2 on the season, defeating both USC (23-6) and Clemson (12-0) along the way. Indeed, during his four years at Furman, the Hurricanes went 3-1 against USC and 2-1-1 against Clemson. Not a bad average. In 1939, they counted a good Georgia team among their victims, winning 20-0.

He was born and raised just outside Union in a little mill community known as Monarch. He was an outstanding end at Union High School and was offered scholarships to both Clemson and Furman. So why did he choose the Hurricanes over the Tigers?

"Well, Clemson was all military back then," he said, "and they tried to sell me on the proposition that wearing a uniform was a great idea, that it made everyone equal. In other words, you couldn't tell the rich from the poor because we were all wearing the same uniform. Well, I knew nobody was as poor as I was, even if we were wearing the same uniform. But I went along with 'em.

"But then I went up and visited Furman. Everybody, of course, was wearing civilian clothes, and I could see they were all just as poor as I was. So I figured that Furman was the place for me. I went up there

Rhoten Shetley, an All-American fullback for Furman in '39, went on to an outstanding career as a Greenville attorney.

with all the other poor folks."

That was in 1936, during the depths of the Great Depression.

"But we always had it good at Furman, despite the Depression. I weighed 162 when I arrived there, but three months later, after eating all those good, regular meals, I went up to 192. Plus they put me to work, working in the chow hall. I waited on tables, washed dishes, scrubbed floors, just whatever. And they paid me $21 a month, which was good money during the Depression."

But how could Furman, a small Baptist college, do so well against major competition back during the thirties? "We had about 450 students when I was there. But I give all the credit in the world to

Shetley runs for Furman's only touchdown of the day as the Hurricanes beat The Citadel 7-0 in 1939.

Coach A. P. "Dizzy" McLeod. I remember one day, for example, I was sitting up on top of a car near the practice field, a total nobody, a total nothing, and old Dizzy walked up to me and said, 'There you are, potentially one of the best fullbacks in the South, and if you aren't careful, you're gonna fall off that darn car and bust your fool neck.'

"Well, like I say, I was a nothing at that point and felt like a nothing. But do you know, before the season was over Dizzy had told me so many times that I was a great fullback that I actually started to believe it! And once you start believing it, you can do it. That's what he did with all the boys. He was practicing psychology before we'd ever even heard of psychology. And that, I believe, was the winning secret of Dizzy McLeod."

In 1939 Shetley served as Team Captain for both the football and baseball teams. Despite Furman's close 16-7 loss to a great Army team in '39, the Black Knights later voted Shetley the most outstanding back they'd played against all year, which is quite an endorsement when it is recalled that Army also beat such powers as Michigan and Notre Dame that year.

He was named All-State, All-Southern, and named to *Collier* Magazine's Little All-American squad. He also started at fullback in the Blue-Gray Game that year. And, in his spare time, he was voted Most Popular by the Furman student body.

Following his graduation in Phys Ed in 1940, Shetley signed with the pro football Brooklyn Dodgers of the old All-American Football League, then coached by Jock Sutherland. All the single players on the team, laughed Shetley, were housed in the Knights of Columbus Hall on Flatbush Avenue, where they could be closely watched by the coaching staff. His best friends with the Dodgers were Bruiser Kinard and Ace Parker, both all-time football greats.

"When I arrived up there," he remembered, "Coach Sutherland told me that if I did a good job calling plays, the starting position was mine. So I went to Ace Parker, and I says, 'Ace, I don't even know the plays, much less how to call 'em.' So Ace says, 'Don't worry about a thing. Just walk by me on the way to the huddle, and I'll tell you what to call.' So that's what we did, and I started every game all season. Coach Sutherland later told me that I was the best rookie play-caller he'd ever had."

Shetley was the Dodgers' number-one quarterback until he was drafted in '42. He returned to pro ball in '46, but after four years of military duty, he says, his legs were gone. Thus he returned home and took a job as football coach at Florence High School.

"As luck would have it," he said, "in 1950 we went undefeated and beat Sumter for the state championship. After the game our fans presented me with a brand new Bel Air Chevrolet. I was so shook up that I couldn't get the darn thing started to drive it off the field. But I loved that car. I finally gave it to my daughter years later when she went off to college."

So, after winning the state championship, how did Shetley suddenly become an attorney? "Well, back then all you had to do was read law in a lawyer's office and pass the bar exam. So I had to have knee surgery that year, and while I was in the hospital I read

Here Shetley throws a long one in Furman's 16-7 loss to a great Army team in 1939. At season's end, the Cadets voted him the most outstanding back they played against all year.

all the law I could get my hands on. Then I went out and talked with a couple of lawyers, passed the bar exam, and they gave me my license. I was the last person in South Carolina to practice law that way."

And so how did he spend his leisure time after retiring from the bar?

"Oh, I just piddle around, try to help poor people in court who can't afford a big time lawyer. In fact, a fellow called me last week, said he needed the best lawyer money could buy. I says, 'How much money you got?' He says, 'I ain't got any.' So I says, 'Well, you sound like my kind of folks.' So I took his case. That's the way things are going now. Just doing things for fun, and keeping up with Furman football."

We sincerely regret the recent death of Rhoten Shetley.

★
Dude Buchanan

He Remains Clemson's All-Time Leading Hitter

The first non-football player ever granted a full athletic scholarhip to Clemson, Buchanan's 1941 batting average of .498 still remains number-one in the Tiger record book.

Henry "Dude" Buchanan left a legacy of athletic excellence at Clemson University that has now stood the test of time for more than half a century.

But that's just typical of Dude Buchanan. Throughout his life, it seems, he has constantly found himself in one tight spot or another. But no matter how dismal the situation, he would inevitably find a way to snatch victory from defeat and make a name for himself in the process.

He was born a poor boy on the mill village in Anderson, S.C. in 1918. Later he would become a star athlete at Boys High, but then in 1935, with the Depression in full swing, life had become so difficult for the Buchanans that he was forced to withdraw from school and take a job at Orr Mills.

It was a tough break for an ambitious lad like Dude, but soon he became the starting first baseman for the Orr Mills baseball team, members of the old Carolina Textile League.

Buchanan received his nickname from Scoop Lattimer, legendary sports editor of the *Greenville News*, who praised his smooth fielding ability, noting that Buchanan was "a real dude" when it came to playing first base.

"In fact, we were sort of a feeder system for the St. Louis Cardinals," he says. "The head man at Orr Mills, Mr. Joe Lyons, was a friend of Cardinal manager Branch Rickey,

In 1936, Joe Lyons, convinced that Buchanan was one of the best pro prospects he'd ever seen, took him on a long train ride to St. Louis to meet with Branch Rickey.

"That was a real thrill for a poor old country boy," laughs Buchanan. "Those were the glory days of the old Gas House Gang. Johnny Mize had just broken in with them. And of course there was Dizzy and Paul Dean, and Pepper Martin and Joe Medwick. I got to practice with them, sit on the bench and listen to them kidding around."

Rickey offered Buchanan $1,500 to sign a Cardinal contract. But Buchanan's father had advised him not to accept a cent less than $3,000.

"Back in those days," says Buchanan, "$1,500 would be like a million today. They were paying Dizzy Dean only about $50 a week. But I told Mr. Rickey what my father said, and he kind of looked at me and said, 'Son, I think you better go back to Anderson for a while.' Which I did."

Standing 6 feet tall and weighing 190 pounds, Buchanan entered Clemson College in the fall of 1937, the first non-football player in the history of Tiger athletics to be granted a full athletic scholarship.

He remembers that it cost $400 a year to attend Clemson at that time, and that no one ever had any money. "But really, we cadets had it pretty good, considering the situation. We were fed all we could eat of roasts, steaks, and so-on. And one of the fellows on the hall had an old beat up automobile.

So on Saturday nights, five of us would chip in a dime each for gas, then jump in that old flivver and drive to Converse or Winthrop to see the girls. Not a bad life at all."

A highly versatile athlete, Buchanan also became a starter at forward on the basketball team in '38, his sophomore season. One of his teammates that season was Great Falls native Banks McFadden, an All-American in both football and basketball. Together they led the Tigers to the Southern Conference championship in 1939.

Today, by the way, after 85 years of intercollegiate competition, the '39 Tigers remain the sole Clemson team ever to win a conference crown in basketball.

But it was in baseball that Buchanan really stole the spotlight. Not only was he a great fielder, he was absolutely murder at the plate. Indeed, during the 1941 season he compiled an incredible .498 batting average for the Tigers (that's right, sports fans, .498!) Which still remains an all-time Clemson record.

His '41 slugging average was an even more incredible .809, which means he got on base four out of every five times at bat! Still another all-time Clemson record.

He also took his degree in textile engineering in '41. Then it was off to war. And as usual, always striving to be the best, Lt. Henry Buchanan volunteered to become a member of the celebrated 503rd Parachute Infantry Battalion.

"I thought the Depression was bad," he says, shaking his head, "but that was before I'd fought the Japanese in the Pacific. Jungle warfare, hand-to-hand combat, that was bad."

Spearheading our efforts to liberate the Philippines, the 503rd made their famous combat jump on Corregidor in early 1945. Lt. Buchanan was among the first Americans to land on The Rock. Weeks later, now fighting up the Bataan Peninsula, he received severe wounds and was taken prisoner by a cruel Japanese enemy. He would remain a POW until the

A starting guard in basketball, Buchanan helped lead the Tigers to the Southern Conference championship in 1939.

Philippines fell months later.

After a total of 39 months fighting in the Pacific, he was finally discharged in '45 as Captain Henry Buchanan. Because of the wounds he'd received on Corregidor, his baseball career was finished.

But as always he found an alternate route to success. He entered the Lowenstein Corporation.'s management program in 1946 and quickly worked his way to the top. In 1980, after many years as manager of two Lowenstein plants in Gaffney, he decided to retire.

He and his wife, the former Louise Alexander, continue to make their home in Gaffney. He is a member of the Clemson Athletic Hall of Fame.

★
Charlie Timmons

This '37 Walk-On Led The Tigers To Victory In The '39 Cotton Bowl

Charlie Timmons, a walk-on for the Tigers in 1937, was named All-Southern for three successive years and later played pro football with the Brooklyn Dodgers. He is a member of the Clemson Athletic Hall of Fame.

In the spring of 1936, at the height of the Depression, young Charlie Timmons felt that he must have been the most unfortunate man on earth. He had been an outstanding athlete at Abbeville High School and had dreamed of going to college on a football scholarship. But no scholarships materialized.

With no where else to turn, Charlie took a job in an Abbeville cotton mill. "I was what they call a spare hand," he recalls with a grimace. "I swept, picked up bobbins and cleaned the store room. I worked 55 hours a week for nine cents an hour. That's $4.95 per week."

Still, he wouldn't give up. Maybe, if he was frugal, he could save enough money to pay his own way to Clemson. To that end, he says, for an entire year he saved every penny he made. Sure enough, in the fall of 1937 he made his big move, he enrolled in college.

"It cost $175 per semester back then," he said. "That included room, meals and uniforms, though we did have to pay for our laundry. It cost a nickel to have a pair of pants pressed. But a nickel's a lot of money—if you don't have a nickel.

"I didn't have a cent of spending money when I enrolled at Clemson, and I was glad we wore uniforms, because I sure didn't have any clothes to wear."

Timmons became a walk-on for the Tigers in '37 with high hopes that Coach Jess Neely would grant him a scholarship if he made the team. And in fact Timmons did make the team, but no scholarship was forthcoming. So at the end of the year, broke again, he told Coach Neely that he could not return to school. At that point, impressed by Timmons' dedication and perseverance, Neely took a deep breath and said, "Okay, son, I just happen to have one scholarship left. It's yours."

Timmons recalls that he was redshirted in '38, but then in '39 he became the starting fullback on a powerful Clemson team that would become one of the most famous elevens in the school's history. At tailback that season was All-American Banks McFadden. Plus the team had such other stalwarts as Joe Blalock at end (he's still the only Clemson football player named All-American twice), Joe Payne at blocking back, Shad Bryant at wingback, and future Clemson President Walter Cox at guard.

The '39 Tigers went 8-1 on the season against some of the toughest competition in the South, their only loss coming at the hands of mighty Tulane by a score of 7-6. Then, as a culmination of this dream season, the Tigers received an invitation to meet undefeated Boston College in the Cotton Bowl on New Years Day. For the first time ever, this little country college from South Carolina would receive national attention.

Indeed, the Eagles' line, considered one of the very best in the nation, had given up only a few points all season. And thus, as one might imagine, Boston College came into the game heavily favored.

Timmons was Clemson's leading ground gainer in the Tigers' 6-3 upset win over Boston College in the '40 Cotton Bowl. Here he breaks out for the touchdown that would give the Tigers their great victory.

But by game's end it was the Clemson defense that made believers out of everyone. Thanks to the incredible punting performance of Banks McFadden (he punted eleven times that afternoon, averaging 45 yards per kick), Boston College had to start almost every drive from within the shadows of their own goal post. And after 60 minutes of play the Eagles had only a single field goal to show for all their efforts. Clemson's offense, on the other hand, managed to bust their great defensive line, and by game's end had a big six points to show for their efforts. Charlie Timmons led all runners that afternoon with 115 yards rushing, and he also scored the Tigers' only touchdown.

It was an incredible 6-3 upset win for the Tigers over a big Eastern power. The news media, along with the 20,000 fans on hand for the game, were incredulous. But there it was, right there on the scoreboard. It was a game that truly put Clemson on the national map for the first time.

Asked how he managed to blitz such a powerful defense for such nice yardage, Timmons answered modestly, "Aw, it was easy for me to run that day. Boston College spent the whole day watching Banks McFadden. And while they were watching Banks, I was running the other way with the football. That was our plan, and it worked."

One of those watching Timmons that afternoon was Frank Howard. Now there are those who firmly believe that God created Frank Howard out of a lump of clay and a squirt of tobacco juice and set him down at Clemson on the eighth day of Creation. In point of fact, Howard was only a humble assistant coach under Jess Neely when Timmons arrived on campus in the fall of '37. It wasn't until 1940 that Howard became head coach. Timmons remembers the night Howard was hired and the rather bizarre way it all came about:

"The Board of Trustees met to hire a successor to Coach Neely, and one Trustee says, 'I nominate Frank Howard.' The Chairman says, 'Do I hear a second to that nomination?'

"Well, there was dead silence from the Trustees, and that silence seemed to go on and on. It was like nobody even heard the Chairman asked for a second. Then, finally, from the back of the room, somebody yelled, 'I second that!' I looked back to see who it was. It was Frank Howard. Well, the Trustees all started laughing, and they hired him unanimously. He rewarded them by winning the Southern Conference Championship that year."

The Tigers went 22-5 during Timmons' three years as a starter at Clemson. He was named to both the All-State and All-Southern Teams for three successive years and was drafted by the Washington Redskins.

But the war was on, and following his graduation in Textile Engineering in June of '42, he immediately volunteered for military duty as a Naval officer. Most of the war, he says, was spent playing service ball at various Navy bases stateside and in Hawaii. Later, with the end of the war, he spent a year playing fullback for the Brooklyn Dodgers of the All-American Football League.

"Then I received a letter from an old friend I'd met in service, and he told me he'd gone to work for the Gulf Oil people and invited me to come on down, said they were hiring engineers.

"Well, my wife, Elizabeth, was expecting our first child at the time, so taking a real job sounded like a good idea. That was in 1947. I retired from Gulf in 1980."

Still, it was hard for Timmons to say goodbye to football. From 1948 until 1965 he became one of the best known referees in football, officiating at games for both the Southern Conference and the ACC.

Charlie and Elizabeth had five children and twelve grandchildren, and made their home in Greenville. He was inducted into the Clemson Athletic Hall of Fame in 1985.

But think about it: 61 years ago Charlie Timmons became a real pioneer, a young man who helped set Clemson on the path to becoming one of the country's finest athletic powers.

Yep, 61 years. That's a lot of water over the old Hartwell Dam.

We sincerely regret the recent death of Charlie Timmons.

★
George Floyd

He Scored Clemson's First Touchdown Ever Under New Head Coach, Frank Howard

It would be difficult to imagine any living human being who has been more actively involved in Clemson football over the past fifty-nine years than Conway's George Floyd. He first donned the purple and orange in 1937, and since that time he has witnessed every moment of Clemson's rise to national prominence.

He was born in Aynor in 1918. Later, during the Great Depression, his father sold their small farm and the family moved to Conway where George's older brother had started an auto parts store. There the family went to work. As for young George, he excelled in athletics at Conway High School, and upon his graduation in '37 he was invited to try out for a football scholarship at Clemson College.

Jess Neely was head coach of the Tigers back then, Frank Howard merely an unknown assistant. Neely liked what he saw in young Floyd and offered him a one-year scholarship. He would, Neely said, become a backup wingback to Clemson's great Shad Bryant.

"They gave us scholarships on a year-to-year basis back then," Floyd said. "If you did well, you'd get a letter the next summer inviting you back for another year of football. If you hadn't done well, then you wouldn't get a letter, and you'd lose your scholarship."

He remembered arriving at Clemson as a freshman and receiving his first scholarship check. "It was registration day at Clemson in 1937, and we football players all lined up to get our scholarship money. I remember Coach Neely handing me a check for $400, which was the most money I'd ever seen in my life. But that paid not only for my tuition the entire year, but also for all my ROTC uniforms, my dorm room, my school books, and three delicious meals a day."

Asked where he parked his automobile, Floyd doubled over with laughter. "Why there weren't half a dozen cars on campus in 1937. One of my roommates, Norwood McElveen from Rock Hill, did have one. His sweetheart's father ran a big car place in Rock Hill, and he let Norwood take this car up to Clemson, so he could come home on the weekends. But any time Norwood didn't go home, he'd let Joe Blalock and me borrow it to visit our sweethearts at

George Floyd is famous for having scored on Clemson's first offensive play of the 1940 season, an 18-yard scamper against Presbyterian College, which just also happened to be Frank Howard's first play since becoming head coach that year.

Lander College."

Floyd played freshman ball in '37, then sat out the '38 season with a broken leg. But in '39 he was ready. And it was that '39 season that put little Clemson College on the football map. With their All-American tailback Banks McFadden running the show, the Tigers lost only one game that season, a 7-6 squeaker to mighty Tulane, before astounding the experts by upsetting big Boston College 6-3 in the Cotton Bowl.

Today Floyd grins when recalling that day in Dallas. "Yep, that was the big one that gave us national attention. I hadn't gotten to play that much in '39 because my leg was still a little gimp. I ran the ball about thirty times all season, I guess. But I averaged 8.9 yards per carry. I still have a Dallas sports article that came out the morning of the game. It called me Ploughboy Floyd and said I was Clemson's secret

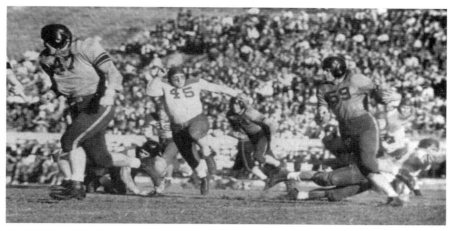

Here Floyd takes off around left end behind big Marion Craig in Clemson's 13-0 loss to Tulane in 1940.

weapon with my 8.9 yards per carry average."

But of all his experiences there was one single moment in Floyd's life that won him a niche high up among the immortals of Clemson football. It occurred on the afternoon of September 21, 1940, during Clemson's season opener at Presbyterian College. (Yes, the Clemson-PC game of 1940 was played at Clinton.)

Coach Jess Neely had resigned after the '39 season, so this was Frank Howard's first game as head coach of the Clemson Tigers. As luck would have it, PC fumbled the opening kickoff, and Clemson recovered at the PC 18-yard line. Howard then sent in a play, his first as head coach. It was to be a reverse, with Floyd carrying the ball.

Floyd recalled the moment: "The ball was snapped to Charlie Timmons. He spun, then pitched the ball back to me coming around. I had Joe Blalock and Wade Padgett in front of me cutting down those Blue Hose, and I went down the sideline all the way for a touchdown."

At that point, having sent in a touchdown play on his very first call as head coach, the irrepressible Howard turned to a sportswriter standing at his side and grinned, "Boy, there ain't nothing to this head coaching business. I wish I'd got into this long ago."

"But do you know," laughs Floyd, "Coach Howard has been telling that story now for the past fifty-five years. And the longer he tells it, the further I ran for that touchdown. I overheard him tell it to a sportswriter last year, and he said I ran eighty yards for a touchdown. When the writer walked away, Coach Howard came over to me and said, 'Say, George, just how far did you run with that durned ball?' In all honesty I really can't remember now

myself. But I think it was eighteen yards."

Floyd also scored Clemson's first touchdown on Big Thursday 1940, thus becoming the first Tiger under Howard to score against Carolina. The team went on then to a 6-2-1 season and won the Southern Conference championship.

As for Floyd, despite the fact that he still had another year of football eligibility, he took his degree and his ROTC commission in the spring of '41. In August of that year he was ordered to report for a year of active duty with the U. S. Army.

"Of course the Japanese bombed Pearl Harbor a few months later, so that so-called year became five years."

At war's end, in 1945, now stationed at Camp Croft near Spartanburg, he met and married Alice Glominski, a school teacher.

George and Alice had four children and two grandchildren and made their home in Conway. He retired as president of the Conway Auto Parts Co.

Still, he could not help but remember that year of eligibility he passed up with Clemson.

"In fact," he grinned, "back in 1990 Clemson celebrated the golden anniversary of our Cotton Bowl team. We had a big banquet that night, and Coach Hatfield spoke to us. He said that Clemson was thin at tailback and said if any of us knew any tailbacks who'd like to play for Clemson to raise our hands. Well, all the fellows started laughing and trying to get me to raise my hand, kidding me about still having a year of eligibility left, you know. But I figured my playing days were about over, so I just kept quiet."

We sincerely regret the recent death of George Floyd.

Moments of Glory
South Carolina's Greatest
Sports Heroes

1940-1949

★
Marty Marion

Not Only Was He The Tallest Shortstop Ever To Play The Game, He Was Also One Of The Greatest

As far as major league baseball is concerned, Marty Marion's done it all—player, coach, manager, and owner—in a career that spanned some forty-six years in the big time. But at heart, he says, he is still just a good ol' country boy.

Back in 1916 he got his start when he was born in the front bedroom of his sister's home in the small farming community of Richburg in Chester County, where his father was engaged in the agriculture business. And even today, despite his status as a prominent citizen of St. Louis, Marty himself owns a farm. Or as he himself puts it, "The acorn doesn't fall too far from the tree."

But then came the Great Depression and his family moved to Georgia when he was just a boy. There he attended Atlanta Tech High School. He remembers going out for baseball his freshman year and being assigned to sit beside Coach Gale Talbert on the bench during the games, what he initially thought was a very important assignment.

"Coach Talbert was an inveterate cigar smoker," Marion explains with a laugh, "and so my job was to jump up about every thirty minutes and run get him a fresh cigar. Still, it was a start."

But over the next three years Atlanta Tech, behind the fielding and hitting of Marty Marion, won the Georgia state championship in baseball. Marion himself was signed to a nice pro contract by the St. Louis Cardinals and assigned to their Class C club in Huntington, West Virginia.

He remembers reporting to their rookie camp in Bartow, Florida. in 1936. He had played third and second base in high school, but here he found a spot for himself at shortstop.

"When I got to the practice field at Bartow there were about ten guys trying out for third and about that many trying out for second, but there was nobody wanting to play shortstop. So I simply trotted out onto the field and told 'em I was their shortstop. Believe it or not, it worked."

Marion made a good decision, and he would play this position with great expertise throughout his major league career.

Born in Richburg, Marty Marion broke in with the St. Louis Cardinals in 1940 and then remained a part of that organization for the next fifty years. Today he is remembered as one of the greatest Big Leaguers of all time.

In fact, at 6-4 Marty Marion remains the tallest shortstop in the history of major league baseball.

"I know people think it's odd that such a tall guy should be playing short. They seem to think that shortstops are quick little guys like Pee Wee Reece and Phil Rizzuto, but I found my height to be an advantage, really. I could reach balls those little guys couldn't get to."

After a year in Huntington, Marty was jumped to Rochester of the Class AAA American Association, where he played for the next three seasons. He also found a wife that year—an Atlanta girl, Mary Dallas, his high school sweetheart.

Then came 1940 and the Big Time. He was called

up by the Cards' manager Bill Southworth. Marty remembers that the era of the famous Gas House Gang was coming to an end the year he broke in, but his list of teammates still reads like a Who's-Who of major league baseball. There was Johnny Mize, Joe Medwick, Mickey Owens, and the ever popular Dizzy Dean.

"Ol' Diz was a great pitcher and one of the most colorful guys to ever play the game," chuckles Marion. "He was a big talker, but he never said a thing he couldn't back up. You remember his famous line 'If you can do it, that ain't bragging'? Well, that pretty well describes Dizzy Dean."

In '42 the Cards won the National League pennant. Then after losing the first game of the World Series, beat the Yankees four straight.

"That was my first World Series," Marion recalls with a smile. "And definitely my biggest thrill in baseball. It's every player's dream to play in a World Series, so I got my wish a little early."

In fact, he says, the '42 Cards were the best team he ever saw during half a century in organized baseball. He also points out that '42 was the year that a young rookie named Stan Musial put in his first appearance.

"Oddly enough, in '42 Stan didn't get to play against left-handed pitchers. We had a guy named Coker Triplett from Boone, N. C. who played left field and was a great hitter. So Triplett played against lefties, and Musial against right handers. It's hard to imagine platooning Stan Musial, but that's the way it was."

If Marion wished for play in the World Series, then he certainly had his hands full over the next few years, as the Cards won the National League pennant in '43, '44, and '46.

Much of their success was attributed to the tall, rangey Southerner from Richburg, and in 1944 Marion received the National League's highly coveted Most Valuable Player Award.

That award, he says today, along with his associations with some "really great guys," represents his fondest memory of his long major league career. Indeed, Marion says he kept no mementos of his playing days—no gloves, shoes, autographed balls, or even old photos. Nothing but his MVP award,

which still hangs on the wall in his St. Louis home.

After fifteen years, in 1951, Marion decided to call it a day while he was still on top. Though he is remembered today for his fine defensive play, it should also be recalled that he was no slouch at the plate and retired with a .263 career batting average. He also played in four World Series and eight All-Star games, and was considered one of the "smartest" players in the game.

So "smart," in fact, that in '51, with the departure of Cards' manager Eddie Dyer to the Dodgers, Marion was named to succeed him as manager of the St. Louis Cardinals. Over the next nine years he would also manage the St. Louis Browns and the Chicago White Sox.

Then in 1960 he moved on to another level of organized baseball when he purchased a Cardinal franchise, the Houston Buffs of the AAA American Association. As owner and president of the Buffs, he jokes, "I got a taste of what it's like to be a front-office boy for a change." Then in '63 he sold the franchise back to the Cards at a nice profit, and soon the Buffs became the major league Astros.

Following that venture, in 1968, Marion and several friends built a private club in the Cards' newly constructed Busch Stadium called The Stadium Club. This club seats 2,000 fans who can, for a healthy membership fee, watch the games surrounded by all the comforts of home.

But finally, in 1985, Marion decided to sell his interest in the Stadium Club and to retire from the game once and for all.

Today, at the age of eighty-two, he and his wife Mary live comfortably in their St. Louis home, surrounded by their four daughters and eleven grandchildren. Marty and Mary will soon celebrate their 61st wedding anniversary.

Asked his plans for the future, Marion quips: "My most immediate ambition is to receive a copy of this book you're doing. I want to see what kind of sports writers South Carolina is turning out now."

Well, prevailing wisdom has it that few things today, including cars, athletes and sports writers, are as good as the old timers. And there's probably some truth in that.

★

Preacher McQueen

This Preacher Was A Holy Terror For The Hurricanes

It will come as a surprise to no one, especially those sadder but wiser victims from the ACC whom the Paladins have rolled over during the past decade, but little Furman University is famous for holding its own against almost anybody in the country. And there was a time, sports fans, back when they were known simply as the Hurricanes, that the mere thought of playing those Furmanites sent icy chills down the spines of the big boys from across the South.

And that brings us to a name that inevitably evokes tears of happy remembrance to those old timers who came along during that simpler era: James R. "Preacher" McQueen.

He remembers being raised on a big tobacco farm down in Mullins. He also remembers his high school years (1935-39) as very tough Depression years.

"Putting in tobacco is hard work," he says, "and we had to scrabble from sunup til dark just to make a go of it and keep the farm from going under. The whole family would have to pitch in and work. But my father would let me off long enough in the afternoons to take part in sports."

He was a high school terror at tackle, and by his senior year he stood 6-2 and weighed 215 pounds. He was highly aggressive, a tough, raw-boned young man with great speed and quick moves. The scholarship offers poured in, but he chose to attend Furman.

"I was recruited by Coach Dizzy McLeod," Preacher explains, "and I thought he was a fine fellow. Despite his nickname, he was a no-nonsense sort of fellow, the sort you always knew where you stood with, and I always got along with people like that. Plus I just liked Furman."

And speaking of nicknames, how did McQueen ever get stuck with a moniker like Preacher? "My father gave all us kids nicknames when we were little," he laughs. "Mine was Preacher. I've been known as Preacher McQueen since I was two years old."

We certainly have no doubts concerning the accuracy of that account, though it is contradicted by McQueen's younger brother, Dan McQueen, a long-

In 1941 James R. "Preacher" McQueen had his education at Furman interrupted by World War II, but he would return in '46 better than ever.

time executive with the Rock Hill Telephone Company.

"The truth is," Dan grins, "that Preacher got a job in a Mullins filling station when he was in the eighth grade. He also had his eye on a certain little girl at school. So every day, knowing that little girl would come by the filling station in her father's car, he'd put on a coat and tie and slick down his hair, then go to

In 1947 McQueen was elected team captain, won the MVP award, and was named to the All-State team. He would remain with the Hurricanes as an assistatnt coach until 1955.

pump gas all afternoon. People at the station would kid him and ask him where he was preaching that night. From that, everybody started calling him Preacher."

Well, so much for the wild tales of little brothers.

McQueen became a starter at tackle for the Hurricanes in 1940. With teammates like Dewey Proctor, Gates Barker, Bill Cornwall, and James Martin, all of whom made the All-State team in 1940, the Hurricanes could boast of big wins over both NC State (20-6) and USC (25-7).

Believe it or not, that same year McQueen played before the biggest crowd ever to witness a Furman home football game when 19,300 fans turned out at Sirrine Stadium to watch the Hurricanes lose a close 13-7 game to Clemson. Incredibly, despite all the great Paladin teams of the past twenty years, not one has ever broken that home attendance figure from fifty-eight years ago.

Then came the war in '41 and McQueen traded in his Purple People Eaters uniform to do service with Uncle Sam. He slogged his way across Europe with the 3rd Infantry Division, participating in some of the most brutal fighting of the war. When discharged in

'46, after some five years in the military, he was more than ready to return to Furman.

Picking up where he'd left off in '41, McQueen again became the starting tackle for the Hurricanes. Over the next two years Furman would take on such giants of the gridiron as Clemson, USC, Georgia, Georgia Tech, Florida, Alabama, Auburn, VPI, and Army. They didn't compile a great won-loss record, but the All-State team for those two years reads like a Who's-Who of former Furman greats.

As for McQueen, he served as team captain in '47, won the team MVP award, and was again named to the All-State team.

He took his degree in biology in 1948, then served as line coach for the Hurricanes until 1954. In '55 he accepted a research position with M & S Chemical Company in Greenville, where he would remain until his retirement in 1992.

He is married to the former Jane Guthrie and they have four children, six grandchildren, and make their home in Greenville.

He is a member of the Furman Athletic Hall of Fame and says he doesn't care whether his old alma mater is called the Hurricanes or the Paladins, he still loves Furman football.

We regret the recent death of Preacher McQueen.

★

Dewey Proctor

He Was Voted Furman's All-Time Greatest Fullback

Born in 1920, Dewey Proctor would one day leave the sandy tobacco country of Dillon County to become one of the finest athletes ever to play football for Furman University. And, despite Thomas Wolfe's comment to the contrary, he would go home again.

Growing up he attended Lake View High School. Due largely to Proctor's talents and leadership, they would win the state championships in both baseball and football in 1937 and '38.

A blockbuster of a fullback, Proctor attracted wide attention from college coaches across the South. But he particularly liked Coach Jess Neely and Clemson College, so he became a Tiger in the fall of '39. But he had always been a hometown boy, and since he knew no one in Tiger Town, he soon came down with a severe case of homesickness. Then he remembered that two of his best friends, Waldo Hinson and James "Preacher" McQueen, boys from Mullins, were playing for Furman.

Thus, after only two weeks at Clemson, Proctor packed his bags and headed thirty miles up the road to join the Purple Hurricanes of Furman and Coach Dizzy McLeod. Of course he had to sit out his freshman year because of his Clemson misadventure, but he has always felt that his move was a wise one. Rhoten Shetley, Furman's All-Everything fullback, had just graduated and thus the Hurricanes were in the market for a new fullback. Proctor hoped he'd be the solution to their problem.

Not only did Proctor make the team his sophomore year, he was also named to the All-State Team. In fact, he remains one of the few Furman athletes ever named All-State for three consecutive years.

In 1942, his senior season, he had an 84-yard touchdown run against Wake Forest, which still remains the third longest scoring run in the Furman Record Book. He was also named to the All-Southern Team in '42.

(It should be noted that the Southern Conference of 1942 included such teams as USC, Clemson, Virginia, UNC, NC State, Wake Forest and Duke. Thus to be named All-Southern back in those days

Dewey Proctor, a Lake View boy, was named to the All-State Team and is today a member of the Furman Athletic Hall of Fame. He was recently voted Furman's all-time greatest fullback.

was quite a testament to one's athletic prowess.)

He was a starter in the Blue-Gray Game in Mobile, Ala. in '42. Then he went high in the draft—to both the New York Giants and to Uncle Sam. Uncle Sam, as usual, won out. And Proctor soon found himself a sailor stationed at Great Lakes Naval Training Station, where the Navy had assembled one of the best football teams in America.

As their starting fullback in '43, Proctor's finest day came against a powerful Notre Dame team that came into Great Lakes undefeated in their past twenty-one games. By game's end, Proctor had rushed for 160 yards, including a 65-yard TD run, as Great Lakes upset the Irish 12-7. Not a bad performance against the number-one team in America.

The next year, in 1944, he was transferred to Bainbridge (Md.) Naval Training Station where he joined Choo-Choo Justice and Lou Sossamon to give

Dewey Proctor scored Furman's lone TD as the Hurricanes fell to mighty Tennessee in 1942.

the Commodores the most feared service team in the country.

During the war years a fierce inter-service rivalry existed for athletic supremacy in America. Thus it was announced that a championship game was to be played between the Army and Navy All-Stars at Pearl Harbor, and Proctor, a Navy All-Star, soon found himself aboard a PBY flying half way around the world to play in a football game. Asked who won that game, he shrugs and says, "To tell you the truth, I really don't remember who won. I was so exhausted from that plane ride that I hardly even remember being there."

At war's end he was signed to a pro contract with the New York Yankees of the old All-America Football Conference. He would become a mainstay at

fullback for the next three years. But then, tired of living out of suitcases in strange hotels, he says, he returned to the land he loved the most, the tobacco country of Dillon County. There, he would serve as a deputy sheriff for the next eight years.

Then he became Chief of Police in Mullins, a position he held for twenty-six years, until his retirement in 1990.

He is a member of both the Furman Athletic Hall of Fame and the South Carolina Athletic Hall of Fame. In a poll recently conducted by the *Greenville News-Piedmont*, he was elected to the All-Time Furman University Football Team.

He has been married since 1947, and he and his family still make their home in Mullins, a world away from the big glamor of New York City. But that's the way Dewey Proctor likes it.

★

Lou Sosamon

He Was Carolina's First True Gridiron All-American

His name is Lou Sosamon, and in the early '70s USC alumni would elect him the Gamecocks' all-time outstanding lineman. But such has not always been his status in the world of athletics. In fact, back in 1936 he was just a scrawny 130-pound second-team center for the Gaffney High Indians.

He remembers playing Boiling Springs High School that year, where the football field, for reasons that remain a mystery, was only 90 yards in length. According to Boiling Springs' special rules, a touchdown was not declared when a team crossed the goal line. Instead, the ball was brought back to the 10-yard line and the team then was given four downs to make the final ten yards in order to have their score.

Sossamon recalls that such was Gaffney's situation in that big game of '36. There were only moments left in the game, and Gaffney was trailing 7-6. They were facing a fourth down at the three when their quarterback spoke to them in the huddle: "Okay, men, this time we're gonna show 'em a thing or two. We're gonna ram it right up the middle." He looked young Sossamon dead in the eye. "Soss, you be sure to shove that big noseguard all the way out of this stadium."

Sossamon gulped and replied, in words that have become immortal throughout the Gaffney area, "I ain't shoved nobody nowhere all day. Maybe we better show 'em a thing or two around end."

"Yep, people still kid me about that," he laughs. He is indeed a very modest man who never boasts about his accomplishments on the gridiron. But those who know him say that the Boiling Springs episode marked the last time he ever begged off from any assignment, no matter how difficult.

The Indians were considered the most formidable team in the state during his junior and senior seasons, and he was chosen to play in the '38 Shrine Bowl Game.

Just recently, Sossamon, along with Clemson's Bobby Gage and UNC's Choo Choo Justice, would be selected for the All-Time Shrine Bowl Team—just one of many All-Time teams he's been elected to during his career.

Lou was born in 1921, the grandson of Ed

Gaffney's Lou Sossamon was named to the AP All American Team in 1942. He would later enjoy a great pro career with the New York Yankees of the All-American Football League.

DeCamp who helped publish the first editions of *The State* newspaper in Columbia in 1894. Then in 1897 DeCamp moved to Gaffney and was instrumental in establishing Cherokee County. He also started a newspaper, *The Gaffney Ledger,* of which Sossamon is publisher today.

His decision to enroll at USC came about sort of casually, he says. It seems that back in 1939 he accom-

Sossamon was featured in this newpaper ad for Carolina's shootout with The Citadel, a game played annually back in those days at the Orangeburg County Fair.

panied his parents, who were reporters for the family newspaper, to Columbia where they attended a press conference at The State House. Just killing time, young Lou strolled over to the USC athletic department to visit with several of his Gaffney friends who were then playing football for Carolina. He himself was still nursing a shoulder broken in the recent Shrine Bowl Game. The first person he met, he says, was Coach Rex Enright, who offered him a football scholarship on the spot. Sossamon readily accepted the offer, and the next four years, as they say, are history.

He was named to the All-Southern Team for three consecutive years, and his senior year he became USC's first bona-fide All-American when he was named to the Associated Press squad at center.

It might be pointed out that these honors came Sossamon's way despite the fact that Carolina won a total of only eight games during his entire 3-year career with the Gamecocks.

Following his graduation in 1943 he enlisted in the Navy and was stationed at Bainbridge (Md.) Naval Training Station, where he became the starting center for the Commodores. For the next two years then the Commodores went undefeated against some of the most powerful service and college teams in America. His old Shrine Bowl adversary Charlie Choo-Choo Justice was the starting halfback for the Commodores.

After his discharge in '45 Sossamon was contacted by Dan Topping, owner of the New York Yankees, who told him that he was forming a profes-

Sossamon, a linebacker for the pro football New York Yankees, manhandles San Francisco 49er John Straykalski in a game at Yankee Stadium. The Associated Press named this the Sports Photo of the Year in 1948.

sional football team, also to be called The Yankees, and that they would play in the newly formed All-American Football Conference. Many outstanding players already had been recruited, Topping said, men whose names would later become synonymous with pro football: Otto Graham, Marion Motley, Elroy "Crazy Legs" Hirsch, Ben Agajanian, Dante Lavelli, Lou Groza, Frankie Albert, Mack Speedie and Ace Parker. Joining Lou with The Yankees would be the great Georgia All-American Frankie "Fireball" Sinkwich, Illinois All-American Buddy Young (as a freshman he had broken Red Grange's touchdown record), Notre Dame immortal Angelo Bertelli and Furman All-Southern fullback Dewey Proctor (a native of Lakeview).

By this time Lou had married his college sweetheart, Kathryn Edgerton of Orangeburg. Not only had Kathryn been a Carolina cheerleader for three years, but she was also the daughter of Dr. Bruce "Red" Edgerton, USC football coach from 1912-15. Her blood truly runneth garnet.

Living in New York during the fall, the Sossamons time-shared an apartment with Yankee baseball great Yogi Berra and his wife, with whom they became fast friends. Later, Sossamon recalls, Yogi would present to Sossamon's son Cody the bat Berra used the night Don Larson pitched his perfect

game for the Yankees. Today the Sossamons regard it as a priceless memento.

The Yankees were an excellent pro football team and consistently outdrew their NFL counterparts, the New York Giants. As a typical example of their popularity, the Yankees in 1947 played the Los Angeles Dons before 83,000 fans in Los Angeles Coliseum, a pro football record crowd at that time.

For four years Sossamon anchored the Yankees' line at center. He weighed only 210 pounds but made up for his lack of bulk with his speed, aggressiveness and hard-nosed play.

Following his retirement from pro football he returned to Gaffney and tackled his journalistic career with the same fervor as he once had tackled opposing running backs. Indeed, the South Carolina Press Association bestowed on him its first Freedom of Information Award, and he would later serve as President of that association.

Today he still publishes *The Gaffney Ledger* and is also a longtime member of the USC Board of Trustees. As Chairman of USC's Intercollegiate Activities Committee he is proud that he played a key role in persuading the SEC to accept Carolina as a member. He is also a member of the USC and South Carolina Athletic Halls of Fame.

He and his family make their home in Gaffney.

★
Bobo Carter

He Is Typical of Those Who Had Their Athletic Careers Disrupted By World War II

Bobo Carter was twice named to the All State Team at tackle and in '42 won the Gamecocks' MVP award. He returned to USC in '46, following the war.

Typical of those college athletes who had their careers disrupted by World War II is Elmore "Bobo" Carter, an outstanding prewar lineman for the University of South Carolina who was forced to trade in his uniform of garnet and black for one of olive drab. For him as for thousands of others, life would never be quite the same again.

A native of Asheville, where he grew up on his father's dairy, Carter was a unanimous All-State selection at tackle his senior year in high school and was named to the 1939 Shrine Bowl team.

"In fact," he says, "we had a heck of a team at Asheville that year and four of us were chosen for the Shrine Bowl. That included Bill Justice, older brother of future UNC All-American Choo-Choo Justice. But Bill was a terrific running back himself and scored all our touchdowns in our 19-0 win over South Carolina in the Shrine Bowl. He went on to play college ball for Rollins College down in Florida."

Carter thought USC Coach Rex Enright was the finest man he ever met, so he decided to cast his lot with the Gamecocks. After a successful freshman season, he became the starting right tackle at USC in '41. He remembers such outstanding teammates as Harvey Blouin, Al Grygo, Lou Sossamon, Kirk Norton, Dutch Elston, Stan Stasica, Bryant Meeks, Earl Dunham, Buford Clary, and Neil Allen.

(Thanks to World War II, by the way, Neil Allen served as captain of the Gamecocks on two occasions, in both 1943 and 1947. Only Ernest Dixon has been accorded this same honor, serving as captain in both 1992 and 1993.)

At 6-1 and 215 pounds, Carter enjoyed an outstanding season in '41 and says that his best game of the year came in their season finale, a 19-12 loss to a strong Penn State team.

"I'd established a pretty good reputation for myself, especially on defense, so the Lions were double-teaming me on every play. But there was this one play where I shoved both blockers back into their backfield. They had me up on their shoulders, but when their ball carrier came flying by, I reached out and grabbed him by the collar.

"So there we were, the ball carrier running in circles, pulling me and my two blockers around and around like a merry-go-round. The refs finally blew the play dead, and they'd lost three yards."

Only eight days after this game the Japanese bombed Pearl Harbor, and for the next three years athletics would become a touch-and-go situation at colleges across America. Carter, luckily, would make it through one more season before becoming an Air Corps lieutenant.

Having been named All-State in '41, he prepared

himself for the '42 season. He recalls that Carolina opened with a shocking 0-0 tie with mighty Tennessee. But it was downhill from there on out, with Carolina's only win coming at the expense of The Citadel.

"When the season opened in '42," he says, "our troops were landing in both North Africa and Guadalcanal. As a result, most of the fellows who played against Tennessee were simply gone to war before our game the next week against North Carolina. That's the way it was during the war years. Here today, gone tomorrow."

Carter had an outstanding year in '42. He was again named to the All-State team and won the team MVP award. But then in February of '43 he received greetings from his draft board. Today he recalls with a grin:

"The Air Corps evaluated my test scores and told me I was mechanically inclined. Which puzzled me, since all I'd ever done was milk cows. But they sent me off to this fancy school to teach me how to keep our bombers flying. Then they handed me a rifle and shipped me off to the South Pacific."

He arrived there just in time to help liberate the Philippines. Then it was on to Iwo Jima, Okinawa, and all those other Pacific islands where the fighting was fierce and bloody.

Peace came an eternity later, says Carter, and he returned to Carolina in time for the '46 football season. He made his presence felt that year and helped the Gamecocks to a good 5-3 season. But he himself says that he never truly attained the level of excellence he'd known before the war.

"To tell the truth, I'd been through some bad times in the Pacific, and my nerves really weren't the best. Football is a violent sport, and I'd just seen enough violence to last me a lifetime. You might say that I'd used up most of my killer's instinct during the war. All I really wanted was peace and quiet."

Following his graduation from Carolina, the Baltimore Colts offered him $5,000 to sign a pro contract. But Baltimore, he says, was too far from home.

"I played a couple of years over there with the old Charlotte Clippers. But really I just longed to return to the tranquility of my father's dairy up in the mountains."

Several years after returning to Asheville, he became a salesman for Biltmore Dairy, a position he maintained until his retirement in 1982. He and his family continue to make their home in Asheville, and Carter says he still wakes up thanking God for the peacefulness of that mountain city.

★
Butch Butler

This Great Tailback Kept Clemson Afloat During Those Dismal World War II Years

As Clemson's new head football coach, Frank Howard in 1940 immediately sought a great tailback to lead his devastating single-wing offense. He finally found one, a young man from Tallassee, Alabama, named Butch Butler.

Marion "Butch" Butler entered Clemson College in 1941 and became one of the finest tailbacks ever to wear the orange and purple. Then came World War II, and from that point on he never knew from one day to the next whether he'd be wearing a Clemson uniform or the fatigues of an army private.

Oddly enough, he frequently wore both.

An All-State performer back in his hometown of Tallahassee, Alabama, Butch recalls that he actually arrived at Clemson some two months before the fall semester began: "I didn't have much money, so Coach Howard paid me to piddle around the athletic department. I'd line off the tennis courts and things like that. The money came in very handy once school started."

Coach Frank Howard, hoping to keep his prize catch happy, even introduced Butch to the young woman who would soon become Mrs. Marion Butler. Howard, who played Cupid in this episode, explains:

"There were only three datable girls on our whole campus. One day Butch came to me and says, 'Coach, I don't like this place at all. Nothing to do. No girls.'"

Howard says that one of the "datable" girls was Rock Rentz, who lived next door to his family in Clemson. So he asked her if she would go out with Butch.

"Well, consequently she did," Howard beams. "She kept him here. Then be darned if that little old boy didn't go and marry her. It almost ruined me. Then I didn't have but two datable girls on campus. The whole football team almost quit."

After a successful year as Clemson's starting tailback in '42, Butler found himself stationed at Fort Jackson in '43, wearing the fatigues of an army private. But Frank Howard was not one to let a little thing like World War II stand in his way of fielding a football team. He arranged with Butler's company commander (a Clemson graduate) for Butler to receive weekend passes so that he could play football for Clemson on Saturday afternoons.

This Butler did, even though he was not enrolled as a student at Clemson (a minor detail). He laughs now and says, "I didn't know a single soul on that team in '43, because the only time I ever saw them was on Saturday afternoons."

Butler played magnificently all year, despite the fact that Clemson fielded their weakest team in history. Indeed, against South Carolina on Big Thursday that year, the Tigers were heavy underdogs. But at halftime the experts were amazed that Clemson held a 6-0 lead, thanks to the slashing runs and booming quick-kicks of Butch Butler.

The Gamecocks eventually won the game, but in

In '42 Butler blasts through the VMI line for good yardage. He would soon be wearing the uniform of a private in the U. S. Army.

later years sports writer Don Barton, who wrote a comprehensive history of the USC-Clemson series, had this to say: "Butch Butler's play that day was perhaps the finest individual performance ever turned in during this long series between the two schools."

And so it went, and by the fall of '45 the war had ended but Butch was still in service. Frank Howard, still desperate for a tailback to run his single wing formation, visited the commanding general at Fort Jackson. Somehow he persuaded the general to give Butler a 90-day pass. (Asked if it is true that a case of gin changed hands in this agreement, Howard says he really doesn't remember.)

So Butch, Rock, and their new baby arrived at Clemson just in time for the '45 football season. He remembers that Clemson merchants were most generous in outfitting him with civilian clothes and that Frank Howard even found a carriage for their baby.

He was instrumental that year in Clemson's impressive wins over mighty Tulane and Georgia Tech, and a 0-0 tie with USC. Still, he was not registered as a student at Clemson. Didn't the NCAA frown on such shenanigans?

Frank Howard dismisses such dumb questions with a wave of his hand. "Nah," he growled. "That was back before the NCAA started meddling in everybody's business. Back then we went by common sense." Howard breaks out with a laugh. "You can just say that Butch Butler was the finest nonstu-

dent tailback in the history of Clemson University."

Butch finally graduated in the spring of '46 and was offered a contract by the Chicago Cardinals. By then he and Rock had two children and, he says, "The last thing I wanted to do was move my family to Chicago."

Instead, he signed with the Miami Sea Hawks of the All-American Conference, who were then training in Asheville. But he was again thrown into a dilemma when told that he was being traded to, of all people, the Chicago Cardinals.

"But about an hour later," Butler recalls with a smile, "I received a phone call from Bob Allen, a Charlotte businessman, who told me he was forming a professional football team in Charlotte, and they wanted me to play tailback. That really solved all my problems."

Bob Allen's Charlotte Clippers bought the Butlers a new home in the Plaza Hills section of Charlotte, plus a brand new '46 Fleetwood Cadillac. Butler was then hired as the public relations director for RKO Radio in Charlotte. He was also paid a healthy salary for playing football on Sundays. Things were indeed beginning to look up for the Butlers.

The Clippers became a part of the Dixie Professional Football League, along with Knoxville, Richmond, Norfolk, Bethlehem (Pa.) and several others.

"Gene McEvers, one of the all-time greats from Tennessee and then coaching at Davidson, became

Butler gave the Gamecocks all they could handle in this 0-0 tie in 1945. He had not been enrolled at Clemson for almost three years when this photo was taken. Frank Howard jokingly called him "the greatest non-student football player in the history of Clemson College."

our head coach," Butler says. "He was assisted by Zip Hannah of the Redskins, who later became chief of police in Gaffney."

The Clippers competed successfully with NFL teams for outstanding players from Southern colleges. "We had Barry Knots and Tommy "Jap" Davis from Duke, Russ Morrow from Tennessee, Arthur Bench and Dave Harris from Wake Forest. Really great guys."

He continues, "The news media and the fans were incredible. Furman Bisher of *The Charlotte News* kept us in the headlines, and the fans packed Memorial Stadium every Sunday."

The league lasted some five years (1947-51), then folded. "Charlotte didn't fold," Butler says, "the league did."

Butch thought of continuing his career in the NFL, but family considerations convinced him it was time to retire. Thus he accepted a position with the J. P. Stevens Co. in Palm Springs, California, where he remained until his retirement in 1989.

He and Rock then returned to Dothan, Alabama, the home of his children and grandchildren. They have been married now for 56 years.

"How time flies," Butch mused after looking back over his career. "It seems like only yesterday. . .only yesterday."

★

Cary Cox

He Served As Captain of Both The Carolina Gamecocks and the Clemson Tigers!

Cary Cox remains the only man on the face of this earth since the beginning of time ever to have served as team captain of both the Carolina Gamecocks and the Clemson Tigers. Only an event as huge as World War II could account for such an incredible twist of fate.

Cox remembers: It was October 21, 1943, Big Thursday in Columbia, and time for the annual Clemson-Carolina shootout that would launch him on the road to his unique niche in history.

Just a few happy months before, Cox had been the starting center for the Clemson Tigers. But on this day, however, through no fault of his own, he would be the starting center for the Carolina Gamecocks.

Cox, a native of Dawson, Georgia, a small community that played 6-man football, arrived at Clemson in the fall of '42 and immediately established himself as the starting center for Frank Howard's Tigers.

Today he dismisses the significance of his foot-

ball scholarship. "During the war years just about any warmblooded animal could get a football scholarship. Everybody else was in service."

In hopes of avoiding the draft until he finished his education, he enrolled in the Navy V-12 Program (a sort of Naval ROTC). Unfortunately for Cox (and Clemson) he was inducted in the summer of '43 and ordered to report immediately to the University of South Carolina, a V-12 training center. His training, as it turned out, also involved playing football for the Gamecocks.

Things went well for Cox at Carolina. He became their starting center and was perfectly happy, until the week before Big Thursday. Then the thought of playing against his alma mater and his former teammates threw him into a "moral dilemma."

Seeking a sympathetic listener, he visited the commander of the V-12 Program and told him of his problem. He quickly learned where he stood.

The commander, a red faced, harried indi-

Cary Cox, a former center for Clemson College, entered the Navy V-12 Program in 1942 and was assigned to USC for training. He was also ordered to go out for football and in '43 was elected game captain for the Carolina Gamecocks on Big Thursday.

Cox returned to Clemson in '46, won back his old center position, and in '47 was elected captain of the Clemson Tigers. To date, he is the only man on the face of this earth to have served as captain of both the Gamecocks and the Tigers.

Big Thursday 1943, a game won by Carolina 33-6. It was in this contest that Frank Howard ran out on the field and in front of 30,000 fans gave Cox a swift kick in the seat of the pants.

vidual with haggard features who had two ships shot out from under him in the North Atlantic, was in no mood to listen to schoolboy problems. He banged the table and proclaimed, "Cox, I won't promise that you'll get your commission if you play Thursday. But I can damned well promise that you sure as hell won't get it if you don't play. Now you got any more moral dilemmas you wanna talk about?"

"It's amazing what a little counseling can do to assuage a troubled conscience," laughs Cox. "So I called Coach Howard up at Clemson and told him I felt bad about playing against Clemson. But old Coach told me to do what I had to do, to go out there and play my heart out."

To deepen Cox's gloom, and assure him a place among the immortals of Carolina-Clemson football, his teammates elected him captain for the game.

As for the game itself, at one point the Carolina offense tried a trick play, lining up in such a way that Cox, at center, became an eligible receiver. Sure enough, Clemson was fooled and Cox caught a pass good for a 24-yard gain. As he was disentangling himself from the ensuing pileup, he felt someone give him a swift kick in the seat of the pants.

It was Frank Howard. "Son, I told you to play your heart out," he yelled, "but I didn't say nothing about catching no pass."

Today Cox shakes with laughter. "Can you believe that Frank Howard would run out on the field in front of 30,000 fans and kick an opposing player? But Coach Howard would do anything for a joke."

The Gamecocks went on that afternoon to take a 33-6 victory over the Tigers. In fact, Clemson did not complete a single pass in this contest, while managing only 8 yards on the ground. (In fact, this game remains Clemson's worst game ever offensively.) Cox's teammates awarded him the game ball following this contest, and today it remains one of his most treasured possessions.

He received his Naval commission not long after this memorable afternoon, then spent the rest of the war in the Pacific as captain of a landing craft. With the coming of peace, he returned to Clemson in '46. In '47 he was elected team captain of the Tigers.

He graduated in 1948, served as an assistant coach with the Tigers for several years, then became a successful investment broker.

Today he is president of the S & M Food Store chain (Starvin' Marvin convenience stores), and he and his family make their home in Atlanta.

★

Earl Wooten

Fans of Textile Ball Still Remember One Name:
Earl Wooten

It would be impossible to mention the names of all those major league baseball players who got their start right here in the South Carolina Textile Leagues back during the thirties, forties, and fifties. But among those fans who closely followed textile athletics there remains one fellow who is still a legend—the irrepressible Earl Wooten.

Wooten was born in 1924 in Pelzer, S. C., and despite his average size (5-10, 150 pounds) he excelled in all three major sports in high school and was offered several college scholarships. But young Wooten grew up during the Depression years and money was tight, too tight to even consider going away to college. Instead, he went to work in a local cotton mill. That mill, very fortunately, was a member of the Carolina Textile League, and Wooten signed on with their baseball team as an outfielder.

In addition to being an excellent hitter, Wooten was also noted for his speed and quickness, and he soon attracted the attention of Zinn Beck, a scout for the Washington Senators. Beck signed him to a contract in 1943, and Wooten was then assigned to the Chattanooga Lookouts of the AA Southern League. There he consistently hit over .300 and was considered a constant threat on the base paths.

"It was wonderful," Wooten remembers today, "for a poor boy from the Pelzer cotton mills. With the Lookouts we always wore coats and ties, traveled by train, stayed in the best hotels, and ate in the finest restaurants. For me, it was a whole new world."

He also loved to play basketball, and thus as soon as baseball season ended, it was right back home to Pelzer where he became a sharpshooting guard on the mill basketball team.

Textile basketball, by the way, was a major attraction back in those pre-TV days, and would be comparable to college basketball of today. In fact, most textile teams were composed of former college players, fellows who didn't make it in the pros for one reason or another.

Wooten recalls that on Pelzer's teams of the forties and fifties there were fellows like Doug

Earl Wooten, like numerous other Carolina athletes, got his start in textile baseball and basketball in the early-forties. In '48 he was called up by the Washington Senators.

Hoffman of Clemson, Jim Slaughter of USC, Jim Baker of Eastern Kentucky, and Truman Hill of Southern Illinois.

They played all the colleges in the state on a home-and-home basis, and were expected to win most of those contests, which they usually did.

In 1954 Wooten averaged a phenomenal 37 points per game, and one old timer who witnessed Pelzer's game that year with Furman University recalls: "I've never seen anything on the court like that Earl Wooten. Against Furman that year he matched

Frank Selvy point for point, and Selvy was an All-American and the leading college scorer in the nation. It's really too bad Earl couldn't have gone pro."

But back to baseball. In 1948 Wooten got that phone call he'd awaited for so long. It was the Washington Senators' home office. Wooten was to report immediately and take his place on the team. Today he still grins when he recalls his first glimpse of Griffith Stadium and his realization that he'd actually made the Big Leagues.

"It was a big jump from AA ball to the majors. But really I felt very confident that I could make it. I was never a power hitter, but I hit for average. And I knew I could handle a glove with anybody up there."

He hit .266 in '48, which was excellent considering Washington's weak lineup. In fact, they were known across the land that year as the "hapless Senators," with Mickey Vernon the only outstanding player on the roster. Thus Wooten almost always had to hit with no runners on base, which meant that the pitcher could concentrate solely on him. Never a comfortable situation.

As for his most memorable experience that year, Wooten says it would have to be the day he hit a homer off Freddie Hutchinson of the Detroit Tigers. "Heck," he laughs, "I didn't even hit home runs when I was in high school. So that homer off Hutchinson would have to go down as my most memorable experience. Certainly it was my most surprising experience."

He says that Ted Williams was by far the finest hitter he ever saw and that players all over the field would stop whatever they were doing to watch him take batting practice before a game. "He was truly awesome. He'd stand there and belt pitch after pitch out of that stadium."

Following the '48 baseball season Wooten returned home and, as always, immediately donned the basketball uniform of the Pelzer mill team. It was a move that would land him in hot water with the Washington Senators.

"You see," he explains, "the Senators pretty well demanded that I not play ball during the off-season because they wanted me to gain weight. So the next thing I know, I received an irate letter from the big brass saying they'd sold my contract to the Boston Braves."

The Braves then assigned Wooten to their AAA Atlanta Crackers club, where he would remain until 1955. That year he led the American Association in hitting with an .346 average. He was also chosen for the AAA All-Star team.

Still, the Braves did not call him up. So, after twelve years in organized baseball, he'd finally had enough. Thus he returned home and accepted employment with the J. P. Stevens Company in Pelzer where he would remain until his retirement in 1986.

Today he spends his time as a part-time Golf Pro at the Saluda Valley Country Club in Williamston where he and his wife Thelma make their home.

★

Doc Blanchard

He Remains The Only Native South Carolinian
Ever To Win The Heisman Trophy

After all those years, there he was, the hero of my youth, the indomitable Doc Blanchard. Had I not known better, I might have guessed that this big, slow-talking fellow with the easy laugh and the ready joke was a prosperous Low Country tobacco farmer. Or maybe a prominent politician.

He is, in fact, Colonel (Ret.) Felix A. "Doc" Blanchard, a former West Point All-American fullback, Heisman Trophy winner, Hollywood movie star, and a native of McColl, S.C.

Yes, Doc was born in 1924 on Tatum Avenue in McColl. His mother was from a prominent family in that area, while his father, a native of Louisiana, was a physician in town (and thus Doc's nickname.)

When he was just a child, Doc's family moved to Bishopville, where his father established both a farm and a medical practice. Then came the Depression and the hated boll weevil. Cotton vanished from the land and money became scarce. Again the Blanchards moved. This time to Louisiana, where Doc finished high school in 1941.

He had proven himself an excellent athlete and was offered a football scholarship to UNC. He eagerly accepted. Why UNC? Doc explains:

"Ah, I was a big kid and pretty brash. I was seventeen and already stood six-two and weighed two-twenty. Plus Jim Tatum was coaching there, and Jim and I were first cousins. Jim was also from McColl, you know."

As for his freshman year at UNC, he says: "I did fine in football, but I really wasn't that academic. In fact, I was worried about remaining eligible for football."

But Doc needn't have worried. In December of

The legendary Coach Red Blaik with his two star running backs, Doc Blanchard and Glenn Davis. They were called Mr. Inside and Mr. Outside, and after fifty years they remain the most famous running duo in the history of American football.

Doc Blanchard shows the form that won him the Heisman Trophy as he glides effortlessly past a bevy of Michigan Wolverines in 1945.

'41 the war broke out, and like most other young men of his era Doc suddenly found himself in the uniform of an Army private. "Yeah, I spent about a year loafing around one Army camp after another, really not doing much of anything."

Then he recieved an opportunity that would change the course of his entire life. He was offered a scholarship to West Point.

"I really wasn't that enthusiastic about all that hotshot military stuff," Doc grins, "but when I considered the alternative, it seemed like a pretty good thing. So I spent several months preparing myself, passed the entrance exams, and became a cadet."

Doc entered the Point in '43. And the rest, as they say, is football history.

Those were the glory years of West Point football, the war years, when so many of America's finest young athletes (most of whom had been stars at other institutions only a year before) were selected to play at the military academies.

With the peerless Coach Red Blaik at the helm, West Point legends became a dime a dozen. And foremost among those legends was this South Carolina farm boy, Doc Blanchard.

Was he concerned about making that fabulous '43 Army team? He looks you straight in the eye (he

always looks you straight in the eye) and says quietly: "No, I wasn't worried about making Army's team. Hell, I could've made any team in the country, and I knew it."

It doesn't come across as a boast but as a simple statement of fact. Or as Dizzy Dean once put it, in his own primordial words, "If you can do it, that ain't bragging."

And Doc could do it. He was a bullish fulllback who ran with the speed of a scatback, a true phenomenon of his era. He could do it all.

His running mate was the fleet Glenn Davis. Together they struck fear into the hearts of all opponents, and soon they became known as Mr. Inside and Mr. Outside, still the most famous running duo in the history of football.

For three years (1944-46) Army went undefeated against the best teams in the country, one of the longest win streaks on record.

Doc says: "My most memorable games, and my best games, too, I guess, were against Navy. Because Navy was the team we most wanted to beat, and the team that always came closest to beating us."

In both 1944 and '45 Doc was named to the All-American team. In fact, in '45 he won almost every major national award given for gridiron excellence. Every one, that is, except for the one most coveted, the Heisman Trophy. That year it went to Glenn Davis. No one applauded more heartily than Doc Blanchard.

Doc won it in 1946.

In 1947, following Army's third consecutive undefeated season, Hollywood came calling. The big money boys had decided that here was a situation that had it all—drama, suspense, the thrilling success story of Blanchard and Davis, and how they had led Army to three undefeated seasons while landing two Heisman Trophies for themselves in the bargain. The movie would be called "Mr. Inside and Mr. Outside" and would actually star Blanchard and Davis playing themselves. Gable and Cooper, the moguls reasoned, would not be better draws at the box office.

Blanchard and Davis were subsequently taken to Hollywood and given a crash course in dramatics. "Or at least they had us sit around reading our lines to a drama coach." After a week the coach threw up his hands in frustration, the director shrugged and said Let's roll 'em, and production began.

Doc chortles at some of the dialogue they had to work with. "It was pretty corny," he says, "not the sort of things we said in real life. " For example, the night before the big '46 Army-Navy game, a worried Glenn Davis is pacing the floor while Doc is silently lying on his bunk staring at the ceiling.

Davis: *Well, Doc, how do you think we'll do against Navy tomorrow?*

Blanchard: *Well, Glenn, Navy is a fine institution, and they have an excellent football team. We will have to play our best game ever just to have a chance against them.*

Despite such immortal lines, Doc and Glenn turned in creditable performances. Plus, for the football buff the MovieTone Newsreel clips of Army's games against the most powerful teams in the country make this movie well worth watching.

Doc says that making the movie was fun, but he had no illusions about becoming an actor. Indeed, from the moment he entered West Point in '43 he has had but one goal in life—to serve his country.

During his military career in the Air Force he served coaching stints at both West Point and the Air Force Academy. He loves football, he says, and he found working with these young men "spiritually rewarding." Yet he refused many lucrative head coaching offers. Always, throughout both the Korean Conflict and the Viet Nam War, Doc was true to his first obligation, the service of his country.

He retired from the Air Force after twenty-five years in 1972. Today he and his wife Jody King Blanchard make their home in San Antonio, Texas, where Doc is an avid golfer and an even more avid fan of his granddaughter Mary Ellen. She is the daughter of Doc's son Tony (he was once a starting end for UNC), and a member of the U. S. Swim Team. Already she holds two American swim records.

But Doc Blanchard has truly done it all. Early in life he became aware of West Point's motto: Duty, Honor, Country, and he has lived his life accordingly. For many of us who grew up in that era, he seemed to personify the very best that America had to offer. Somehow, after the passage of half a century, he still does.

★
Cally Gault

He Helped Build A Half Century of Athletics in South Carolina

Cally Gault, a member of the South Carolina Athletic Hall of Fame, devoted almost fifty years of his life to his beloved alma mater, Presbyterian College.

He retired as athletic director at Presbyterian College four years ago. But for over fifty years Cally Gault functioned as a football player, coach, and athletic director on his way to becoming a major influence on athletics in South Carolina.

Born in 1928, he's the son of Marvin Gault, a star athlete himself at Erskine College and a member of the Erskine College Athletic Hall of Fame.

Young Cally began his own athletic career at the age of fourteen at Greenville High School under coaches Speedy Speer and Slick Moore.

Then in 1944 it was on to Presbyterian College, where he played quarterback under coaching legend Lonnie McMillan. "I have to laugh about it now," he says, "but I was one of those wartime athletes. I was only sixteen at the time. In fact, the whole team was composed of boys too young for the service and a few 4-Fs."

Gault remembers that Coach McMillan and his Blue Hose pulled off one of the major upsets of the century when they defeated the mighty Clemson Tigers 14-13 in 1943. "But then Clemson got their revenge two years later. It was our opening game of the '45 season, and the temperature was about 93-degrees. We were wearing our blue wool jerseys and long wool socks, and of course we had to play the full sixty minutes back in those days. We almost died."

The final score, by the way, was 76-0, Clemson's favor, and the worst defeat in history for PC.

But Gault is an optimist. Of that drubbing, he says, "We learned a valuable lesson that afternoon. Coach Mac said we should never fear anything again for the rest of our lives. If we could cross Death Valley the way we had that afternoon, and do so without a single fatality, then we were pretty good men."

Gault says that the news media picked up on Coach MacMillan's reference to Death Valley, and Clemson's stadium has been known by that name ever since.

Gault remembers that there was a beautiful girl named Joy Godfrey whose family lived right across the road from his dorm. Every day he'd watch from his window as she rode her horse up and down the road. He dreamed of meeting her.

Years later, as fate would have it, he took his first coaching job. Soon afterward, just by accident, he met Joy Godfrey. Then they were married.

Which is a good example of how Gault works.

In 1953 he became head coach at North Augusta High School and went on to compile one of the best winning records in the state. Indeed, in 1955 his team began a 42-game winning streak that wasn't broken until late in 1958, the year North Augusta beat Lancaster for the state title.

In 1963 he was offered the head coaching and athletic director jobs at his old alma mater, Presbyterian College. He agonized over his decision.

"I talked it over with Joy, and I even prayed about it. One night, sure enough, I was awakened by a voice telling me to go to PC. I just knew it was the Lord speaking to me.

"Later on, after I found out about all the problems up here, I decided maybe it wasn't the Lord speaking after all. Maybe it was Joy whispering in my ear. She's from Clinton, you know."

Most of the problems he encountered, he says, were attitude problems. He says that his players asked him not to mention to their professors that they were on the football team because there was so many negative feelings towards the football program.

"So I made it a point to visit every faculty member, and I told them that if football was not an asset to the college, if it were not a part of the overall educational process, then I'd be the first to suggest dropping it. In other words, it was my job to change attitudes."

Later, during the '63 season in a game against a strong East Carolina team, there occurred his most memorable coaching experience.

"It was just before halftime, the score was tied, and the Pirates had a first down at our three. Well, they tried to punch it across four times, but our boys held. Then the half ended.

"As our boys ran off the field, the fans went wild. They were jumping up and down and gave us a standing ovation. Many of them followed us off the field and down through the tunnel to the dressing room.

"I knew then that the old PC spirit was not dead."

Gault said that PC eventually lost that game, but he knew the football program had won back its self-respect. "It's been great up here ever since."

In 1984 Gault gave up his coaching position to devote more time to his duties as athletic director. "It's not like the old days," he says. "Being athletic director now means you stay busy. Besides, I'd reached the point where I no longer found our victories as thrilling nor our losses as devastating as in the past. So it was time to let a younger fellow take over."

Since 1963 the Gaults have made their home in Clinton. They have three children, a son (now deceased) and two daughters. Plus four grandchildren.

After half a century, Cally Gault was recently inducted into the South Carolina Athletic Hall of Fame.

★

Bryant Meeks

He Served As Captain of Carolina's First Great Bowl Team

Bryant Meeks served as captain of the 1945 Gamecocks, and like many players of that era of college football, he has a great sense of humor and can rattle off one amusing anecdote after another. One such story concerns his nickname. Some called him Junior, while to others he will always be simply Meatball.

"Life on the gridiron back in those days wasn't nearly as regimented or formal as it is today," he observes. "Back then, football was played for fun, and we kidded around a lot. Most players even had descriptive nicknames. I remember you met a lot of Bulldogs back in those days."

As for Junior, he explains: "My father was also named Bryant Meeks, so I was always Junior at home and to my friends. But later, when I was a senior at Macon High School down in Georgia, our basketball coach was scrimmaging with us one day, and I went up high for a rebound. When I came down my elbow caught him right on top of his bald head.

"I laughed and said, 'Watch out, Shorty, you can get hurt in this game.' So he gave me a poke in my belly and said if I didn't watch my weight they were going to start calling me Meatball. So that's the inspirational story of how I became Meatball Meeks."

At 6-1 and 195 pounds, Meeks initially enrolled at the University of Georgia and became the starting center for Wally Butts' Bulldogs in '42. But then, with the war in full swing, he signed up for the Naval V-12 Program. Sure enough, he was drafted, spent two years on active duty, then was assigned to USC for officers training. He also went out for football and in 1945 became the starting center for the Carolina Gamecocks.

Carolina's longtime head coach, Rex Enright, was still on active duty with the Navy in '45, serving as athletic director at the Jacksonville Naval Air Station, and in his place stood interim head coach Johnny McMillan, who would later go on to a successful coaching career at Erskine, Presbyterian College, and The Citadel.

McMillan guided the '45 Gamecocks to a 2-4-3 season, which really wasn't that bad, considering all the negative factors that existed during the war years.

Bryant Meeks was named All-Southern and won the Jacobs Blocking Trophy in '45. He is a member of the USC Athletic Hall of Fame.

What is incredible is the fact that the 2-4-3 Gamecocks received not one bowl bid that year but TWO. One came from city fathers in Jacksonville. They were starting a new bowl game and planned to call it the Gator Bowl. The other came from city fathers in Columbia and they wanted USC to play

Carolina captain Bryant Meeks meets his Wake Forest counterpart for the coin toss in the 1946 Gator Bowl, a game won by the Deacons 27-14. Meeks later signed with the Pittsburgh Steelers and remains the smallest linebacker ever to play pro football.

host in a new bowl game they planned to call the Tobacco Bowl.

Yep. The Tobacco Bowl. Columbia city fathers, it seems, dreamed up this idea in '45, hoping to match the champion of South Carolina against a suitable out-of-state opponent. Thus they invited USC. Subsequently, unfortunately, USC decided to accept the bowl bid to the Gator Bowl, and since it was then too late to find an alternate state champion, city fathers announced that the inaugural Tobacco Bowl would be postponed until 1946. (To date, nothing further has been heard from our city fathers, though it still sounds like a good idea.)

Many sports observers were frankly puzzled as to how the '45 Gamecocks might have received an invitation to the Gator Bowl or anywhere else. But rumor had it that Rex Enright, now a power in Jacksonville, had used his influence with the Gator Bowl Committee to finagle a bid for his beloved Gamecocks. Lacking a better explanation, this one sounds as good as any.

Earlier in the season, on Thanksgiving Day, Carolina had managed to hold a good Wake Forest team to a 13-13 tie, and so now the Gator Bowl folks were convinced that a re-match would be a natural. Such a game would, they hoped, draw numerous fans to their inaugural Gator Bowl game, perhaps even thousands.

As it turned out, Carolina played a respectable game, even holding a 7-6 half time lead. But in the end the Deacons were too much and walked away with a 27-14 victory. It might be noted, by the way, that Carolina's celebrated halfback, Dutch Brembs, set an all-time Gator Bowl record that afternoon, one that has survived now for over half a century, when he intercepted a Deacon pass and returned it 90 yards for a touchdown.

At season's end, Meeks' outstanding play was recognized when he was named to the All-Southern Football Team.

"Oh sure, I still have great memories of that game," he says. "In fact, I still have the silver dollar we tossed to see who'd win the kickoff prior to the game. But honestly, I think my most vivid memory concerns our Big Thursday game of 1946."

That was the day when some enterprising counterfeiters sold 10,000 bogus tickets to Carolina and Clemson fans all over the nation. When the stands were filled that day, the gates were closed. Which was fine—except for the 10,000 furious fans milling around outside the stadium. At that point, they stormed the gates and swarmed into the stadium like killer bees. They filled every inch of the stands and stood five-deep around the playing field.

"It was so bad," says Meeks, "that they spilled out onto the playing field. Every time either team

Dutch Brembs set an all-time Gator Bowl record when he returned this Deacon pass 90 yards for a touchdown in 1946.

In 1946 10,000 counterfeit tickets were sold to the Carolina-Clemson football game. Irate fans stormed the gates, then filled every inch of space in the stadium (including the playing field).

would want to punt, the police would have to clear the fans off the opposite end of the field. Otherwise, the safety man would have gotten lost in the crowd."

After an outstanding career at Carolina, Meeks took his degree in physical education in '47, then played pro ball for the next two years with the Pittsburgh Steelers. He was the smallest linebacker ever to play professional football.

"I retired after the '48 season, and with good reason. In our final game of the year, versus the Philadelphia Eagles, a guy named Kilroy gave me a shot in the mouth with his elbow and knocked out five of my teeth. I came home and promised my wife I'd never play again, and I didn't."

He coached at Sarasota (Fla.) High School for five years, then went into the petroleum business, managing nearly two hundred LP gas stations around the country.

In 1981, wishing to go into business for himself, he purchased five businesses in Sarasota and continues to manage those today.

He has been married to the former Jacqueline Fay Griffis for forty-seven years now, and they have a son, a daughter and two grandchildren.

★
Ray Clanton

Clemson Became His Real Life O. K. Corral

Maybe you remember that notorious gang known as the Clanton boys, those bank robbing cowpokes who got done in so handily by Sheriff Wyatt Earp in that old Hollywood movie, *Gunfight At O.K. Corral.*

Well, Ray Clanton, though no relation to that Western branch of the Clanton clan, was once described by a badly bruised South Carolina player as "…the meanest doggone son of a gun I ever saw. They oughtta lock that boy up."

But that was way back in 1948 when big Ray Clanton was considered one of the finest guards ever to play for the Clemson Tigers. And lucky for us he was not "locked up," for today he comes across (having obviously been rehabilitated) as a congenial, soft spoken gentleman who harbors nothing but the warmest memories of his long-ago gridiron adversaries.

Born in 1927, he attended Darlington's St. Johns High School where he was an all-around great athlete. At 6-2 and 200 pounds, he was a shoo-in at fullback for the Shrine Bowl game, and had numerous scholarship offers. He chose Clemson over all the others.

"I really liked Coach Frank Howard," he recalls. "He was a small town sort of fellow and always gave it to you straight. Plus I loved the town of Clemson. In fact, if Darlington should vanish off the face of the earth, there's no place I'd rather live than Clemson."

There was one other factor in his decision to don the purple and orange. "You know, I'd forgotten this until you asked the question, but we had a teacher at St. Johns, a Miss Aggie Rigsby. She was engaged to Clemson's great All-American tailback Banks McFadden, and every time Miss Rigsby would see me she'd tell me all about what a wonderful school Clemson was. She really influenced my going there."

(Note: Miss Aggie Rigsby and Banks McFadden recently celebrated their golden wedding anniversary.)

"But when I entered Clemson in the fall of '45, the war had just ended, and we had some of the

Ray Clanton was the starting guard for Clemson during their great undefeated '48 season. In later years Frank Howard would name him to his all-time Clemson Dream Team. Today Clanton owns Clanton Auto Auction in Darlington.

oldest, meanest looking fellows you ever saw, those old war veterans, come out for the team that year. They were fellows who had enrolled there before the war, then went in service and fought through the war and were now back to complete their educations. I think Bobby Gage and I were about the only two kids on the whole team."

It might be noted, by the way, that Frank Howard was famous for recruiting high school fullbacks, then converting them to pulling guards once they reached Clemson. They were big and fast and could lead the blocking on those end sweeps that Clemson became so famous for back during their single-wing days.

Clanton became a starter at left guard his junior year in 1947. But it is the year 1948 that still stands out in his memory. That was the year that Clemson ran undefeated through ten regular season opponents before upsetting a good Missouri team in the Gator Bowl. And little wonder, considering their magnificent lineup in '48.

From end to end, their line featured such stalwarts as John Poulos, Tom Salisbury, Ray Clanton, Gene Moore, Frank Gillespie, Phil Prince and Oscar Thompson.

And in their backfield there was Bobby Gage, Fred Cone, Ray Mathews, and Bob Martin.

(Let us pause for a moment of silence here while the Tiger faithful try to regain their composure.)

Indeed, many who are knowledgeable about such things still consider the '48 Tiger team to be perhaps their most outstanding in history, not excepting even their great national championship team of '81. Gage, Cone, and Mathews, for example, would all become consensus All-Americans and then go on to great pro careers.

As for Clanton and Gillespie (he was All-Southern in all three major sports), both would later enjoy the distinction of being named to Frank Howard's All-Time Dream Team (1931-69).

Still, going undefeated in '48 was not a simple matter, says Clanton. "Our win streak almost ended at one that year, thanks to NC State. We were tied 0-0 with only two minutes remaining, and it looked as though that's how it would end. But then Bobby Gage took a State punt at our 10-yard line and ran it back 90 yards for a touchdown, and we got by 6-0."

Clanton also remembers a tough Auburn team that year. "We played down in Alabama, and it had been raining torrents for the past 24 hours. By game time the field was a virtual quagmire. They took a 6-0 lead early in the game, and it looked as though that's the way it was going to wind up. Neither team could move the ball.

"Then with only moments left in the final quarter, we faced a fourth down at the Auburn five, and we knew it was do or die for us at that point. Bobby Gage switched positions with Ray Mathews on the next play, a sweep right, because Gage was a twinkle-toes type runner while Mathews was real heavy footed. And it worked. Mathews slogged his way through that mud and bulled his way into the end zone. We won 7-6."

And who was leading the blocking on that sweep? Well, let's count 'em. There was Thompson, Clanton, Gillespie, Gage, Cone and Bobby Martin. To Auburn it must have looked like the entire Clemson student body was coming around that end.

Clanton took his degree in history from Clemson in '49, then returned home to Darlington to oversee his father's business, Clanton's Auto Auction Sales, which for many years now has been famous with car dealers throughout the Southeast.

"In fact," he says, "my father started this business in 1943, so we've been here now for over fifty years. We're now one of the ten largest auto auction dealers in America, and of course being next door to the Darlington International Raceway gives us a lot of publicity."

Ray married his high school sweetheart, the former Mary McFadden, and they have two sons and four grandchildren. They make their home in Darlington.

★
Billy Poe

This Great Tailback Still Holds A Clemson Rushing Record

Billy Poe was one of those exceptionally talented young athletes who came along just as the world exploded in war. At Greenville High School he had excelled in football and track and graduated in June of '41, just six months before the Japanese bombed Pearl Harbor.

In September of that year he enrolled at Georgia Tech with visions of becoming the Wrecks' starting tailback for the next four years. But after a week in Atlanta he began to experience those debilitating homesick blues so common to incoming freshmen.

"I'd been there for just a few days when several friends from Greenville stopped by," he says. "We sat around in my room and talked for a while, then they finally said they had to be getting back home. I remember them standing up to leave and me walking them to the door. Then, out of the blue, I said, 'Hold it, fellows. Let me grab my suitcase. I'm going with you.'

"So I packed my bags and said goodbye to Georgia Tech. That was on Friday. On Monday I enrolled at Clemson where I had friends and could go home whenever I felt like it."

Poe had scholarship offers from Tech, Furman, and USC. But at 6-2 and 150 pounds he was considered just too small to fit in with Coach Frank Howard's brand of hardnosed football. But when he walked into Howard's office that Monday afternoon, Howard told him a scholarship was waiting if he still wanted to play for the Tigers.

I played freshman ball in '41," Poe says. "Then they red-shirted me in '42. In fact, I still remember that '42 season and us leaving old Riggs Field to play our first game at Clemson Memorial Stadium. We beat Presbyterian College that day in front of about 5,500 fans. Students, I recall, were charged a quarter, Boy Scouts in uniform were let in for free."

In '43 Uncle Sam informed Poe that the U. S. Army had another scholarship awaiting him. So for the next eleven months he spent his time pulling KP and guard duty at a military base in Alabama. Then, for reasons that still remain unclear to Poe, the Army suddenly notified him that he was to receive a medical discharge because of a bad knee.

Billy Poe (called "Tweetie" by his teammates) played tailback for Clemson back during those tumultuous war years.

"You bet I was happy," he says laughing. "I was as patriotic as the next fellow. But anybody who tells you he wasn't happy to be discharged during World War II, well, he simply isn't telling the truth."

Oddly enough, he says, he arrived home the very Saturday that Clemson was playing Georgia Pre-Flight (a service team) at a site in Greenville. So Poe decided to take in the game.

"I went by to see Coach Howard after the game, and he did everything he could to persuade me to suit up the next week and play against Georgia Tech. So there I was, I hadn't been enrolled in school for almost a year, totally out of shape, but Coach Howard really wanted me to play.

"I said, 'Coach, I got a medical discharge, but that doesn't mean there's anything wrong with my head. I'd have to be crazy to get out there next week.'"

Poe played college ball back when nicknames

Here Poe skirts end in Clemson's 0-0 tie with Carolina in '45. He averaged an amazing 7.2 yards per carry that season, still an all-time Clemson record.

were common on most teams. At Clemson, for example, there was Mavis "Bull" Cagle, Marion "Butch" Butler, Bobby "School Boy" Gage, Tom "Black Cat" Barton, and Wyndie "Dumb Dumb" Wyndham. As for Poe, his teammates were surprised to hear a fellow of his size with such a soft spoken voice and immediately dubbed him "Tweetie Bird" or simply "Tweetie."

Today Poe grins at the memory. "Really, I think if you asked any of my old teammates about Billy Poe, they wouldn't know who you were talking about. But football is a tough sport, and the nickname thing just demonstrates the easy comradeship that existed among members of the team, and brought us closer together.

"But the nickname was sort of an inside joke. I'm sure Wyndham might have been offended if an outsider had called him Dumb Dumb, but it was fine coming from Coach Howard or his teammates."

Led by Poe, Ralph Jenkins, Bull Cagle, Jim Reynolds, Alton Cumbie and Butch Butler, the '45 Tigers posted a respectable 6-3-1 record and were ranked 18th nationally by the Associated Press.

Among their triumphs that year was an amazing 47-20 win over national power Tulane, a game in which Poe (now playing at a more respectable 190 pounds) scored three touchdowns. But most of all,

he still remembers the Tigers' 0-0 tie with Carolina on Big Thursday that year.

"Coach Howard was really put out that we didn't win that game. So on Friday, the day after the game, a day we normally would have had off, guess where we were. Yep. Coach Howard had us out on that practice field for a full scale scrimmage. We practiced from three o'clock that afternoon until nine that evening. It was a while before any of us wanted to see a football again."

In 1945 Poe averaged an incredible 7.2 yards per carry. For understandable reasons, this is a Clemson record that has now stood the test of time for half a century. In fact, no other Clemson runningback has ever even approached this record.

In fact, Poe was so successful in '45 (his junior year) that he was drafted by the Chicago Bears. "But I told them that I hadn't even finished college yet. They said that was no problem, that they'd send me to the University of Chicago. But really I just didn't want to go to Chicago. Besides, my knees were too bummed up to be playing pro football."

Today, after taking his degree in textile engineering in '46, Poe is a stockbroker with Payne-Webber in Greenville. And he says he had no plans to retire, but is just getting his second wind in the business world.

★
Lou Brissie

This War Hero Went On To Become One Of America's Greatest Major League Pitchers

It was 1944, and he was only 19 years old, a young American soldier fighting in Italy, when he was hit by an enemy artillery round.

He awakened days later in a field hospital, his body riddled with shrapnel, the bones in both feet and his left leg shattered. The doctors said they'd have no choice but to amputate.

He wept and pleaded, and at last the doctors relented. Still, they said, he'd never walk again.

He was Cpl. Leland Victor Brissie, who would later become known throughout the baseball world as Lou Brissie, southpaw pitching ace for the Philadelphia A's and the Cleveland Indians.

Born in 1924 in Ware Shoals, Lou broke into organized baseball when he was only 14, pitching for the Ware Shoals Regals of the old Central Carolina Textile League, a circuit composed mainly of college and former professional players.

Which was pretty heady company for a young teenager. But Brissie already stood 6-3 and had developed a blazing fastball. Three years later, in 1941, Chick Galloway, coach of the Presbyterian College Blue Hose and a scout for the A's, escorted him to Philadelphia to meet with the legendary Connie Mack.

"Coach Mack felt I needed a year or two of seasoning, and advised me to enroll at PC, where Coach Galloway could sort of bring me along," recalls Brissie. "That was fine with me. I was only seventeen and really wasn't ready to get too far from home."

Brissie pitched for the Blue Hose until 1943, when he was drafted and sent to Italy. There he received the wounds that should have ended his career.

But he refused to give up. From his hospital bed he wrote Galloway: "I'll play again, but it will be quite awhile. If God lets me walk again, I'll play. That's my ambition. I'll be OK in time."

In 1946, after two years in the hospital and 23 operations, with his left leg now 5 inches shorter than his right, forced to wear a metal brace, Brissie at last was back on his feet. It was then that he received a letter from Connie Mack telling him that if he still wanted to play baseball to report to Savannah of the South Atlantic League for spring training.

Lou's answer was obvious. He threw his cane into the nearest trash can.

It was incredible just to watch him walk to the mound under his own power. More incredible, he won 23 games for Savannah in '46 and struck out 278

Here Lou Brissie (top row, center) poses with his PC Blue Hose teammates in '42.

batters, both figures representing all-time Sally League records.

As a reward for his amazing performance, the A's brought him up to pitch the final game of the '47 season against the league champion New York Yankees. Brissie remembers that night this way:

"It was Babe Ruth Day, and the Yankees had brought back all those great old timers from the Ruth era in honor of the Babe. There was Ty Cobb, Honus Wagner, Tris Speaker and of course Babe Ruth himself.

"So there were all those great legends I'd heard about all my life sitting there in the Yankee dugout, which was quite an audience for my first start in major league baseball."

Brissie pitched a respectable game that evening, though the A's lost 5-2. Following the game, in fact, Connie Mack stated to the press: "Lou Brissie is potentially a greater pitcher than Lefty Grove."

Lou opened the '48 season for the A's against the Boston Red Sox and the great Ted Williams. He scattered four hits in that contest (Williams went hitless) and won the game 10-1. That game, he says, still remains one of his greatest thrills, that along with winning a pitching dual later in the season against the great Bob Feller.

Lou won 16 games in '48 and was named to the Rookie All-Star team. And the American Sports Writers Association named him America's Most Courageous Athlete.

Still, pain was his constant companion, and in the late innings the fans would become hushed as they watched him limp about the mound, pushing off with that shattered left leg, his face contorted with pain. They knew they were watching a symbol of man's indomitable will to win against all odds, a monument to faith, courage and determination.

In '49 he was named to the American League All-Star team. Then in '51 he was traded to the Cleveland Indians and played for manager Al Lopez. On the mound with him in Cleveland were such baseball immortals as Bob Lemon and Bob Feller. For the next three years he would again be named to the American League All-Star team.

Brissie also enjoyed a phenomenal career batting average of .260, despite his obvious difficulties in running the bases.

He retired from baseball in '54 and became the National Commissioner for American Legion Baseball. To promote the game, he once toured South America with a team of American Legion All-Stars, and later, representing the International Education Commission, he visited Australia, where he introduced baseball to the Australian public schools.

In 1948 Brissie won 16 games for the Philidelphia A's and was named to the Rookie All-Star Team. Also that year the AP named him America's Most Courageous Athlete.

Entertainment moguls from MGM offered him a fat contract to let them make a movie of his life, but Brissie refused.

"I just couldn't do it," he says. "I felt guilty about capitalizing on my war wounds when there were so many others who were hit just as bad or worse and hadn't made a cent from it."

He remembers Ted Williams and Joe DiMaggio as the two greatest players he was ever associated with. And thinking back to his days at PC, he says: "I honestly can't think of an institution that's been more fortunate in its choice of people to lead its athletic programs than PC. They've always had quality people up there, including their former athletic director, Cally Gault."

Brissie recently retired from the S. C. Board of Technical Education, and today he is writing his memoirs. He and his family make their home in North Augusta.

In 1974 he was inducted into the S. C. Athletic Hall of Fame.

★

Bobby Gage

Clemson's All-Time Mr. Football

If there was a Most Versatile Award for Clemson University football, it would doubtlessly have to go to old no. 77, tailback Bobby Gage.

Gage played from 1945-48 and led Clemson to their finest season ever, an 11-0 mark in '48, that included a 24-23 upset win over Missouri in the Gator Bowl.

Incredibly, after the elapse of some fifty years, his name is still right up there at the top of most offensive statistics in the Clemson Record Book. During his career with the Tigers, for example, running out of the old single-wing formation, Gage completed 123 of 278 passes for 2,448 yards, a school record 8.8 yards per attempt. Indeed, even today he still ranks as Clemson's third all-time most efficient passer, trailing only Mark Fellers and Mike Eppley.

Note also: against Auburn in '47 he threw four touchdown passes and collected 374 yards in total offense. Both figures still represent all-time Clemson records.

In addition to his passing proficiency, he led the Tigers in rushing yardage in both '46 and '47, and his 3,757 yards in total offense remains fourth in the Record Book behind only Steve Fuller, Rodney Williams, and Homer Jordan.

He also had 491 yards in kickoff returns and 469 yards in punt returns. In his spare time, so to speak, he punted 89 times, averaging 38.1 yards per kick. Not a bad overall performance.

Incredibly enough, despite his impressive offensive credentials, Gage was actually considered better on defense than on offense. He intercepted ten passes and in 1948 was named to the Associated Press All-American Team as a safety.

A product of Boys High in Anderson, Gage played in the Shrine Bowl of 1944 and attracted the attention of Clemson's Coach Frank Howard. Howard recalled the clever way he recruited Gage:

"I couldn't wait for the game to end, so I could recruit that boy for Clemson. So after it was over I went down to the dressing room and told old Gage that we'd sure like to have him up at Clemson. Well, he just looked at me and said, 'Coach, my uncle's a math professor at Clemson, and my parents have planned to send me there all my life. In fact, they've

Bobby Gage, a product of Boys High in Anderson, is still remembered as one of the finest football players in the history of Clemson University, a true All American.

already paid my tuition so I can enter next fall.' Later, after old Gage became the best tailback in America, I told 'em, I says, Yeah, it took some real smart recruiting efforts on my part to get that boy up to Clemson."

Gage remembers trotting onto the practice field for the first time back in August of '45 and finding himself surrounded by dozens of the hardest looking fellows he'd ever seen.

"The war had just ended, and those fellows were all old war veterans," he says. "They'd fought through the war, and most of them looked like they were in their late-twenties. I, on the other hand, only shaved about once a week back then. They were really some pretty tough looking fellows."

Because of his obvious youth, he was immediately dubbed School Boy Gage, a name that stuck. "Yeah, he was just a kid," Coach Howard remembers, "but he was the best tailback in America."

Gage stretches for a touchdown in Clemson's 13-7 win over USC in 1948. Incredibly versatile, not only was he one of the finest offensive players in America, but on defense he intercepted ten passes and was named to the Associated Press All-American Defensive Team.

In 1946 he broke in as Clemson's starting tailback. In his first game, versus Presbyterian College, he dashed 88 yards for a TD the first time he carried the ball. In the next game, against Duquesne, he returned the opening kickoff 89 yards for a touchdown.

But the real big year for Gage and the Tigers was 1948. "That '48 team was no fluke," he says. "That was something Coach Howard had been planning since 1945. But in '48 it all came together. In the backfield we had Fred Cone, Bob Martin and Ray Mathews. And in the line we had John Poulos, Ray Clanton, Gene Moore, Frank Gillespie, Tom Salisbury, Phil Prince, and Oscar Thompson. They were a great bunch of guys."

That season Clemson blanked five opponents, yet won five games by a touchdown or less. Against NC State, for example, Gage returned a punt 90 yards for a touchdown with two minutes to play to win 6-0 and keep Clemson's win streak alive. When reminded of this spectacular play, Gage, who personifies modesty, replied: "It was really nothing. With all my great teammates out in front of me leading the blocking, anyone could have done it. All I had to do was follow their blocks.

"But that '48 season really set the stage for Clemson," Gage says. "Nothing succeeds like success, and over the next ten years Clemson won a lot of football games and played in five bowls.

"But mainly I credit our success to Frank Howard. People don't realize what a shrewd man he really is. Every move he made was done with an eye to the future. He used to let Boy Scouts in the game for free because he knew that some day those boys would grow up to be loyal IPTAY men. He had what they call vision."

Following his graduation in 1949 Gage was chosen in the first round of the pro draft by the Pittsburgh Steelers, where he played for the next two years.

"That was before television and the money just wasn't there," he explains.

Today he is retired from Chemiturgy Products in Greenville, where he and his family have made their home for the past forty-five years.

In 1976 he was inducted into the Clemson Athletic Hall of Fame.

★
Frank Gillespie

He Remains The Only Clemson Athlete
Ever Named All-Conference In Three Major Sports

"To put it bluntly," chortles Clemson's Coach Frank Howard, "that boy'd give Horace Greeley himself an inferiority complex."

Howard was speaking of Frank Gillespie, one of the most successful athletes ever to enroll at Clemson University. Gillespie was a star lineman under Howard from 1946-48, but his incredible story actually began years earlier.

"My father owned forty acres and a mule in Tam, West Virginia," Gillespie says. "That's where I was born back in 1924, but then a big mining company came in, and we were forced to sell out and move a few miles away to Beckley. My father went to work in the mines then, and I started to school."

By the age of fifteen Gillespie began spending his summers working in the mines. He enrolled at Mark Twain High School, where he excelled in athletics. His senior year, in 1942, he was named to the All-State football team.

"I had some scholarship offers from several schools, but my dad liked the way Frank Howard talked," Gillespie says. "Old Coach never pulled any punches. He always gave it to you straight. He was the sort of fellow who could get along real well with coal miners."

During a recent interview, Frank Howard's face brightened at the mention of Gillespie: "I wrote him a letter and told him to come on down to Clemson, and I'd give him a tryout. Well, he came. So I put on some pads, and he put on some pads. Then we went out on the field, and I got down like a lineman, you know, and told Gillespie to try to knock me out of the hole. Well, that boy knocked me winding.

"It took me a minute to clear my head, then I says, 'Okay, Buddy, that's enough. Let's go in and get all those papers signed.'

"He says, 'I thought you said you was gonna give me a tryout.'

"I says, 'Hell, you already did.'

"You see, I weighed about 230 back then, and I figured anybody who could knock me around like that was good enough to play for Clemson. My backbone liked to have killed me for a week."

A 1948 sports cartoon advertising Gillespie's prowess as both a student and an athlete.

Gillespie's initial stay at Clemson was brief. World War II was in full swing in 1943, and he was drafted in December of that year and assigned to Patton's Third Army. He won three decorations for bravery in the Battle of the Bulge.

Returning to Clemson in '46, he became a mainstay at right guard for the Tigers. He remembers Clemson's undefeated season in 1948 and their big 26-19 win over Boston College that year.

"After the game those big Boston newspaper reporters wearing their three-piece suits approached Coach Howard for comments," Gillespie grins. "Without cracking a smile, he's try to force a chaw of tobacco on them. Their jaws would go slack, and they'd pull back like they'd been burned. All the boys got a kick out of that."

Gillespie was also a starting guard in basketball, and the starting third baseman in baseball. In fact, he was named to the All-Southern Team in all three

Frank Gillespie was named All-Southern in football, baseball and basketball, the only Clemson athlete ever to be named All-Conference in three major sports, and Conference Athlete of the Year. He was also a straight A student and president of his senior class.

sports. To date he still enjoys the distinction of being the only Clemson athlete in history to be named all-conference in three major sports.

He earned eleven varsity letters and was named all-conference on seven different occasions, still more Clemson records.

Even today he remains the only Clemson athlete in history to be named Conference Player of the Year, an honor bestowed on him in 1948.

As though those accolades were not enough, in 1949 he graduated from Clemson with a straight-A average in a tough Electrical Engineering course. In his spare time, so to speak, he also served as President of the senior class.

As an engineer with IBM, the big money rolled in. But still, says Gillespie, there was something missing in life.

"Life was hard down in the coal mines. Even in good times life was hard. In bad times, when the mines closed or what not, times were terrible. During those times, we had only one thing to sustain us and see us through—and that was our religion. Somehow, no matter where I was or what I was doing, I could never get it out of my mind that I really wanted to become a minister."

And that's exactly what he did. Stationed in Louisville with IBM, Gillespie began studying theology in his spare time at the Southern Baptist Seminary. Several years later he became an ordained Southern Baptist minister.

Today, retired from IBM and semi-retired as a minister, Gillespie and his family make their home in Valrico, Florida. But he is still learning, he says, and commutes several days a week to Rice Seminary in Jacksonville where he pursues a graduate degree in theology.

He is a member of the Clemson Athletic Hall of Fame.

★

Joe Landrum

He Was Clemson's First All-American Baseball Player

Today Joe Landrum is a successful semi-retired businessman, and Columbia has more high schools than you can shake a stick at. But half a century ago, when young Joe Landrum was first beginning to feel his oats as an outstanding athlete, Columbia had only one high school and it was called, appropriately enough, Columbia High. They were known as the Capitals. That was in 1941.

Like millions of other Americans coming along during that era, Landrum had not only World War II to contend with, but the Great Depression as well. How tough was it? Today Landrum quips: "Well, I'm sure those were tough years. But I didn't realize it at the time because I'd never known anything better. Back then we didn't have TV to tell us how bad off we were."

By 1945 Landrum had established himself as one of the top prep pitchers in the state. He received numerous scholarship offers, including one to USC. But he chose to attend Clemson—at his own expense.

"I'd always been a devoted Clemson fan," he says. "But I'd never even laid eyes on the place until that day in September of '45 when I got off the Greyhound bus. I remember I staggered off the bus with my big footlocker on my shoulder, then had to struggle up that long hill to the admissions office to get enrolled. But I'd rather pay to go to Clemson than to go anywhere else for free."

He remembers his first start as a Tiger pitcher. It came his freshman year, in March of '46, and it would be a memorable one.

"I'd been in the infirmary for two days with strep throat, but they let me out that morning. Coach Randy Hinson told me I was going to start that afternoon against Erskine College and he wanted me to go for as long as I could. Gosh, I felt awful."

In his very first start for the Tigers, Landrum pitched a no-hitter. In fact, it's still recorded in the Clemson Record Book as the first no-hitter ever tossed by a Clemson pitcher. (In fact, even today Landrum remains one of only ten Tiger pitchers ever to throw a no-hitter.)

During the '46 and '47 seasons, despite the fact

He was the first Clemson baseball player ever to be named All American. He later played with the Brooklyn Dodgers.

that Clemson played a total of only 56 games, Landrum himself won 22 of them, thus making him the fourth winningest pitcher in the history of Clemson baseball. Indeed, his 1.07 earned run average in '46 remains second only to Billy O'Dell's 0.79 in 1954.

He recalls that Clemson's pitching staff during that era consisted of himself and a young man from Woodruff named Joe Hazle. And that was it. But on the strength of their great pitching arms Clemson won the Southern Conference championship in 1947. They then traveled to New Haven, Conn. to take on Yale in the Eastern Regional Championship where they lost a close one.

By way of explanation, Landrum says, "Our second baseman was Lyn McMakin from Pacolet, S.C., a fighter pilot during the war who'd been shot down on two different occasions. His legs had been hit by shrapnel, and he simply couldn't bend down in cold weather. Well, it was cold as the dickens that day up in New Haven, and Lyn just couldn't scoop up those ground balls. We finally got beat."

Landrum laughs when he recalls that the first Yale hitter he struck out that day was a hot-fielding first baseman, who would later go on to enjoy some prominence in American politics, a young fellow named George Bush.

Following his sophomore season, in '47, Landrum was named to the Associated Press All-American Team. He was the first Clemson baseball player ever to be so honored.

At that point the Brooklyn Dodgers came calling and Landrum signed a fat pro contract. "They also signed Joe Hazle, which means that Brooklyn wiped out Clemson's entire pitching staff."

Oddly enough, several years later Hazle, who still had a year of collegiate eligibility left, retired from the Dodgers and joined the pitching staff at Wofford College. At season's end he was named to the Little All-American Team.

After three seasons with Ft. Worth of the Texas League, Landrum was called up to the big leagues in 1950. Today he rattles off the names of his Dodger teammates like a mad monk chanting his hourly prayer beads, truly a roster of all-time Brooklyn greats—Gil Hodges, Jackie Robinson, Pee Wee Reece, Billy Cox, Duke Snyder, Carl Furillo, Andy Pafko, Roy Campanella and Carl Erskine.

Though he did well his rookie season in Flatbush, Landrum was dismayed to find his country again at war. This time it was in Korea, and so he quickly returned to Clemson to complete his degree in engineering and to receive his ROTC commission. Still, he did manage to play the last half of the '52 season with the Dodgers and says that he had a ringside seat to watch the classic '52 World Series between the Dodgers and the Yankees.

Then for the next two years it was off to war. And that, for all practical purposes, was the end of the pro baseball road for Joe Landrum.

And who was the toughest hitter faced in the majors? Landrum shakes his head. "Anybody who brought a bat to the plate was tough. There are no easy outs in the majors."

Following the war he returned to Columbia and opened an electronics business. Eighteen years ago, following his retirement, he became the assistant to the CEO of the Duquesne Corp., a position he continues to hold on a part-time basis.

And does he spend his retirement time fishing and golfing, as most people dream of doing? "Nope. I haven't done either in twenty years. Take my word for it, fishing and golfing aren't that great if you don't have to slip off from work to do them. I do enjoy a little gardening now and then."

He is married to the former Rose Marie McCutcheon of Kingstree, and they have four children and four grandchildren. (His son, Bill Landrum, is a former outstanding major league pitcher.)

"Bill pitched for USC in college," jokes Landrum, shaking his head in disbelief. "But I always kid him and tell him if he'd been a little smarter I could have got him on at Clemson."

Landrum is a member of the Clemson Athletic Hall of Fame.

★
Bishop Strickland

He Was Named All-State For Four Consecutive Years

It was 1947 and with the arrival of high school sensation Bishop Strickland, the University of South Carolina would boast that it now had one of the most potent backfields in the South. But it wasn't until the next year, 1948, that the Gamecocks would learn what a truly great backfield was. That was the year that Steve Wadiak arrived on the scene.

Thus with Strickland at one halfback position and Wadiak at the other, the Gamecocks fielded what many considered the finest running duo in Southern football and one of the best in the nation.

Their cheerleaders' favorite chant that year was "If the right one don't get you, the left one will," and many opponents can attest to the truth of that prediction. Put another way, how the heck do you pitch to Lou Gehrig when you've got Babe Ruth on deck?

Football fame was no stranger to Strickland. He was born in Mullins in 1929, played high school ball under Coach Joe Cox, and led the Auctioneers' football team to three consecutive state titles. He scored 27 touchdowns his senior season (then a state record) and was a unanimous selection to play in the Shrine Bowl.

He could have attended any college in America, but he opted to remain instate and chose the University of South Carolina. He immediately won a starting position with the Gamecocks and would start in 36 consecutive games over the next four years.

More impressive, he was named to the All-State team each of those four years, still the only running back ever to earn such a distinction.

At 5-9 and 200 pounds, and with a low center of gravity, the speedy Strickland was a fire hydrant of a ball carrier, tough to catch and ever tougher to bring down.

Against Clemson his freshman year, he raced 49 yards for a touchdown the first time he touched the ball. Against Wake Forest that same year, in a game played in Charlotte's Memorial Stadium, he scored the game's only touchdown, giving the Gamecocks' a 6-0 win.

He also enjoys the distinction of having played in USC's first televised game, a 13-13 tie with Marquette University in 1949. Strickland, by the way, scored

Bishop Strickland was named All Southern in 1950, finishing his career with a total of 1,965 rushing yards, an average of 5.2 yards per carry. He would later enjoy an outstanding career with the San Francisco 49s. He is a member of the USC Athletic Hall of Fame.

both Carolina touchdowns in that contest.

But his most memorable experience, he says, was being the running mate of the legendary Steve Wadiak, a native of Chicago who never played high school ball. "In fact," says Strickland, "Steve was playing semipro football in Chicago when Coach Enright discovered him.

"We didn't advertise it, but Steve was already a pro when he came here. In fact, I remember the first time we practiced somebody knocked him down, but then he jumped up and ran for a touchdown. That was legal in pro ball back then but not in college ball. Coach Enright had to step in real fast and stop him from doing things like that."

Looking back, Strickland laughs and shakes his head. "Yeah, old Steve was a good boy and a great ball

Strickland goes over for the winning TD in Carolina's 7-0 win over Furman in 1948.

carrier. But he couldn't block worth a darn. Any time I took off on an end sweep, I figured I was pretty much on my own."

Oddly enough, despite their vastly deferent backgrounds, Strickland and Wadiak soon became almost inseparable off the field as well as on. "I can't explain it," Strickland says. "Steve was a big city boy while I was from the country, but we were both sort of laid-back, easygoing, informal types. We just sort of hit it off and always ran around together."

As most fans are aware, Wadiak, who neither drank nor smoked, was killed in a tragic automobile accident his senior year, in 1952, only months after being named to the Associated Press All-American Team.

Despite being somewhat overshadowed by Wadiak, Strickland himself remains one of the top ten greatest runners in USC football history, finishing his career with 1,965 yards on 365 carries for a 5.2 per carry average. He was named All-State, All-Southern, and 2nd Team All-American by the AP.

In '51 he was signed by the San Francisco '49ers, where he became a teammate of such all-time greats as Y. A. Tittle, Joe "The Jet" Perry, Lee Nomalini and Frankie "One Eye" Albert.

Asked how Albert, one of the greatest quarterbacks ever to play the game, received such an intriguing nickname, Strickland explains:

"Well, Frankie was a southpaw, you know, and he had a funny way of cocking his head way to the side when looking down field. To us receivers, it looked like he was peeping at us out of the corner of his right eye, like he didn't have a left eye."

So there you have it, sports historians!

As a '49er, Strickland rushed for 460 yards his rookie season, for 570 the next year, but then following a severe injury in '53 he decided to return home. He then began his own construction business in North Augusta (Strickland Construction Company), which he continues to operate today. He has been active in civic affairs in that area, serving as President of both the JCs and the Chamber of Commerce.

In 1977 he served as President of the USC Alumni Association, and he is on the Board of Directors of the North Augusta Country Club.

He and his wife have two daughters and a grandson. His grandson, he says, was named Bishop in his honor. Strickland called it "the greatest honor I've ever received."

★
Tom Wham

Determination Took This Furman Ace
From Poverty to Fame

TOM WHAM! With a name like that he could hardly miss! And indeed Tom Wham did come in for his share of fame and glory, first with Furman and later with the Chicago Cardinals of the NFL. But his rise from dire poverty wasn't easy. In fact, after hearing his life story, we're convinced that if he had a nickname it should be Tom "Grim Determination" Wham.

He was born in 1924 and spent his early years growing up on a bleak mill village in Greer. As though things were not already bad enough, when Tom was ten his father died unexpectedly. And now, with the Depression in full swing, and with very little family income, his mother was forced to place Tom and his younger brothers, Don and Bradley, in Thornwell Orphanage in Clinton.

"The people at Thornwell were wonderful," he recalls. "And under Coach Walter Beaman we had some truly great athletic teams. My senior year there, in 1942, we won the state championship in football."

At 6-3 and 195 pounds, young Tom was offered a football scholarship by Carolina's Rex Enright. He accepted it, but then, following a visit to Carolina and taking a look at all the great material the Gamecocks had on hand, he suspected that he wouldn't get much playing time in the near future. Thus he rejected the scholarship and decided to enroll at Presbyterian.

But before he could become a Blue Hose he received a draft notice from Uncle Sam, and soon he was wearing the uniform of the U.S. Navy. While home on leave during Christmas of '42 he married his high school sweetheart, Azilee Allen, also a resident of Thornwell. For the next three years then he saw heavy combat duty in both the North Atlantic and the South Pacific. Truly, life was moving very rapidly for Tom Wham.

In 1946, following his discharge, he and Azilee settled in Greenville and Tom entered Furman University on the GI Bill. That was the year that Furman resumed football after a three-year hiatus because of the war. Tom decided to give the team a try.

"I was running as a fifth-string end to start, but then our starting end was injured one day and Coach

Tom Wham is still remembered as one of the finest ends in the history of Furman football. He would later go on to an outstanding pro career with the Chicago Cardinals.

Bob Smith yelled over to where we rinky-dinks were going through our drills for an end to come over. So, since I had nothing to lose, I trotted on over.

"I had a pretty good practice and after it was over Coach Smith said to me, 'Wham, you like that defense pretty good, don't you.' And I said, 'I like defense and offense, but you haven't given me a chance to prove it.' Well, Coach Smith just laughed." The next day Smith listed Wham as Furman's starting end. Three days later the Hurricanes opened their season—against Alabama.

"We got beat 20-7, but that wasn't too bad considering it was Alabama, and that this was the first football team we'd fielded since '42. I did okay, so for the next three years I missed very few plays, on either offense or defense."

Furman played a killer schedule including teams like Alabama, Auburn, Army, USC, Clemson, Georgia, and Georgia Tech. "Really, to look at our schedule," says Wham, "you'd have thought we were members of the SEC."

In '53 Wham became line coach at Furman, a position he would hold until taking a job with the Department of Corrections. He recently retired as State Director of Community Services. He is a member of the Furman Athletic Hall of Fame.

One of his fondest memories was the Clemson game of 1946 when he intercepted a Dick Hendley pass for a touchdown.

"Actually," laughs Wham, "Bobby Gage was Clemson's quarterback that day while Hendley was their halfback. Later Hendley joked to me that he'd had big dreams of becoming a star quarterback himself when he hauled off and threw that bomb that day, but that I'd burst his bubble with that interception. He said he knew right then that he'd just have to go through life as a mere halfback."

Also in '46, which was turning out to be a real memorable year for the Whams, Tom's younger brothers left Thornwell and returned to Greenville to live once again with their mother. Then the next year, in 1947, Don and Bradley were named the most outstanding athletes at Greenville High School, and that fall both entered Furman on football scholarships.

"It was really great having the family back together," beams Wham. "But the folks at Thornwell were fine people, and we owe them so much for taking us in when we had no where else to turn."

Wham was named to the All-State team in 1948

and '49, and became a draft pick of the Chicago Cardinals, then coached by Buddy Parker and Curley Lambeau.

He remembers such teammates as Paul Chrisman, Elmer Angsman and Charlie Trippi. Wham spent the next three years as their starting defensive end.

"I loved every minute of it," he says, "but back then there was really no future in pro football. We were paid about $6,500 a year and had no job security whatsoever."

So he returned home in 1953 and became line coach for his old alma mater, a position he would hold until he finally decided to take a position with the S.C. Department of Corrections. A few years ago he retired as State Director of Community Services.

Today he is a member of the Furman Athletic Hall of Fame. He and Azilee, his wife, make their home in Greer.

He was asked if he has any advice for young people struggling to better themselves, and he responds: "Don't ever give up. Don't ever quit. Don't ever get discouraged. No matter how bad things get, just keep plugging away and sooner or later things will begin to fall into place. But don't ever give up."

★

The Bronze Derby

This Is What Makes College Football
The World's Greatest Sport

Presbyterian College and Newberry have been going at one another on the gridiron now for the past 84 years, but a special name for their game, The Bronze Derby Game, didn't originate until 1947. And there's an interesting story as to how that came about.

Cally Gault, who was a fixture as both coach and athletic director at PC for many years, was a runningback for the Blue Hose in that very first contest in '47, and he furnished most of the following details.

In the winter of '46 several hundred Presbyterian students traveled just a few miles down the road to Newberry College to watch a basketball game between the Blue Hose and the Indians. Since a great many of these students were studying for the Presbyterian ministry and therefore just full of love for their fellow man, they thought it would be a wonderful gesture on their part to hang a huge banner from the Newberry gym ceiling which imparted the following inspirational message: BEAT HELL OUT OF NEWBERRY!

But the Newberry students, a great many of whom were studying for the Lutheran ministry, somehow took umbrage at the PC boys' attempt to reach out to them. After a great deal of prayer and meditation, they resolved that the banner should come down.

The problem, since the ceiling was some forty feet above the floor, was how to take the banner down without disrupting the game now in progress. Finally, the Lutherans went outside and secured a long ladder which they placed against an upstairs window. One hardy fellow then scaled the ladder, reached inside the window, grabbed a handful of banner and gave it a strong jerk. Down came that banner and off went the Lutherans across campus, the banner trailing in their wake.

The gym emptied and the Presbyterians gave chase. They finally caught up with the fleeing Lutherans, which proved a terrible mistake. A deep discussion then ensued, interrupted periodically by wild slugging contests. A full-blown riot was averted when officials from both schools arrived on the scene.

The captain of Newberry College turns over the Bronze Derby to his PC counterpart after the Indians fell to the Blue Hose in 1948.

During all this hullabaloo three Presbyterian students were seated in a '46 Buick convertible parked just outside the gym, gleefully watching the debate unfolding before them. The driver was wearing a derby hat.

As luck would have it, a Newberry student emerged from the melee at that point nursing an enlarged lip. He walked straight past the Buick containing the laughing PC students (Gault was sitting in the back seat) and the driver with the derby hat.

Very deftly, his arm shot out and he grabbed the derby from the amazed driver's head, then fled to the safety of his dorm, his prize in hand.

A few days later Charles McDaniel, sports information director at PC, phoned Frank Kinnard, student editor of the Newberry College newspaper, and suggested the incident be transformed into something positive. Why not bronze the purloined derby and present it to the winner of their annual football game?

Kinnard said he thought it was a great idea. He then contacted The Mad Hatter, as the daring Newberry raider was now known all over campus, and persuaded him to surrender his trophy.

Thus was born one of the great traditions in Palmetto State football, the Bronze Derby Game.

★

Blake "Kilo" Watts

He Remains One of PC's All-Time Great Runningbacks

It was late afternoon, September 17, 1949 and the heat inside Memorial Stadium was almost unbearable as Coach Frank Howard stood before a dozen sweating reporters at his weekly postgame press conference. His Tigers had just demolished the Blue Hose of Presbyterian College 69-7, and Howard was in a jovial mood. As is usual with football coaches, he commended the opposing team, especially their great fullback, Blake Watts.

"That Watts boy is some ball player," Howard growled. "He gained 210 yards against us this afternoon and scored a touchdown. They oughtta call that boy Kilo, Kilo Watts, 'cause he's about a live wire if I ever saw one."

Today Watts is a good natured individual with an easy laugh. He smiles when reminded of Coach Howard's compliment. "Do you know that nickname stuck? For almost half a century now, thanks to Coach Howard, I've been Kilo Watts to everybody. Even my wife calls me Kilo. Even my business cards bear that name."

He is a product of Bishopville, which also happens to be the hometown of Army's great 1940s All-American, Doc Blanchard.

"Doc Blanchard was my idol back when I was in high school," he says. "This is hard to believe, but we had a big cow pasture back home and every Sunday afternoon we'd have a baseball game out there. Whenever Doc was home on leave from West Point, he loved to come out and play with us. But there was a four-foot barbed wire fence around the pasture, and I've seen him hop that fence like it wasn't even there to go after a fly ball. He was a great athlete."

Following Watts' graduation from high school in 1943, he served two uneventful years in the Merchant Marines, then returned to high school in '46. So why would he go back to high school if he'd already graduated?

"Well, I know that sounds odd, but they'd added another year of high school while I was away. I was older and bigger in '46 and I hoped I could play football again and win a college scholarship."

And that's exactly what happened. By this time he stood 5-10 and weighed 175, still not a giant by any means. But his greatest asset was his speed. He ran a 9.8 100-yard dash, which is extremely fast, even by today's standards. He was offered a scholarship by USC's Rex Enright and planned to go there, but after

Fullback Blake "Kilo" Watts and his '49 Blue Hose teammates. He averaged 7.4 yards per carry that season and was named to the All State team.

visiting a friend at Presbyterian College, he decided to throw in his lot with Coach Lonnie McMillan's Blue Hose.

His freshman year, 1947, he became a starter at fullback, joining such other PC greats as Walter Gooch, Ken McCutcheon, Bill Jolly, and George "Chop Chop" Fleming. Together they formed what is still remembered as PC's famous Ten Second Backfield.

"In fact," says Watts, "we all ran the hundred in less than ten seconds. All except Bill Jolly, but he was our quarterback, and so we didn't count him anyway."

Watts still has fond memories of Presbyterian's legendary Walter Johnson, who had served as head coach from 1915 until 1940 and then was named athletic director.

"Coach Johnson was quite elderly by 1949, and I remember he came down to the sideline just before kickoff in our big game with Furman that year and gave us a highly emotional pep talk. Well, all the boys started crying," Watts says. "Then Bill Jolly reached down and got a handful of sand and started rubbing it on his face. We saw what he was doing, and we started doing the same thing. We kept doing it until the blood began dribbling down our chins. When all the boys were bloody, we looked up at Coach Lonnie Mack and told him we were ready."

Apparently it was a good idea.

"That was a great Furman team," Watts continues. "They'd already beaten USC and had lost to Florida by one point. But be darned if we didn't go out there and upset them 20-13. Our faces were pretty sore for the rest of the week, but it was worth it."

By the end of his junior year, 1949, Watts had carried the ball 116 times for 856 yards (during a nine-game schedule). His incredible average of 7.4 yards per carry remains an all-time PC record.

Not only was he named to the All-State team that year—along with such other greats as USC's Steve Wadiak, Clemson's Fred Cone, and Wofford's Sammy Sewell—he was also chosen for the Little All-American Team. He even drew attention from pro scouts.

Indeed, he remembers sitting in the dressing room just before the final game of the '49 season when he was approached by a well dressed stranger. The stranger stared at him for a moment, as though taking his measure, then asked, "Watts, can you pass?"

A little unnerved by being stared at and surprised by the question, Watts replied, "Well, I'm doing okay. I've got a high C average."

The stranger guffawed. "I mean can you throw the ball? If so, the Green Bay Packers would like for me to sign you to a contract."

But as fate would have it, Watts severely injured a knee in the final quarter of that game, and that was the end of his football career.

Today, some forty-nine years later, Watts is still a live wire whose only speed is wide open. A longtime resident of Hickory, N. C., he is a financial planner, active in civic affairs, and holds a national office with the Chamber of Commerce. He is also a member of the N. C. Alcohol Beverage Control Board and an elder in the First Presbyterian Church. In his spare time, he founded the booster club for Hickory High School. He is married to the former Alice Miller and they have two sons.

Looking back, he says, "I'm more grateful to Presbyterian College than I can ever express for what they did for me. The education and experiences I gained there have given me the foundation to accomplish everything I've ever wanted to do in life."

★

Fred Cone

"He was the best football player I ever coached."--Frank Howard

Frank Howard simply cannot talk about Clemson football without extolling the virtues of the man he calls his finest football player ever, Fred Cone. And with good reason. Cone performed so many incredible feats as a Tiger fullback (1948-50) that he could easily fill up his own personal record book.

In 1950, for example, he averaged a phenomenal 6.1 yards per carry and averaged scoring 10.1 points per game. Both these figures, after the passing of almost half a century, still remain number-one in the Clemson record book.

For his career he gained a total of 2,172 yards (the first Clemson player ever to go over the 2,000 yard mark) and scored 30 touchdowns (still number-two in the Tiger record book).

Indeed, he was so good for so long, as both a collegian and as a pro, that many just naturally assume that he must have been a highly sought after All-American out of Gargantuan High in Ohio or some place.

But not so, sports fans. Cone was born in 1926 in the small farming community of Pineapple, Alabama, a few miles south of Montgomery. He was never a noted high school football player for the simple reason that Pineapple High didn't field a football team.

"In fact, we could hardly get enough guys together to play a game of checkers," he laughs. "But like a lot of country boys growing up at the time, I used to listen to college games on the radio. I would have given anything to be able to play myself."

Cone finished school in 1943, but his dreams of attending college and playing football were cut short when he was drafted into the U. S. Army. He volunteered for duty as a paratrooper with the elite 11th Airborne Division, saw heavy action in the Pacific, then spent a year with our occupation forces in Japan.

By 1946 his family had moved to Elmore, Alabama, and Cone joined them there, taking a job stacking lumber for his father's business. Still, he harbored dreams of playing college football.

Like a great many Southerners, Cone is a friendly,

Fred Cone averaged 10.2 points per game for Clemson in 1950, still a scoring record in the Clemson record book. As the starting fullback with the Green Bay Packers he led the NFL in field goal scoring in 1955. He remains one of the few players in history named to two all-time NFL teams (Green Bay and Dallas).

gregarious sort of fellow and the only thing he enjoys more than hearing a good story is telling one himself. He relates one of his early athletic misadventures:

"I read in the *Montgomery Advertiser* that Auburn University was holding spring tryouts. So a buddy of mine and I jumped in my old Model-A and took off for Auburn. Gosh, I can't believe how naive we were. But we really thought we'd drive up to Auburn, make their team, then be back home in time for work Monday morning with a couple of big football scholarships in our pockets, despite the fact that neither of us had hardly even seen a football at the time."

Cone (#31) goes in for his second TD of the day to put Clemson up 14-0 over Missouri in the '49 Gator Bowl.

Auburn, as it turned out, had invited 60 highly recruited high school stars to spring tryouts. Cone and his friend simply walked up and got in line with all the others.

"None of the coaches knew who we were, and they kept giving us funny looks. But none of 'em said anything because they were afraid that maybe they were supposed to know who we were, and they didn't want Coach Carl Voyles to know they didn't know who we were."

On the final day of practice Cone badly twisted his ankle. He was carried off the field and past Coach Voyles. "I yelled, 'Hey, Coach, how about my football scholarship?'

"He looked at me like where in the world did this thing come from, then mumbled something about Auburn would be in touch. But that was the end of my career at Auburn."

That was in the spring of '47. That summer he visited his sister in Biloxi and experienced one of those incredible coincidences that changed his life forever.

It just so happened that his sister lived next door to, of all people, Hazel Howard, the sister of Clemson immortal Frank Howard. Hazel Howard, in fact, was Cone's sister's best friend.

Frank Howard recalls subsequent events this way: "I got a letter from Hazel down in Biloxi, said I ought to give a football scholarship to her neighbor's little brother. Said the boy never had played football, but she'd seen him down at the swimming pool and he sure looked like a football player.

"Well, I just happened to have one scholarship left over that year. And I thought the world of Hazel, so just as a favor to her I wrote old Cone and told him that if he wanted to come to Clemson and play football, I'd give him a scholarship.

"I'd never even heard of the boy before. Later I told people that landing Fred Cone was an example of my great recruiting ability."

Cone spent the fall of '47 working out with the B-team and learning the game. But by '48 he was ready. "Or at least," he laughs, "I learned that the guys wearing the orange jerseys were the good guys."

Indeed, 1948 marked a milestone in the history of Clemson football, a Golden Era of sorts. The Tigers enjoyed their first undefeated season since 1900 and wound up in the nation's Top Ten for the first time in history. It has been said that had it not been for the blocking and running of Fred Cone, none of those good things would have happened.

It was Cone, for example, who scored Clemson's first two touchdowns in their big 24-23 upset win over Missouri in the Gator Bowl that year.

Tough Fred Cone bulldozes his way to daylight as Clemson and USC tied 14-14 in 1950. The Tigers would go on to upset Miami 15-14 in the Orange Bowl on New Years Day.

In 1950 the Tigers again went undefeated and played a highly favored Miami team in the Orange Bowl. Cone rushed for 81 yards in that contest (then a Clemson record for rushing yardage in a bowl game) as the Tigers upset the Hurricanes 15-14.

He was elected captain of the Tigers that season and won the team MVP award. He was also named All-Southern and won the Teague Award as the best athlete in the Carolinas. Not bad for a young man from Pineapple, Alabama.

But the highlight of his college career came against Auburn in 1950. Remembering how he had been brushed aside several years earlier, Cone rushed for 163 yards on 33 carries as the Tigers blasted the War Eagles 41-0. Pay back time was sweet.

In 1951 he was taken in the third round by Green Bay, and would become a mainstay at fullback for the Packers for the next seven years. He taught himself to kick field goals ("just to fortify my position with the Packers," he says), and, incredibly enough, in 1955 he led the NFL in field goal kicking.

He retired from pro ball in 1957. But then three years later, in 1960, he received a call from Coach Tom Landry of the Dallas Cowboys. It was their first year in the NFL and they needed a place kicker. Thus Cone spent one more year in pro football before finally retiring for good in 1961.

He was recently named to the All-Time All-Star teams of both the Green Bay Packers and the Dallas Cowboys, one of the few players in history to be named to two all-time NFL teams.

In '61 he joined the Clemson coaching staff as head recruiter, a position he held for 27 years until his final retirement in 1988.

Today he and his wife Judy make their home in Blairsville, Ga., just a few miles down the road from Clemson's Memorial Stadium. He is a member of the Clemson Athletic Hall of Fame and the South Carolina Athletic Hall of Fame.

"But life takes some funny bounces," he says now, looking back over his career. "If my sister hadn't lived next door to Hazel Howard, and if I hadn't gone to visit her that summer, I guess I'd still be stacking lumber down in Elmore. It's kind of scary when you think back over all the ifs in your life."

★

Fulton Hines

This Ex-Globetrotter Now Leads the Senior Olympics

Fulton Hines' professional athletic career lasted for not quite one year. But the nature of that experience was so unique, and the pleasure so intense, that this Florence resident will remember it forever as one of the highlights of a long and very fulfilling life.

The other highlight concerns the U. S. Senior Olympics. But more about that later.

Growing up in Plainfield, N. J., he was such a tall, gawky lad that even his parents considered him a poor athletic prospect.

"Well, let me put it this way," he smiles, "I was built like Ichabod Crane. Not exactly the type to get coaches real excited."

Then came the war, and in 1944 Hines was inducted into the army where he began to put flesh on his 6-4 frame. Just on a whim he went out for the post basketball team, a squad of mainly former college players. Incredibly enough, he nailed down a starting position at center and helped his team win the 6th Army championship. But this was merely a dress rehearsal for the experience of a lifetime that was waiting just around the corner.

Discharged in '48, he returned to Plainfield. His father, meanwhile, just chanced to attend a Harlem Globetrotters' exhibition game at about that same time. Following the game he collared the Trotters' team manager and told him all about his son, what a great asset he could be to any team in America.

The manager, amazed at being nabbed by a fan out of the stands, mumbled his telephone number and said for young Fulton to call him the next day.

Fulton did—and was invited to Philadelphia for a tryout.

"Everything happened so quickly at that point," Hines remembers. "I tried out, was handed a contract, tossed a uniform, and told to jump on the bus. We were headed for Oklahoma City. In fact, my father had to ship my clothes to me by Greyhound bus."

Hines recalls that the first three Trotters he met on the bus that afternoon were Marcus Haynes, Goose Tatum and Nat "Sweetwater" Clifton, national heroes who could have played for any pro team in America.

They gave their new teammate a warm greeting.

Today Fulton Hines is a leader in the Senior Olympics, but years ago he knew the thrill of playing forward for the world's finest basketball team, the Harlem Globetrotters.

Then, after a brief conference, they announced that, since everyone had to have a nickname, Hines' would be Foo Foo (after a popular comic strip character). And so for the next year he would be billed as Fulton "Foo Foo" Hines.

"On the court," he says, "those guys were really magicians with that ball. Off the court they were just regular guys, just like any other group of athletes. Our conversations usually revolved around girls and food. We played two or three exhibitions a week, so we were always on the road. But any spare time we had was spent getting our routines down pat."

Hines relishes every golden moment he spent with the Trotters, though segregation did present a problem back in those days.

"We were rarely allowed to stay in hotels. Usually the coach would call ahead to wherever and make arrangements for us to stay in privates homes. And the same is true of restaurants. Our deluxe cuisine generally consisted of hot dogs and hamburgers we'd pick up at the rear window of some greasy spoon cafe."

Also, Hines points out, as a rookie with no experience, the Trotters paid him only expense money. "So there I was, no place to sleep, no place to eat, constantly broke, but still young and crazy and having the time of my life."

Cut by the Trotters the next year, he decided to marry and settle down. But then came another war, and for the next two years he would see heavy combat duty with the 24th Infantry in Korea. Discharged in '53, he entered Rider College and four years later received a degree in accounting.

Today, in addition to being a former Globetrotter, Hines takes great pride in the fact that he is considered the father of the U. S. Senior Olympics in South Carolina. He participated in the Senior Olympics in St. Louis in 1984, then later was distressed to learn that South Carolina had no such chapter. He immediately set out to remedy that situation.

Debbie Wall, manager of the Florence Recreation Department, says: "We wouldn't have had a Senior Olympics if not for Fulton Hines."

Hines himself, now a CHAMPUS Claims Counselor with Blue Cross and Blue Shield, is a resident of Florence and a member of their Senior Games board of directors. He urges any senior citizen interested in the games to give them a try.

"People who don't even know each other get together at these things," beams Hines. "It's really great to see that many people in that age group getting together and doing their thing. They're doing something that younger people should be doing, just having good clean fun."

★

John McKissick

He Remains Football's Winningest Coach Ever

Talk about great football coaches and such names come to mind as Amos Alonzo Stagg, Knute Rockne, and Bear Bryant. Well, folks, you can just put those illustrious fellows on a back burner for a while. As wonderful as they may have been, their gridiron accomplishments pale in comparison with those of a fellow we know right here in South Carolina. His name is John McKissick, and he just completed his forty-fourth year as head coach at Summerville High School.

In case you've been held incommunicado somewhere for the past few years, McKissick, as of this writing, has now won 425 football games, making him the winningest coach in the history of American football.

No, you didn't just find a terrible typographical error in this little book. McKissick has now won 425 football games, and all at Summerville High School. (The previous record holder, by the way, was Gordon Wood of Brownsville, Texas, with 405 wins to his credit.)

But think about it. You would have to win ten games per season every year for forty years to amass 400 wins. Few coaches even last forty years, and certainly they don't win ten games per season while doing it. (In fact, very few people ever win 400 arguments during their lifetime.)

But McKissick, who grew up during those tough Depression years in Kingstree, learned early to latch on to whatever came his way and to make the best of it.

"My father was the youngest of fifteen children born to a Methodist minister in Greenwood," he says. "I don't know when Grandpa had time to preach, but he did have fifteen children. My own father lost his business during the Depression, and we moved to Kingstree."

McKissick finished high school in 1944 and entered Clemson College. But then in December of that year, with World War II in full swing, Uncle Sam stepped in and McKissick suddenly found himself wearing the uniform of an Army private. Luckily he survived the war, and, discharged in 1948, he enrolled as a student-athlete at Presbyterian College, playing

Today, after forty-five years, John McKissick is the winningest coach in the history of American football with an incredible 425 wins (at last count) to his credit.

fullback on their varsity eleven.

"I majored in economics and upon graduation went to work for a finance company. They told me that with my degree I'd be working as an auditor for the company, which really sounded wonderful. But then I found that all I did was run up and down the highway trying to run people down to collect money out of 'em."

A highly rewarding, fulfilling career, obviously.

"I hated every danged minute of it. So I applied for a coaching job up in Clarkton, N. C., about ten miles east of Whiteville. That was in 1951. I didn't know it when I took the job, but Clarkton is a little tobacco community, and they played six-man football up there. Heck, we didn't have but about ten boys on the whole team."

The next year McKissick was hired at Summerville, and the rest, as they say, is history. He still retains vivid memories of his first football game at Summerville in September of '52.

"My only experience at that time was in six-man

John McKissick as a Blue Hose fullback in 1950.

football, so I was extremely nervous about coming here, not knowing whether I had the know-how to meet the challenges of real eleven-man football. Believe me," he laughs, "that field looked awfully crowded with twenty-two players out there at the same time."

Does he remember the details of that first game? McKissick doesn't bat an eye. "Absolutely. we beat Wade Hampton by a score of 27-0. That was the most important game of my career. If we'd lost that night I might have been forced to start chasing people down for that finance company again. No," he says, tapping his forehead, "that game is forever stamped indelibly right here."

So now, after forty-five years and 425 victories, what is the secret of his success? "Well, I have seven very dedicated assistant coaches and a certified athletic trainer. Plus we try to work harder than other coaches do."

McKissick served as head coach of the Sandlappers in the 1961 Shrine Bowl, a game in which his team beat the North Carolina All-Stars 19-3. And of course he's had many offers to enter college coaching.

"I might consider a college job if somebody started a college right here in Summerville. But my family and I wouldn't leave Summerville for anything. We've always been in love with this community."

He is married to the former Joan Carter of Kingstree, and they have two daughters and four grandchildren.

He also points out that he's had dozens of players who've made it big in college and pro ball. Two who come immediately to mind are the Jennings brothers, Keith who plays with the Bears, and Stanford with the Bengals.

Asked why he didn't retire ten years ago, McKissick expresses surprise at the question. "Retire? Well, I don't know what I'd do with myself if I did retire. Coaching is the greatest pleasure in the world, and I'm getting paid to do it, and you can't beat that. I can honestly say that after forty-five years, I still can't wait to get up in the mornings and go to work."

In 1987 the good folks in Summerville paid McKissick the ultimate tribute. They named their football stadium John McKissick Field in his honor.

As for the future, he says, "I've just started my next 400-game winning streak. I figure I should get there about the year 2033."

★

Ray Mathews

Clemson Tiger or Pittsburgh Steeler, Ray Mathews Remains One of the Greatest

Ray Mathews' stature as a backfield ace with the Clemson Tigers and the Pittsburgh Steelers is a matter of legend. And for good reason.

He accounted for thirty-nine touchdowns as a Tiger (1948-50), a figure surpassed only by Steve Fuller.

His 3,128 all-purpose rushing yardage has been surpassed by only Kenny Flowers, Buddy Gore and Raymond Priester.

He remains the only player in history to lead the Tigers in both rushing and passing yardage during a single season (1949).

He remains one of the few players in history to be named to Clemson's Athletic Hall of Fame in both football and baseball.

He remains the only Steeler ever to score four touchdowns in a single game.

He remains fifth in career receiving with the Steelers and sixth in rushing yardage.

Recently he took time out from harvesting pumpkins on his big farm near Harrisburg, Pa. to tell us his story.

He was born in 1929 and graduated from McKeesport (Pa.) High School, in a senior class of more than one thousand students, where he starred in all three major sports. "Back then you had to play all three major sports if you wanted to keep the same sweetheart all year," he laughs. But football really was his favorite.

He was a standout and was offered scholarships by just about every major college in America. In fact, he still retains fond memories of a visit to Tulane and being their guest at the 1947 Sugar Bowl between North Carolina and Georgia.

"Yes, it was really something to watch Charlie Trippi and Choo Choo Justice perform on the same field that afternoon. But Louisiana was just too far from home. You see, I knew all along that I wanted to go to Clemson."

He says that as a youth he'd spent his summers working on his grandfather's farm, tending cattle and picking vegetables, and that he'd decided by his junior year in high school that farming was the life he wanted to pursue. And his grandfather told him that

Ray Mathews accounted for 39 touchdowns during his career at Clemson, a figure surpassed by only Steve Fuller. He remains one of the few Tigers in history to be named to the Clemson Athletic Hall of Fame in both football and baseball.

Clemson would be the place to study agriculture.

Plus he was impressed by Clemson assistant coach Walter Cox. "I thought Coach Cox was the finest man I'd ever met. If everybody at Clemson was as nice as Coach Cox, then that's where I wanted to go."

Mathews also says that Coach Frank Howard was the world's greatest con man. "I had been recruited as a tailback, but once I arrived at Clemson I knew I wasn't going to replace Bobby Gage. He was the best in America. So one day during preseason drills I was piddling around with the subs and Coach Howard walks up to me and says, 'Ray, can you think of anybody who'd like to make our first team? Somebody who'd like to make a real splash in the football world by playing wingback for us? If you can think of a likely person, let me know.'

"Well, of course I was jumping up and down and

Here Mathews goes for big yardage against USC on Big Thursday 1949. He is still the only Pittsburgh Steeler ever to score four touchdowns in a single game.

tugging at his sleeve and begging How about me, Coach? How about me? Which is exactly what Coach Howard wanted to hear."

For the next four years, then, Ray Mathews was the wingback in Clemson's devastating single-wing formation. And there was never a better one. Not in America, anyway.

Mathews recalls some of his great teammates with the Tigers: Bobby Gage, Billy Hair, Dick Hendley, Fred Cone, Wyndie Wyndham, Billy Hudson, Dan DiMucci, and Jack Miller. He recalls that a shaky 1947 season almost cost Coach Howard his job, but then the Tigers beat everything that moved in '48, won the Gator Bowl, and thus Howard's job was safe for another twenty years.

He recalls that many of the same players who made '48 such a great year were still around to lead Clemson to an undefeated season again in 1950, including a victory over Miami in the Orange Bowl.

Following his senior season in 1950, he was a first-round draft pick of the Pittsburgh Steelers. And, sure enough, his rookie season he played for the Steelers as though he'd been born in a gold and black uniform.

He was named to the NFL All-Star Team in '52, '53, and '54. His best game, he says, the one that still stands out in his mind, came in a win over the NFL champion Cleveland Browns in 1953. Mathews scored four touchdowns that afternoon, still a Steeler record for TDs scored in a single contest.

Following his retirement as a player in the NFL, he coached for a couple of years with Calgary of the Canadian Football League.

"But it was awfully cold up there, so I finally decided to quit football to do what I'd always really wanted to do. And that was farm. So I bought a little spread up here near Harrisburg, which is in Amish country, and I got me some cows and horses, and started raising lots of vegetables. It's similar to what my grandfather used to have.

"But today about all I do is raise pumpkins. And I still think a lot about the old days at Clemson. Those were some great days."

Mathews is a member of the Clemson Athletic Hall of Fame.

★

Jim Slaughter

At 6-11 He Was USC's First Giant of the Hardwood

Jim Slaughter averaged 16.5 rebounds per game in 1951, a new USC record.

Way back in 1934 the Carolina Gamecock basketball team went 18-1 on the season, still their best season ever on the hardwood. They had a center that year named Freddie Tompkins, who was named to the Converse All-American Basketball Team, the first Gamecock ever to be so honored.

Some seventeen years would then elapse before Carolina could boast of another All-American. His name is Jim Slaughter, and he is from Roanoke, Va. It was in 1951 that Jim Slaughter would delight Carolina fans throughout the Free World by being named to the Associated Press All-American Basket-

ball Team. That despite the Gamecocks' mediocre 14-10 won-loss record.

This was back in the days when people didn't seem to grow taller than 6-4. Indeed, if a team had a center who measured in at 6-5, he was called a BIG MAN, and he would become the talk of the Southern Conference.

But then Jim Slaughter casually strolled into the gym one day, and all those BIG MEN had to jump mighty high just to touch the top of his head. Yes, at 6-11 he was considered a physical phenomenon, literally a giant among men, when he first jogged onto the hardwood for the Gamecocks in 1947.

He had played both football and basketball in high school and says that football was actually his favorite sport.

"I liked football and thought I was pretty good," he says. "But my high school coach didn't think I was so hot, and since it's his opinion that counted, I decided to concentrate on basketball."

He played his senior year (1946-47) at Augusta Military Academy in Staunton, Va., where his coach just happened to be best friends with USC coach, Frank Johnson.

Johnson took one look at Slaughter and knew immediately that here was a center he had to have. Thus he offered Slaughter a full scholarship to play for the Gamecocks. Which doesn't seem that surprising today, but Slaughter says he was the first USC basketball player ever given a full scholarship. Prior to his arrival, basketball players at Carolina were given partial scholarships.

"Back in those days basketball was considered a minor sport, a cold-weather activity intended to keep the tall, skinny kids off the streets."

To say that he made the team his sophomore season is a great understatement. He took the team, the opposition, and Carolina fans by storm. By his junior year he was truly coming into his own, and, thanks to his offensive and defensive efforts, the humble Gamecocks went 12-5 in the Southern Conference, enjoying wins over such traditional powers as Duke, Maryland, and Wake Forest. More importantly, perhaps, they beat Clemson twice that year.

Slaughter finished the season averaging 20.1

The 6-11 Jim Slaughter towers over his '49 Carolina teammates (L-R): Don Cox, Chuck Prezioso, Jim Slaughter, Bob Kahle, and Al Munn. In 1951 he was named to the Associated Press All American Team.

points and 15 rebounds per game.

By his senior year he had established himself as a force to be reckoned with. He averaged 22.1 points per game that season while accounting for 413 rebounds, an incredible average of 16.5 rebounds per contest (after half a century, this figure is still number-two in the USC Record Book!).

For his career with the Gamecocks, Slaughter scored a total of 1,521 points. Only four other players in history have ever scored more—John Roche, Alex English, Jimmy Foster, and Brian Dunleavy. So Slaughter again finds himself in good company.

He took his degree in '51 in physical education, hoping to become a high school basketball coach. "But things never worked out that way," he says. "After college I was drafted by the Baltimore Bullets and played a couple of years up there. Then I came back to Carolina."

Like so many young athletes of his era, Slaughter found an attractive alternative to retirement in the textile leagues of the Carolinas. And so for the next five years he played textile ball for various mill teams in the Greenville area.

"Back then," he says, "the mills even had their own basketball gyms. Textile ball was really big stuff back in those days. We played two nights a week, and I don't know how many people our gym held, but it was always packed."

Slaughter retired five years ago. Today he and his wife, the former Virginia Riggins of Pendleton, make their home in Clinton.

He is a member of the USC Athletic Hall of Fame.

★
Bobby Starnes

A Memorable Player During A Memorable Era of Wofford Football

Bobby Starnes describes himself as just a poor boy from Chester who only wanted a chance to show what he could do. He got that chance in 1948, and he hasn't slowed down since.

At 5-9 and 175 pounds, he was an all-around athlete at Chester High and was named to the All-State Football Team his senior year.

"In fact," he recalls now, almost half a century later, "Chester won the state championship in '47, and we were invited up to High Point, N. C. to play the North Carolina state champions in the Sealtest Bowl. I don't remember now who we played, but I do remember that we won the game and that it was as cold as the dickens that night and that everybody, especially the players, was happy when the game ended and we could get back to that warm dressing room."

One of the premier tailbacks in the country that year, Starnes was recruited by Coach Carl Snavely and the University of North Carolina.

"Coach Snavely wanted me as a backup to Choo Choo Justice. So I went up to Chapel Hill and stayed about a week. But UNC, despite being a wonderful school, was just a little too big for my tastes, and it was definitely too far from home."

Pondering his situation, Starnes decided that if he wanted to remain within easy driving distance of Chester, Wofford College would be the place to go.

"Coach Phil Dickens would go on to fame at Wyoming and Indiana, but at that time he was head coach at Wofford. I phoned him, and he told me to come on down and he'd fix me up with a scholarship."

Starnes soon found himself running backup to Wofford's legendary Slinging Sammy Sewell, Everybody's Little All-American tailback. And of course back in '48 Wofford was still running from the single-wing formation, and in the single-wing the tailback was *the man* who made it all tick, the equivalent of the quarterback in more modern formations.

He had the good fortune to enter Wofford during a football era that remains their most memorable in history. In 1948, for example, the Terriers stunned the football world when they tied their first

In 1949 Bobby Starnes returned a punt 97 yards for a TD against Tennessee Tech, still an all-time Wofford record. But he is best remembered for helping Wofford to their record setting five consecutive ties in 1948.

five games of the season. This performance remains an all-time national record, one never even approached by any other football team in America. In fact, their 4-0-5 record that year won them more national recognition than Clemson's 10-0 record that same year. After all, they were undefeated!

And Starnes played a starring role in the Terriers' string of ties. "As a backup tailback to Sammy Sewell, I came in late in the fourth quarter in every one of those games, and in every one of them we were trailing by a touchdown. Somehow, I managed to score a touchdown in every one of them, so that we walked away with a tie instead of a loss."

It should be noted that the Terrier defense in '48 gave up a total of only 45 points, an incredible performance that still remains an all-time record at Wofford.

But Starnes' big year came in '49, his sophomore season, when he became Wofford's starting tailback. Now it should be noted that the 1970 Terriers went 10-0 on the season, which is not a bad record. But the '49 Terriers went 11-0, the best record in school history. Five of those wins, by the way, were shutouts, still another all-time school record.

Against Eastern Kentucky that year Starnes completed an 81-yard TD pass to Jack Whitted, still the longest TD completion in team history. And against Tennessee Tech he ran a punt back 97 yards for a touchdown, yet another all-time Terrier record.

By season's end, Wofford had scored 353 points to only 67 for the opposition and were undefeated. They then accepted an invitation to Tampa's Cigar Bowl, where they finally lost a close one to Florida State, 19-6.

As for 1950, the Terriers kicked off a good 7-2-1 season with an astounding 19-14 upset win over mighty Auburn, a game the Wofford faithful still chuckle over.

Indeed, during Starnes' four years at Wofford (1948-51) the Terriers went 28-11-7, while Starnes himself was named to the All-State Team both his junior and senior years.

Following his graduation in June 1952, he accepted an ROTC commission and became an Army pilot, flying combat missions in a L-20 reconnaissance plane in Korea.

Discharged in '56 but still in love with flying, Starnes was hired as a pilot with Eastern Airlines and assigned to Miami. It was a job he would love for the next thirty years, until his retirement in 1986.

"I guess the most exciting times I had as a pilot was flying over those Andes Mountains in South America and having to land at such high altitudes," he says. "Some of those landing strips were at an altitude of 13,000 feet."

Today Starnes and his wife, the former Donna Latimer of Mississippi, have nine children and make their home in Nokomis, Fla., their home situated right on the Gulf Coast where Bobby can take his boat out for the fishing he so dearly loves.

So, everything considered, we'd have to say that Bobby Starnes got his chance, and he parlayed one opportunity into still another. Today he owns 500 acres of oranges and 500 head of beef cattle which he raises on 2,000 acres of prime pasture land.

Not real bad for a poor boy from Chester.

★
Steve Wadiak

To Gamecock Fans, Wadiak Is Still The Greatest

Many who saw him play still regard Steve Wadiak as the greatest Gamecock ever. In 1948, his freshman season, he averaged a phenomenal 8.2 yards per carry, still an all-time USC record. Against George Washington in 1950 he ran 96 yards for a TD, still another USC record.

For most Gamecock fans, even after the passage of forty-five years, the late Steve Wadiak still personifies all that is good and great about Carolina football. Sure, there have been many great runningbacks in the history of Gamecock football, but just ask any of the old timers. Wadiak was the greatest.

He was born a poor boy on the wrong side of the tracks in Chicago in 1929, and was once quoted as saying, "Any side of the tracks was the wrong side in my neighborhood."

But Steve's parents were good people, and he grew up appreciating all the right things in life. He attended a vocational high school that had no football team (kids in his neighborhood were not expected to go to college). Still, he had great natural athletic ability. And after graduation he signed a contract to play with a semi-pro team in the Windy City.

It was during one of those knock-down-drag-out semi-pro games that Fate stepped in. It just happened that former Carolina great, Bill Milner, who was playing with the Chicago Bears, just happened to have a few minutes to kill one afternoon, so he parked his car, took a seat in the stands, and began watching the semi-pro game then in progress. Milner watched in amazement as Wadiak ran wild from his left half position and decided that this kid must be one of the finest football players he'd ever seen. In fact, said Milner later, he stayed for the entire game, just to watch Wadiak. Then he ran to a phone and called Coach Rex Enright down in Columbia and suggested that he sign Wadiak to a scholarship as quickly as possible. Enright did so.

And the rest, as they say, is history.

Wadiak stepped into a starting role immediately as a USC freshman in 1948, joining the irrepressible Bishop Strickland in the Carolina backfield. After only a few games opponents, who were stymied when trying to stop these two Carolina dynamos, were reminded of the old saying— If the right one don't get you, the left one will!

Wadiak was only 5-10 and 180 pounds, but he was great to watch (if you weren't the opposing coach), running with a smooth, effortless glide. And his speed was deceptive. He would seem to be just cruising along, then he would suddenly throw it into overdrive and vanish in a burst of speed, leaving befuddled defenders grabbing thin air. This earned him the nickname Wadiak The Cadillac.

After forty-five years it seems incredible that his name is still right up there at the top in most rushing categories in the Carolina Record Book. For example, he rushed for 2,878 yards during his career, which is still fourth in the USC record book . This despite playing on a USC team that rarely beat anyone. Indeed, the joke back then was that the Gamecocks should change their name to the Carolina Quakers, since they were so opposed to violence.

In 1950, his junior season, he averaged 110 yards per game, again second in the Record Book only to that of George Rogers. Against Clemson that year he amazed fans everywhere when he ran for an incredible

In 1950 Wadiaks streaks 73 yards for a touchdown as the Gamecocks tied Clemson 14-14. He rushed for 256 yards in this game, an average of 13.5 yards per carry.

Wadiak (#37) and teammates celebrate with Coach Rex Enright Following their upset win over West Virginia in 1951. Note: Lip LaTorre is standing to Wadiak's right. He would serve as a pallbearer at Wadiac's funeral a few months later.

256 yards (a record later surpassed by Brandon Bennett). Included in those 256 yards were touchdown runs of 66 and 73 yards.

Even more incredible, perhaps, is his 8.2 yards per carry record set in 1948, his freshman season. Even George Rogers never approached that effort.

He also holds the record for the longest touchdown run from scrimmage, going 96 yards for a score against George Washington in 1950. Ninety-six

yards! Which really doesn't leave much room for improvement, which means that this record might stand for another century or two.

But fame never touched Wadiak. His running mate, both on and off the field, Bishop Strickland, says, "Old Steve was a big city boy, while I was just a little country boy from Lake View. But we always hit it off and ran around together.

"I don't know, we were both just relaxed, easy

going fellows, and we enjoyed a good movie anytime to going out to one of those big night clubs. One thing, neither one of us liked to dress up. We'd get up in the mornings, put on our khaki pants and t-shirts, and we'd be set for the day."

Wadiak was a high draft pick of the Steelers in '52, and those who know about such things say he would doubtlessly have made a fine pro runningback.

But it was not to be.

Harold Lewis, now a Methodist minister, was a fledgling quarterback in 1951, who roomed on the same floor in the dorm with Wadiak. Today he remembers that fateful morning in March of 1952.

"It came about five A.M. in the morning, the ringing of the pay phone out in the hallway, waking me from a deep sleep. I answered it, and it was a deputy sheriff down in Aiken County. He wanted to know how to get in touch with Coach Enright.

"I then asked him what was wrong. For the rest of my life I'll remember his words. He said that Steve and some friends had been out joy riding in a car down there, and the car had gone out of control on what he called Dead Man's Curve. No one else in the car was even scratched, but Steve was killed instantly. My heart turned to ice."

And Tom Price, retired sports information director at USC, remembers talking to Wadiak the day before his death.

"My son was about a year old at the time, and we were walking down the street right there in front of the Claire Towers when Steve came up and we started talking. Then Steve reached out and took my son out of my arms and started playing with him.

"He was a great guy and extremely sensitive to the feelings of others. If there was ever a little unknown guy in the room, Steve would go out of his way to seek that guy out and make him feel noticed and welcome. That's just the way he was."

Wadiak, the man nobody could stop, was dead. Just like that.

His friends and teammates served as his pall-bearers: Bayard Pickett, Bob Kahle, Harry Steward, John LaTorre, Charles Prezioso, and Larry Smith. At his funeral, it is said, grown men cried openly.

His jersey, number 37, was immediately retired by the University. But they needn't have bothered. No one else is big enough to wear it anyway.

★
Wofford College

Those '48 Terriers Couldn't Win For Tying

Even the old timers, those who remembered every football game played in the Palmetto State since Reconstruction, shook their heads in disbelief. It was one of the darnest things they'd ever heard of.

One old fellow from Monks Corner said it was even more amazing than USC's inspirational 89-0 win over Welsh Neck Academy (now Coker College) in 1903. But that may have been stretching it a bit.

But this wasn't USC. It was Wofford College. It was 1948, and the Terriers had just established one of the most incredible records in the annals of college football: five consecutive ties on their way to an undefeated season.

Today, some fifty years later, that record has still not been broken. In fact, it remains a record that no other team in America has ever even approached!

No less a personage than Bill Stearn, the legendary sports announcer, broadcast Wofford's story on national radio, and people across America then turned their attention to the Terriers, waiting to see how long their incredible tie streak could continue.

Bob Prevatte, now retired and living in Gaffney, who starred as a runningback on Wofford's 4-0-5 team, recalls that '48 season:

"Our coach was Phil Dickens, who gained fame at Wyoming and Indiana. He stressed defense; nobody ever scored more than one touchdown against us that year."

Game One came against Hampton-Sydney, who was led that year by former Navy star, Lynn Chewning, and Wofford was a decided underdog going into this contest.

But after trailing 6-0 for fifty-eight minutes, Wofford, led by the running of John Clabo and the passing of Bobby Starnes, finally scored. Vernon Quick missed the extra point, and the game ended in a 6-6 tie.

Prevatte quips with a laugh: "Vernon got the ball rolling for us, you might say."

Game Two came against Northwestern Louisiana State, who had lost by a single TD to LSU the previous week.

Both teams played extraordinary defense, with a number of goal line stands by both teams. Recog-

The workhorse backfield of the '48 Terriers: Del Wiles, Bobby Starnes, Bill Glenn, and Sammy Sewell.

nized for their great defensive play following this game were Harvey Moyer, Jim Clary, Elby Hammett and Bill Creech. The game ended in a 0-0 tie.

"We were 0-0-2 at that point," says Prevatte. "We were happy to be undefeated, but you remember what Coach Frank Howard once said about a tie being about as exciting as kissing your sister? Well, that's true."

In Game Three, against Catawba College, the Terriers again trailed by a score of 7-0 most of the contest, but with only seconds left, Wofford's great All-State tailback, Sammy Sewell, scored from three yards out. Vernon Quick was true with the extra point and the game ended, a 7-7 tie.

At that point Wofford had tied their first three opponents, and Terrier fans were beginning to look askance at one another.

Even the editor of Wofford's student newspaper, a fellow affectionately known to his peers as Bill "Jughead" Rone, posed the question: "What's wrong with the Terriers? They can't seem to win for tying."

Well, sports fans, you ain't seen nothing yet.

Against Furman the next week, in Game Four, Wofford was again rated a big underdog. But

The Wofford Terriers of 1948 set an all-time football record when they tied the first five games of the season. No other team has ever even approached this mark.

Sewell's 54-yard scamper for a TD in the third quarter gave the Terriers a 7-0 lead that would hold until late in the game. Then Furman scored on a disputed 4th down play.

Disputed or not, the play stood, and the game ended in a 7-7 tie.

It was then, after tying their first four games of the season, that the Terriers began to attract national attention. Coach Dickens was a guest of the Bill Stern Sports Hour, a nationally syndicated radio show.

And Ken Alyta of the Associated Press wrote in a syndicated column: "Wofford is possibly the most interesting team in the country this week. Their fourth consecutive tie has given them more publicity than any victory could ever have give them."

Game Five the next week came against a highly touted team from Davidson College. The game, as one might expect, was sold out by Monday afternoon. Then Saturday evening, just before kickoff, Wofford's cheerleaders, in a fit of levity, led the fans

in yelling: "Tie Davidson! Tie Davidson! Tie hell out of Davidson!"

As for the game itself, Doug Loveday and John Clabo led the Terriers to a fourth quarter touchdown which—of course—knotted the score, and the game ended in a 7-7 tie. Wofford had now tied their first five games of the season!

Sadly, their streak ended the next week with a 12-0 romp over Newberry. Still, the Terriers had established their place in football history. Numerous teams have tied three games in a single season, but not one team in the history of the sport has ever tied five games in a single season. Wofford, of course, tied five consecutive games in a single season!

Some may say that the Terriers had earned the all-time football Dubious Achievement Award. But as Bob Prevatte says, "Any way you look at it, the '48 Wofford Terriers went undefeated. We're proud of our four wins, and we're proud of our five ties."

★
Art Baker

He's Done It All—And Better Than Anyone Else

From a professional standpoint, Art Baker is one of those rare individuals who has always known the best moves to make and the best times to make them. Call it common sense, or intuition, or whatever, but his rise from obscurity to prominence in the world of athletics has been both rapid and seemingly inevitable.

That's not to say that he hasn't suffered setbacks. He has. Many times. But Baker is a man whose confidence borders on audacity, who learned early in life the knack of turning adversity to advantage. In other words, if he couldn't go around an obstacle, he would go over it. But eventually he would get there. Plus his cordial personality is one that Dale Carnegie himself would envy.

Today he serves as Special Consultant to Coach Brad Scott of the Carolina Gamecocks, a position to be envied by anyone's standards. But he traveled a long road in getting there.

A native of Sumter, Baker attended Edmunds High School where he was elected captain of the football team in the spring of 1946. "Unfortunately," he says, "that fall we had some old war veterans return to school, and I got beat out for my quarterback position by this old guy who had fought throughout the war. Somehow he came up with this miracle birth certificate which said that he was still only eighteen and thus eligible to play. So for the rest of the season I'd go out before the kickoff for the coin toss, then I'd go sit down on the bench for the rest of the game. Sort of an awkward situation."

The following summer, in 1947, a family friend, a retired Air Force officer, persuaded young Art that he should go in service before the GI Bill expired. So Baker, now only sixteen years old but with an independent nature that would stagger a wildcat, joined the Army and soon found himself taking basic training at Ft. Bliss, Texas. "I spent three of the loneliest months of my life out there," Baker says. "Then, wanting to make more money, I volunteered for airborne training. But at that point my mother stepped in and said that her child would not be jumping out of airplanes for anybody, GI Bill or not, and so she blew the whistle on me. The next day the

Art Baker served as head coach at Furman, The Citadel, and East Carolina before becoming Executive Director of the Gamecock Club. He is now Special Consultant to Coach Brad Scott.

Army had me on a train bound for home."

Baker returned to Edmunds High for his senior year only to find that he had been declared ineligible to play football. "But Coach Larry Weldon told me that if I'd coach the B-team, he'd help me get a scholarship to Presbyterian College. So there I was, at the age of seventeen, head coach of Edmunds B-football team. I had some great little guys on that team, and we went 10-0 on the season. I decided then and there that coaching was the easiest way in the world to make a living, and that's what I wanted to do forever."

In the spring of '48 Coach Weldon sent Baker and four other players up to PC to try out for scholarships. The legendary Coach Lonnie McMillan offered scholarships to the other four but not to Baker, who weighed in at about 150 pounds. But the boys, loyal to one another as only teenage boys can be loyal, told McMillan he'd have to take all five or none.

"So Coach McMillan called me in his office," laughs Baker, "and gave me this very sincere look, as

Art Baker (#20) as a star halfback with the Blue Hose in 1951.

though he were about to offer me the college library. But he did offer me a scholarship. It consisted of a bed down in the dank basement of the gym and free school books. In return, all I had to do was practice football in the afternoons and wash dishes seven mornings a week over at the chow hall. It sounded wonderful, so I gladly accepted."

Unfortunately for young Art, he performed better on the football field his freshman year than he did in the classroom, and thus found himself ineligible to play his sophomore season. So, facing a forced vacation, he spent that year working in Columbia where he gained valuable experience playing quarterback for the Brooklyn-Cayce All Stars, a semi-pro team that went 10-0 on the season.

In 1951, now back at PC and on a full scholarship, Baker asked to be shifted to a runningback position where he could get more playing time. "I had so much frustration that I hadn't had a chance to play and that truly motivated me to do well." For the next two years he would be the team's leading ground gainer.

His senior year, as though he didn't already have enough to do washing dishes, going to class and practicing football, he married his high school sweetheart, Edith Edens from Dalzell. "I originally met Edith at the beach during the spring of my senior year in high school. In fact, after meeting her, I stayed a few days longer at the beach than I should have, and the coach tossed me off the baseball team for skipping practice."

Back in those days all students at PC were required to take ROTC their first two years at the college. "We had drills at 7 AM every morning. So I'd get up, run to ROTC drills, then run to the chow hall to wash dishes, then run to class. One morning during my junior year my basement roommate, Cedric Jernigan, and I were standing there in the chow hall, up to our

necks in dirty dishwater, and he said to me, 'Say, Art, let's dump this ROTC business, and we can start getting a little sleep in the mornings.' Well, I had worked my way up to sergeant by then, but I reluctantly agreed to retire from the ROTC. Later, when I entered the Army as a private, I regretted that move."

In June of '53, after taking his degree in History, Baker was drafted and suddenly found himself a resident of Ft. Jackson in Columbia. He was now Private Art Baker, a position he would hold for the next two years.

Following his discharge in the summer of '55, he took the head coaching job in McColl, S.C. It was then and there that this writer had the honor of serving as captain of Art Baker's first football team (which should give the reader a pretty good idea of the tremendous talent he had to work with that year).

But Baker's coaching took off once he arrived at Eau Claire High School in Columbia, where he recruited what must have been the finest high school coaching staff in America. Guys like Buddy Sasser, Jimmy Satterfield, Steve Robinson, and Dick Sheridan, all who have made their mark in college athletics.

Then, in 1965, having just coached the Shrine Bowl team to victory, he received a phone call one morning about 6 AM, rousing him from a deep sleep. "The voice on the other end of the line was one that anyone would recognize," he grins. "It was Coach Frank Howard up at Clemson. He said, 'Hey, Al, I need a new freshman coach. You want the job, Al?' I told him my name was Art, but that my wife and I would like to come up and speak with him about it. He said, 'Now wait a minute, Buddy. I didn't say nothing about putting your wife on the payroll.' But to make a long story short, I took the job and spent five delightful years with Clemson and Frank Howard."

Then in '73 Baker was named head coach at Furman University where he was again joined by Satterfield, Sasser, Robinson, and Sheridan. Following his 7-4 season that year sports writers voted him Coach of the Year in South Carolina.

After a few years as head coach at The Citadel (it was while at The Citadel that Baker hired a young assistant named Brad Scott) and following a stint as offensive coordinator under Bobby Bowden at Florida State, Baker accepted the head coaching job at East Carolina, a school with a perennial killer schedule.

But Baker soon tired to living the life of a kamikaze, and in 1988 he became associate athletic director at USC and executive director of the Gamecock Club, a position he would hold until 1995 when he eagerly leaped from behind his desk to get back down on the playing field as Special Consultant to Coach Brad Scott.

★
Tom "Black Cat" Barton

He Was A Frank Howard Favorite

Tom "Black Cat" Barton was a young man of humble origins whose vision and manhood combined to make him not only one of the most outstanding athletes in the history of Clemson football, but also one of this state's most successful educational leaders.

The son of a carpenter, Barton was born in a small cottage in Lancaster in 1929, the year the stock market suffered its resounding crash. Still, says Barton, it is not the poverty of his childhood that he remembers. It is being blessed with caring parents who fulfilled his need for security and imbued him with a determination to succeed in life.

He played high school ball under Coach Paul Gaffney during the war years. Then upon his graduation in 1946, he entered the Navy. It was then, he recalls, while home on leave in 1948, that some old friends told him they'd formed a sandlot football team and were going to Columbia to play a squad from that area. Young Tom said he'd like to go along.

As inconsequential as that event may seem, Barton remembers it today as one of the pivotal moments in his life. For among the spectators at that pickup game that afternoon was an influential Clemson alumnus. He was impressed with Barton's aggressive line play, and immediately after the game phoned Coach Frank Howard and advised him to contact Barton.

Sure enough, a week later young Barton was surprised to receive a letter from Frank Howard. The Bashful Baron promised he would be in touch as soon as Barton was discharged from the Navy.

"And that's exactly how it went," he recalls. "Following my discharge, I returned to Lancaster and went to work stringing lines for the power company. I had just about forgotten about Clemson when one day there came a knock at the door. It was Coach Howard's main assistant, Goat McMillan. He invited me up for spring tryouts. So I went up in the spring of '49 and tried out. I loved Clemson from the moment I set foot up there."

Barton quickly became one of Coach Howard's favorite people and the object of some of Howard's

Black Cat Barton was a starter on two of the greatest Clemson teams ever, playing in both the Orange and Gator Bowls. He served as team captain in '52 and was named All American that same year. He would go on to become Doctor Tom Barton, President of Greenville Technical College.

most outrageous anecdotes. There is, for example, Howard's explanation of how Tom Barton became Black Cat Barton. Says Howard:

"It was 1952 and we was playing College of Pacific out in California. They had this big black guard playing across from old Barton. I mean that boy was broader between the eyes than Barton was between the shoulders, weighed about 300 pounds. So after a while Barton comes to the sideline and says, 'Coach,

Tom "Black Cat" Barton (#37) and Clemson's defensive eleven of 1952.

that black cat's about to beat me to death out there. I gotta have some relief.' Well, at half time Barton kept talking about that black cat beating him to death out there. So the boys all got tickled and after that they started calling him Black Cat. That's how he got his name."

Barton, in all justice, vigorously disagrees with this version of how his nickname came to be. He says: "No, Coach Howard is mistaken. I got that name the first day I arrived at Clemson. We were running up and down the hill at the far end of the practice field during practice that morning. Going up and down on our hands and knees, that is. Well, I have black hair and dark features, so Coach Howard yelled, 'Hey, Barton, you look just like a black cat scampering down that hill.' And that, really, is how it came to be."

He made the Tigers' starting lineup in '49. But the real highlight of his freshman season came, he says, when he met and married Jean Yarborough, the sister of Clemson's all-time basketball great Bill Yarborough.

Indeed, Barton was a starter on some of the greatest Tiger teams ever, and had the pleasure of playing in both the Orange Bowl and Gator Bowl. He was twice named to the All-Southern team at guard, and his senior year he received the greatest honor of all when he was named to the Associated Press All-American squad.

He started for the College All Stars that year against the NFL champion Detroit Lions at Soldiers Field in Chicago. He'd been a high draft pick of the Pittsburgh Steelers, but a knee injury suffered in the All Star game ended his football career.

Not one to mope long over what might have been, Barton turned his energies to coaching on the high school level for several years and says that he truly loved working with young people of that particular age group. But his real ambition, he says, was to become a college administrator.

Like many men of varied talents, Barton is not satisfied to merely dream. Once he's made up his mind, he can't rest until he's seen that dream become a reality. Thus he entered Peabody College and earned his masters degree in 1962. In 1971 he received his doctorate from Duke.

He was named President of Greenville Technical College in 1962, a position he still holds today.

He is a member of the Clemson Athletic Hall of Fame and a Director of the South Carolina Athletic Hall of Fame.

He and Jean now have four children and three grandchildren and make their home in Greenville. Asked to comment on his rise from obscurity to prominence, a thoughtful Barton replies:

"Growing up, I always knew that education was my key to success, and I used my athletic ability to get that education. If it had not been for football, God only knows where I'd be today."

★

Nield Gordon

"If Furman's good enough for Nield Gordon, it's good
enough for me." —Darrell Floyd

Nield Gordon, former Furman University basketball star and successful coach at Newberry College and Winthrop University, says he was born with a love for the game. It was a love he nourished during his spare time when growing up in Brunswick, Maryland.

He remembers constantly dribbling a basketball in the yard, and even on the den floor inside his home at night, driving his parents to distraction.

But in the end his dedication paid off.

In 1949 he was recruited by University of Maryland head coach Flucie Stewart. But after some deliberation, Stewart decided that young Gordon, a 6-6 center, needed a little more seasoning before becoming a Terrapin.

Nield didn't know it then, but this was a decision that would change the course of his entire life.

Stewart put in a call to Coach Danny Miller at Wingate Junior College and arrangements were made for Gordon to head south.

Gordon wasted little time in making Miller happy that Stewart had called. His freshman year he led Wingate to a 29-6 record and led the nation in scoring with a 22.3 average.

Then, his sophomore year, he led Wingate to the National Junior College Championship with a 40-3 record, while he himself was named to the Junior College All-American Team.

Gordon had been joined that year by another Junior College All-American, Darrell Floyd, a future Furman great. Today Floyd recalls: "Nield was the first guy I ever saw dunk a basketball. His leaping ability was truly incredible."

Gordon agrees: "I wasn't much of a shooter, but I was pretty good under the basket."

Finally Gordon's two years were up at Wingate, and he was troubled to learn that Stewart had departed Maryland, which meant that he was now a free man with no scholarship looming on the horizon. Thus he began to shop around.

"I had been heavily recruited by all the schools in the Southern Conference," he says. "So I narrowed

In 1953 Furman University became the first college ever to average over 90 points per contest, thanks largely to Nield Gordon and his average of 25.1 points per game. After several years with the Knicks, he would go on to a successful coaching career.

my choices to Duke and Furman. But mainly I wanted to go where I'd have a chance to play, and since Furman had gone 3-20 the previous year, I felt that might be my best option."

(The reader should note that this took place in 1952, back when the schools that now comprise the Atlantic Coast Conference were still part of the Southern Conference.)

"Again, as far as Furman was concerned, I also thought that Coach Lyles Alley was one of the finest men I'd ever met. That's what really decided me to go to Furman."

Gordon started at center for the Hurricanes in 1952. They went 18-6 that year and were voted the

Gordon demonstrates his leaping ability in Furman's 105-62 win over USC in '52.

most improved team in America.

With Gordon at center and Frank Selvy in the backcourt, Furman quickly became a team to be reckoned with. Then, as though Gordon and Selvy were not blessing enough, in '53 they were joined by the nation's "other" hotshot guard, Darrell Floyd. It was as though Coach Alley had truly put together a team of college all-stars.

When asked by the press why he chose Furman, Floyd quipped, "If Furman's good enough for Nield Gordon, it's good enough for me."

That year, in 1953, Furman became the first college basketball team ever to average over 90 points per game. As for Gordon, he himself averaged 25.1 points per game, tenth best in the nation.

He and Selvy were both named All-Southern, and both were named to the Conference All-Tournament team, the first time in history that two players from the same college had been so honored.

Upon graduation, Gordon spent a year with the New York Knicks before being drafted by Uncle Sam. After two years in service, in 1956, he became head coach at Belmont Abbey. At the age of twenty-five, he became America's youngest collegiate head coach.

He left Belmont Abbey (he was replaced by Al McGuire) to take the job as freshman coach at Furman. Then in '61 it was on to Newberry College where he would remain until 1976. That year the Indians were 36-1 and ranked number-1 in NAIA competition, and Gordon was voted NAIA Coach of the Year.

He left Newberry that year to become head coach and athletic director at Winthrop University, a position he held until his retirement in 1986.

Nield Gordon has been named to the S. C. Athletic Hall of Fame, the NAIA Hall of Fame, the Furman Hall of Fame, and the Wingate Hall of Fame. Which would seem to cover most bases.

Today he is active with Sports Tours as Director of Basketball Tournaments, and he is also a partner in Chattooga Family Camp Grounds in Mountain Rest, where he and his wife Susan make their home.

Moments of Glory
*South Carolina's Greatest
Sports Heroes*

1950-1959

★

Paul Anderson

"With God's Help, Anything Is Possible."

Born in 1932, Paul Anderson was a small, sickly child who was never allowed to go out and roughhouse with the other children. But that condition lasted for only a while. By his senior year at Toccoa High School, he was considered one of the top football prospects in the state of Georgia.

Indeed, in 1949 he was offered football scholarships from colleges across the South. But young Paul liked what he saw at Furman University, and in the fall of 1950 he was enjoying an outstanding freshman season when tragedy struck. He was blindsided during the Wofford game, and he heard an awful crunch as his left knee buckled under him. He had to be carried from the field.

As part of his physical therapy, Coach Bill Young directed Anderson to the weight room. At first, he says, he found lifting weights to be hard work, and he dreaded going to those lengthy sessions. But eventually he discovered that he had a talent for lifting. At a burly 5-9 and 340 pounds, he amazed his teammates by lifting weights they could only dream of.

Returning home to Toccoa that summer, Anderson turned his father's garage into a gym of sorts and fashioned himself a set of weights from an old tractor axle. It was a crude setup, but it worked.

A year went by and Anderson's progress was remarkable. "Actually, I could have won the world championship from 1952 on," he says today. "But the first competition I ever entered was the North American in Montreal in 1953. And I won the North American Championship there."

Following that achievement, it was on to the Soviet Union, where weight lifting is considered the national pastime. But Anderson was there as a mere substitute for the American champion who had been taken ill. Tonight he would face 15,000 exuberant Soviet fans in Moscow's Gorky Park, a daunting prospect by anyone's standards.

"I remember the Russian announcer was very disturbed because I didn't have a jersey with my name and number on it, and he was afraid the audience wouldn't know who I was. In fact, I was called to make the trip at the last moment, and my

In the '56 Olympics, Anderson brought home the gold medals after breaking the world's record with lifts totaling 1,104 pounds. This despite having a fever of 105 degrees.

name wasn't even on the program." But Anderson confidently told the announcer, "Don't worry. When they see me lift, then they'll know who I am."

The Soviet champion lifted an incredible 330.5 pounds in the two-handed press. Applause reverberated throughout the hall. Indeed, the audience assumed that Anderson would not even attempt such a super effort. There came an audible gasp when he calmly called for 402.5 pounds, a weight that exceeded the world record by 20 pounds.

Anderson recalled the moment: "I succeeded in lifting it on my first try. There was dead silence in the hall for a full ten seconds. Then it was as though the place exploded. The audience went wild, applauding, screaming and stamping their feet. It was truly a very electric moment for me. In

Paul and wife Glenda. In the background is their Youth Home where they've experienced remarkable success rehabilitating young men who were headed in the wrong direction.

fact, they were always very nice to me in Russia."

The following day the news media labeled him "The World's Strongest Man."

Then it was on to Australia for the '56 Olympics in Melborne. By now it was a foregone conclusion that Anderson would bring home the gold medals—unless he somehow became too ill to compete.

And that, unfortunately, is exactly what happened. A week before he was to lift he came down with a severe ear infection which affected his balance. By competition day his weight had dropped by thirty pounds and he awakened with a 105-degree fever. The team doctors told him they might not allow him to lift that night.

"Lift!" Anderson exclaimed. "I can't even stand up!"

Fortunately, he was not scheduled to compete until midnight. Throughout that day, he says, he prayed fervently for the strength to mount the stage when his time came. Sure enough, by midnight he was feeling better.

He had to make three lifts. After two he had a total of 690 pounds, and needed 414 more on his final lift to take the gold medal. He would have to break his own world record by 18 pounds to enjoy the sweet taste of victory.

Again he prayed. "More than at any time in my life I felt God's presence. I knew with His help I would be able to do it."

And he did. He brought home the Olympic gold medal.

"But as I look back," said the introspective Anderson, "getting sick was the best thing that ever happened to me. It gave me a feeling of great humility, and proved to me that with God's help anything is possible. If people would only learn to put their lives in the hands of God, they could achieve miracles."

Anderson says that he experienced a religious conversion that night that has grown stronger with the passage of time. Indeed, it is his faith, a faith shared by his wife Glenda, that led him to create what he considers his finest achievement: The Paul Anderson Youth Home in Vidalia, Ga.

Since 1961 the home has provided an alternative to penal institutions for young men ages 16-21. More than 1,200 young men have graduated from that home, and Anderson says it success rate has been astounding.

"Here, Glenda and I have acted as parents to these boys and given them the love and teaching they never received at home. But of course the real key to success with these young men is giving them love and religious faith."

Anyone wishing information concerning the Paul Anderson Youth Home can write to P.O. Box 525, Vidalia, Ga. 30473, or call 912-537-7237.

We sincerely regret the recent death of Paul Anderson.

★

Buck George

This Young Indian Lad Became An Outstanding Tiger

Buck George, a former Clemson great, takes pride in his Catawba Indian heritage and today spends much of his free time collecting and preserving the history of his people.

Life was tough for everyone back during the days of the Great Depression. But for young Buck George, a Catawba Indian lad growing up on a Rock Hill mill village, life was more than tough. Still, through it all, he somehow always knew the good life was waiting just over the horizon. He had only to work hard and persevere, and someday he would become a star player in the Great American Dream. Indeed, George says, he always tries to treat adversity as simply a challenge to be met head on.

Of his childhood, he remembers, "My father had only recently left the reservation to work in the cotton mill, and we were very poor. Nothing came easy."

Nothing, that is, except running with a football. At Rock Hill High he played under Coach Walter Jenkins and ran wild from his tailback position in the old single-wing formation. In 1950 he was named All-State, All-Southern and was a starter in the Shrine Bowl.

Scholarship offers rolled in, but Buck's mother,

delighted at her son's opportunity to escape both the reservation and the cotton mill, insisted that he attend Clemson. Buck explains: "Coach Howard was a real student of human psychology. While the other coaches sat in the living room with my father and me explaining what a wonderful education I would receive at their schools, Coach Howard sat in the kitchen with my mom telling her how he always took the boys to church on Sundays and to prayer meetings on Wednesday nights. After a while I heard my mother call, 'Come in the kitchen, son, we just made our decision.'"

Buck laughs at the recollection. "You'd be surprised how many boys at Clemson I heard tell that same story."

He enrolled at Clemson in '51 and immediately stepped into the starting lineup at wingback. He recalls that in his first college game, versus Presbyterian College, he entered the contest almost in shock from frayed nerves.

"I remember, for example, that I was supposed to block for our punter on fourth down. As the ball was snapped, the PC linebacker broke through—and he was flying. I recognized him immediately as my old friend and teammate from Rock Hill, Buddy Neely. I was so happy to see a familiar face that I almost threw my arms around his neck instead of blocking him."

But George says that seeing a young player in shock was not too unusual. He recalls a game against Georgia, for example, in which quarterback Don King was injured and rookie Charlie Bussey came in, facing a third-and-fifteen situation.

"It was Charlie's first college play. His eyes were glazed. He opened his mouth to call the play but nothing came out. He was in shock. Well, we looked at one another, then Billy O'Dell said, 'Heck, Charlie, just pitch it out to Buck around left end. We'll block for him.'"

The play worked for a first down, says George. "The funny thing is, the sports writers all congratulated Charlie for having the presence of mind to call such an imaginative play on third and long. Charlie just smiled very modestly and said it wasn't anything."

George still holds the Clemson record for the

George turns the corner in Clemson's 13-0 win over Boston College in 1952. He still holds the Tiger record for the longest TD run from scrimmage, a 90-yarder against Furman in '52. That same year he carried the ball 15 times against PC for 204 yards, an average of 13.6 yards per carry, yet another Tiger record.

longest run from scrimmage, a 90-yard TD run against Furman in 1952. That same year he rushed for 204 yards against PC, a 13.6 per carry average, still another Tiger record.

In 1954 he served as team captain, then played in the North-South Shrine Game in Miami. He was a high draft pick of the Washington Redskins, but was forced to pass up pro ball because of a leg injury suffered in the Shrine game.

For many years now Buck and his family have made their home in Rock Hill, where he works in the engineering department at Hoechst-Celanese. Both he and his daughter, prominent Rock Hill dentist Dr. Wenonah Haire, are active in cultural affairs at the new Catawba Indian reservation.

★
Billy Hair

He Was A Great Tailback Who Made The Tigers Clinck

Those were the golden years of Clemson football, the late '40s and early '50s, when big Frank Howard reigned supreme as king of the Clemson Hill, the Tigers wore orange jerseys and purple pants, and they still clung to that hard-nosed single-wing formation (which Howard once described as "our come-and-get-us offense") and ran it with devastating effectiveness against all comers.

It was the tailback who made the single-wing click, and Howard's list of all-time great tailbacks reads like a Who's Who of Clemson immortals. Guys like Billy Poe, Bobby Gage, Jackie Calvert, and the irrepressible Billy Hair.

He was a starter at tailback for the Tigers for three glorious years ('50-'52), and even today the Clemson Record Book still ranks him at seventh in total touchdowns (running and passing) with thirty-one, and sixth in total offense with 3,464 yards in 616 carries, an incredible 5.62 yards per carry average.

But Hair distinguished himself early as a tailback at Walterboro High School, where he played under Coach George Dailey, an alumnus of Notre Dame University. In fact, Notre Dame was one of more than thirty colleges that held out big scholarship offers to Hair his senior season.

"But really, I never seriously considered anybody but Clemson and Tennessee, because they were two of the few schools still using the single-wing formation," Hair says.

Following Hair's brilliant performance in the '48 Shrine Bowl (U. S. Representative Floyd Spence was a teammate), Howard became a permanent fixture in Walterboro.

Hair grins: "I remember one night Coach Howard dropped in, and he had Peahead Walker and Bear Bryant with him. My parents invited them in, and we all sat down at the kitchen table, and Mom poured us all a cup of coffee, and they started talking. Everybody was a little formal at first, but those fellows couldn't hold back for long. So finally Peahead told a funny story on Coach Howard, and then of course Coach Howard had to come back with a funny

A native of Walterboro, Bill Hair was an All Southern tailback for Clemson and led them to two bowl games.

story about Peahead. Then Bear Bryant chimed in with an outrageous story about Peahead and Howard, and pretty soon everybody was talking and laughing and we were all just about rolling on the floor."

Hair became Clemson's starting tailback in 1950. That was the year that Clemson went undefeated and played Miami in the Orange Bowl. Hair remembers that the game became a grudge match after Miami expressed disappointment that a fine team like the '50 Hurricanes should be paired with a bunch of hicks from a hick school like Clemson, never mind that half of Clemson's "hicks" hailed from Pennsylvania and Ohio.

But thanks to the fine play of Billy Hair, complemented by that of Fred Cone, Ray Mathews, and Wyndie Wyndham, the Tigers held their own for most of the game. But then with only two minutes of play left on the clock, Miami scored and went ahead 14-13. It looked as though the Tigers were going to lose a heartbreaker.

Two minutes later, however, Miami again had the ball, this time at their own 5-yard line, and were running down the clock. Miami fans, in fact, were loudly counting off the seconds: nine-eight-seven. . . . It was then that the Hurricanes tried an end sweep. It was an unfortunate play call, one that has haunted them now for the past forty-seven years.

For just as the Miami halfback took the toss, Clemson's Sterling Smith, a second-string guard, shot the gap, totally untouched, and nailed the runner behind the goal line for a safety. Final score: Clemson 15, Miami 14.

Hair remembers that it was all work and little play for the Tigers that week as they prepared to meet Miami.

"I think they took us downtown to a couple of movies, but that was about it," he says. "But a few of the boys decided to go out on their own to taste the Miami night life. And sure enough, Coach Howard caught them—sort of early in the morning, you might say. And he was furious, or pretended to be. But then, everybody played well the next day, so no real harm was done."

The next year, 1951, was not quite as good for the Tigers. They went 7-2-1 on the year and played a rematch with Miami in the Gator Bowl.

This game began with a bang as Hair raced the opening kickoff back 74 yards before getting bounced out of bounds at the Miami 26-yard line. But in the end the day belonged to the Hurricanes as Clemson went down by a score of 14-0.

Clemson, by the way, accepted this bowl invitation in direct violation of Southern Conference rules and was thus placed on probation. It was this frustrating situation that led to the formation of the

Here Hair runs for yardage against Miami in the 1950 Orange Bowl, a game won by the Tigers in an upset 15-14.

Atlantic Coast Conference the next year.

Hair was named All-Southern in both '51 and '52 and became a high draft pick of the Green Bay Packers. But a crippling knee injury suffered his senior year prevented further play.

For many years now he has been employed in the engineering department of the Lockheed Corp. at the Naval Weapons Station in Goose Creek. He and his wife, the former Nell Sease of Lexington, have three sons and make their home in Summerville.

He is a member of the Clemson Athletic Hall of Fame.

★

Roland Barefoot

He's Strictly a Furman Man—Always!

Roland Barefoot, everyone agreed, was indeed a most deserving lad. He was always prepared when he entered the classroom, he appeared on time for work at the local grocery every afternoon, and he could hardly wait to attend Sunday School on Sunday mornings. His only limitation, it seemed, was money. Like many young men of his day his parents were not well off. Thus, upon his graduation from Lancaster High School in 1950 he stayed at home and went to work. Attending college was out of the question.

Earlier he'd had high hopes for an athletic scholarship. At 6-2 and 190 pounds, he had led Lancaster High to the state high school basketball championship. And in football he'd been named an All-State end and chosen to play in the Shrine Bowl. But he'd broken his ankle in that game and lost all hope for a big college career.

But then, just before Christmas, just when things seemed darkest, he was at home one evening stringing lights on the family tree, when there came a sudden knock at the door. Young Roland was flabbergasted to find Lyles Alley, Furman's legendary basketball coach, standing there.

"Boy, that really cheered me up," Barefoot recalled recently. "I also remember that Coach Alley mentioned that he'd just signed one of the best players in America, some fellow from Corbin, Kentucky named Frank Selvy. I got real excited then. I truly wanted to become a part of that team. He then went on to say that he'd see me in a couple of months, and hopefully sign me to a scholarship then."

Then, to compound (and complicate) Barefoot's good fortune, just three days later he received another surprise visit. This time it was Bill Young, head football coach at Furman. "Coach Young wanted me to sign a scholarship right there and then, and so I did," says Barefoot. "As a result, I missed out on playing with Frank Selvy, Darrell Floyd and all those other great Furman players of that era. But I truly have no regrets."

The following fall Barefoot reported to Furman for preseason drills. "I was one more scared

Roland Barefoot started 36 consecutive games at end for the Hurricanes, and served as team captain in 1954.

freshman, and I thought they'd at least let me get my feet wet before throwing me to the wolves. But Coach Tom Wham, our end coach, saw something he liked in me and immediately stuck me up there with the starting defensive unit."

And so how did it go? "The first time we scrimmaged, Coach Wham told me to crash on the quarterback on the next play. I didn't know what he meant by crash, but I wasn't about to tell him so. So on the next play I just floated out, the way I'd been taught in high school. Now Coach Wham had been an All-Southern end at Furman and had played for years with the Chicago Cardinals. He was the nicest fellow you'd ever want to meet out in real life, but down on that football field he was as mean as the dickens.

"Well, he didn't say anything to me, but then on the next play our quarterback came optioning down the line and Coach Wham hauled off and gave me a big kick in the seat of my pants. I went

Here Barefoot goes in for the touchdown that upset a great West Virginia team in 1952. It was the Mounties' only loss of the season.

about six feet in the air and came down right on that quarterback's shoulders. Coach Wham yelled, 'That's it, son. That's exactly what I want you to do.' Under my breath I said, 'Thanks, Coach, I never had anybody explain it to me that way before.'"

Between 1951 and 1954 Barefoot started 36 consecutive games for the Hurricanes. He had some great teammates during those years, and they played against some of the best teams the South had to offer.

He especially remembers 1952 and upsetting a great West Virginia team led by future all-pro linebacker Sam Huff. The Mounties lost only to Furman that year before going on to win the Sugar Bowl. The Hurricanes also upset a good Florida State team that year.

Then came 1953. This edition of the Hurricanes has been called one of the finest in Furman history, losing only to USC and Army, while beating both Wake Forest and Florida State on their way to a great 8-2 season.

In '54 they claimed NC State among their other victims, but the game Barefoot remembers most vividly from the '54 season is a 51-14 loss to Miami.

"It was our opening game of the season, played in the Orange Bowl, and Miami really went all out to make a special occasion of it. There were parades and banquets and speeches, and they were just old pie to us. And we had a wonderful time, except for the game itself. But on game day we knew we were in for trouble when Miami came out for pregame warmups. They weren't wearing pads, and they were bigger than we were without them."

In 1954, in addition to serving as team captain, Barefoot was named to both the All-State and All-Southern teams.

Then, following graduation, he would spend the next thirty years operating his own trucking business, a very profitable enterprise.

But in 1984 he gave it up to return to his beloved Furman University where he became Director of Planned Giving. "It's the best job there is," he says. "I get to talk with Furman alumni all over the world, and there are really some very interesting people out there. But best of all, this job gives me an opportunity to repay Furman for some of the wonderful things they did for me. In fact, if it weren't for Furman, I might still be a bag boy down at the local grocery."

Roland is married to the former Ann Collins of Lancaster, and they and their two sons make their home in Greenville.

★
Don King

He Set Two All-Time Clemson Rushing Records

Back in 1951 Don King was one of the most highly sought after high school quarterbacks in the country. He had made the All-State Team both his junior and senior years at Anderson's Boys High School, was a starter in the Shrine Bowl, and named to the High School All-American Team.

Today King attributes much of his high school success to another Boys High alumnus, all-time Clemson great Bobby Gage.

"I was fortunate that Bobby Gage, who was playing for Clemson when I was in high school, would come down in his spare time and work with me on my passing and punting," King says. "There wasn't a better tailback in America than Bobby Gage, so I got some pretty good pointers."

King pauses for a moment, then continues: "As for the running part of it, you can't teach somebody to run. Either they can or they can't."

He entered Clemson in the fall of '52, the year before Clemson switched from the single-wing to the T-formation.

"Billy Hair was our starting tailback that year, and I was his backup. But Billy injured his shoulder against PC in our first game of the season, so I got quite a bit of playing time."

In November King got his first start. It came against Fordham University, the number-one team in the nation, in a game played in New York City. Was he just a little nervous about his first start?

"You bet!" he says simply.

But King says he soon settled down and did what he had been taught to do in practice. And by game's end, he had rushed for a phenomenal 234 yards, a Clemson single-game rushing record that would stand for the next thirty years. He carried the ball 33 times that afternoon, averaging 7 yards per carry, more Clemson single-game rushing records.

In addition, he scored both of Clemson's touchdowns, one of them a 74-yard run in the fourth quarter that tied the score at 12-12. Which is how the game ended, one of the upsets of the '52 season.

Recalling his record-setting exploits running the ball that afternoon, King says: "It was awfully cold that day, and the wind was gusting at 40 mph. So there really wasn't much passing I could do. So

Like Bobby Gage, Don King was a product of Boys High in Anderson, S. C. He is still remembered as one of the finest quarterbacks ever to play for Clemson.

it developed into a running game for both teams." King finished his freshman season as the Tigers' leading scorer.

A list of King's teammates during his four years at Clemson will bring tears to the eyes of the toughest Tiger fan. Guys like Joel Wells, Joe Pagliei, Jim Shirley, Billy O'Dell, B. C. Inabinet, John Grdijan, Earl Greene, Wingo Avery, Red Whitten, Dreher Gaskin, Bill McLellan, Nathan Gressette, Walt Laraway, Buck George and Tom "Blackcat" Barton.

Yet, despite their all-star lineup, the Tigers went 2-6-1 in '52. By way of explanation, King says, "Well, I was always a better runner than passer. But I had bum knees that year and couldn't go at full speed. So we were in pretty tough shape physically. But actually, the whole team was plagued with injuries the whole year."

In '53, now converted to a quarterback in Clemson's new T-formation, King led the team in both rushing and punt return yardage.

It was in '54 that he had his most memorable experience as a Tiger, and that came against the tough Hurricanes of Miami. King starts to laugh even before he begins the story: "We were in the fourth quarter of a very close game when Joe Pagliei went back to punt from our own 10 yard line. But instead of punting the ball, Joe got a sudden inspiration to run it out. Well, he took about two steps and got nailed. Miami then took over at our ten.

"We trotted off the field, and Coach Howard's face looked like he was having a stroke. He ran over and grabbed Pagliei and started shaking him and yelling and having a fit in general. But Pagliei, who was a real unforgettable sort of character, just looked him straight in the eye and very calmly said, 'Coach, football is just like horse racing—sometimes you have to take a chance.'

"I honestly believe that's the only time I ever saw Coach Howard speechless. He stood there with his mouth hanging open, watching Pagliei walk away."

But the game he can never forget, King says, came against Maryland his senior year. They were playing for the ACC crown and the right to play Oklahoma in the Orange Bowl. Clemson, he remembers, jumped off to a 12-0 lead, but then the Terrapins came back to win the game.

"That's the game I remember most," he says. "We had it in our pocket and let it get away. I still replay that game in my mind about once a week. I threw an interception at a crucial point, and that has always stuck with me, wishing I could call back that bad throw. Yep, after all these years, that's still the game I remember most."

Following his graduation in 1956, King returned to Anderson and opened a Shell Oil Co. distributorship. He went into semi-retirement several years ago, he says, but continues to dabble in real estate and land development.

His two sons, Don and Mark, are also Anderson businessmen, and his daughter, Brandi, who was homecoming queen at T.L. Hanna High several years ago, is a graduate of Columbia College.

In his first start as a freshman in 1952, against Fordham, the number-one team in the nation, a jittery Don King simply ran for 234 yards, a rushing record that would stand at Clemson for the next thirty years.

★

Harold Lewis

At the Age of 16 He Became One of the Youngest
USC Quarterbacks Ever

Harold Lewis, a native of Aynor, led the Gamecocks to an incredible 34-20 upset win over a powerful Army team in 1954. He still grows sad when reminded of his old teammate, the late Steve Wadiak.

Harold Lewis was only sixteen the first time he trotted onto the grassy playing field at Carolina Stadium, making him one of the youngest quarterbacks ever to take a snap for the Carolina Gamecocks.

He was born and raised in Aynor and was not even old enough to qualify for a drivers license when he finished high school in 1951. "Actually I was attending Carlisle Military Academy back then," he says. "I remember I played football my junior year at 5-8 and 138 pounds. But then by my senior year I'd shot up to 6-1 and 190 pounds. Still, I've always wished I'd had another year or two to grow and mature before I entered Carolina."

The great Steve Wadiak, who was a senior at Carolina during Lewis' freshman year, remains one of his all-time heroes. "In fact, Steve and I lived in the same dorm, and I remember the pay phone in the hallway outside my room ringing about five one morning in March of '52. It was an Aiken County deputy sheriff, and he told me that Steve had just been killed in a car wreck and to call Coach Enright. You can imagine the shock. It was truly one of the darkest days of my life."

Of all the games that Lewis played from '53 to '55, there are two that still stand out in his mind. The first concerns Big Thursday of '53.

As usual, there was a capacity crowd of 35,000 on hand to watch this annual Carolina-Clemson shootout. As for Lewis, now eighteen and playing backup to the great Johnny Gramling at quarterback, he watched anxiously from the bench as the Gamecocks repeatedly turned back Tiger threats to take a 7-0 lead into the locker room at halftime.

But then early in the third period Gramling went down with a shoulder injury and Harold Lewis was thrown into the breach. He would disappoint no one.

It was late in the third period, he remembers, with the 'Cocks still nursing their 7-0 lead, when Lewis led them on a long drive down to the Clemson 21-yard line. Then, looking at third and long, he faked a handoff to Carl Brazell that fooled everyone in the stadium. Then he looked downfield and there, running all alone towards the corner of the Tiger end zone, was Joe Silas. Lewis rifled the ball to him, and suddenly the score became 14-0.

Later, with time running out and Clemson trailing 14-7, Lewis again saved the day for USC when he intercepted a Don King pass in the USC end zone and ran it back to mid-field. And that was the game.

The other contest that stands out in his memory is the Army game of '54, a game that the experts still recall as one of the greatest wins in the history of USC football. But for Lewis this game represents more than just a big win.

"That game with Army was the first game I ever started at Carolina, and it was played on my father's birthday. My father was extremely ill by that time, and it was the last game he'd ever see me play. I remember, I asked him what I could get him for his birthday, and he told me a win over Army would be the finest gift he could ever receive."

As the first quarter got underway West Point fans sat in stunned silence as Lewis and his underdog Gamecocks passed their way to an early 7-0 lead. But then, just before half time, Army tied the score when they intercepted a Lewis pass and ran it back for a touchdown. Lewis left the field with his head down, feeling that he'd let his teammates (and his father) down with that poorly thrown ball.

But his dejection didn't last long. To begin the third quarter the Gamecocks took the ball at their own three, in the shadow of their own goal posts. It was not an enviable position. But with Carl Brazell and Mike Caskey ripping off nice gains around end, and Harold Lewis tossing the ball, the Gamecocks marched 97 yards over the next five minutes for another score. And from that point on, the Gamecocks dominated. Final score: USC 34 - Army 20.

Following his graduation, Lewis served two years in the Army at Ft. Jackson, where he played on the post football team and worked as a chaplain's assistant. It was a job that would change the course of his life. For upon his discharge he entered Emory University and was ordained a Methodist minister in 1961.

Today he is pastor of the Belin United Methodist Church in Murrells Inlet. He and his wife Edna have two sons and a daughter and make their home in Garden City.

★

Carl Brazell

Proverbial Paper Boy Becomes
An All-Time Great Gamecock Runningback

Carl Brazell is still remembered as one of the finest running backs ever to wear the garnet and black. During his four-year career at USC he averaged 5.7 yards per carry, a record that has stood now for over forty years.

Horatio Alger had nothing on University of South Carolina football great Carl Brazell, a true success story by anyone's standards.

A lifelong resident of Columbia, Brazell began chipping away at life's fortunes as a seventh grader at Hand Junior High. He remembers rolling out of bed every morning at 4 AM, gobbling down a quick breakfast, then mounting his bike to deliver newspapers throughout the Five Points area. "It didn't matter whether it was raining, sleeting, snowing, or whatever," he says, "those newspapers had to be delivered. And it had to be done every morning. I finally resigned as a carrier five years later, the day I graduated from Dreher High School."

Despite his diminutive size (he stood 5-8 and weighed 150 pounds), he became a star in all three major sports at Dreher and was named to the All-State team in both football and baseball his senior year in 1951.

Yet no colleges came calling.

Undeterred, Brazell drove up to Clemson to try out for a scholarship (tryouts were legal in those days). After a brief scrimmage, Coach Frank Howard motioned Brazell to the sideline. Trying to be as tactful as possible, Howard gazed down at the little Brazell and somewhat hesitantly asked:

"Carl, uh, just how big is your daddy, son?"

"Oh, I guess I'm about an inch taller than Daddy," Brazell answered.

Howard's face fell. "Well, thanks for coming up, son. We'll be in touch."

It was the same story at both Furman and Presbyterian College. Brazell was just too small to play college football. Then, just when it seemed that young Carl would spend the rest of his life delivering newspapers, Coach Rex Enright granted him USC's last scholarship of 1952.

"Coach Enright said that he wanted me because of my good attitude. But I'm pretty sure he did it just as a favor to my coach at Dreher."

Brazell remembers how it was when he reported for preseason practice drills at USC. "I wasn't even given a uniform or a jersey number. After they'd given out equipment to everyone else, they'd just toss me whatever was left over."

His big break came on the Saturday before Big Thursday in a scrimmage game for the JVs against Georgia Southern. Despite wearing a uniform that looked as though it had been designed to fit King Kong, Brazell amazed everyone by running back two punts for touchdowns. Then later in the game he dashed 80 yards from scrimmage for another score. Following that impressive performance a delighted Rex Enright ordered him to report to the varsity on Monday afternoon.

"They actually gave me equipment that fit,"

In USC's '54 opener at Army, Carl Brazell took this Harold Lewis pass and ran it the distance for a TD and a 7-0 USC lead.

laughs Brazell, "and issued me a real USC jersey."

Four days later, on Big Thursday, he dressed out with the rest of the team to meet the Clemson Tigers. "But really, that didn't mean anything," he recalls. "I just thought I'd get to sit on the bench with the team and watch the game for free."

Just prior to the kickoff that day Coach Enright gathered the Gamecocks together in the locker room. At the conclusion of his pep talk, he said, "If we win the toss, I want Carl Brazell to run it back."

"I remember I was sitting there minding my own business, maybe thinking about what I was going to do after the game, when I heard Coach Enright mention my name. I'm not kidding, it was like sirens suddenly went off inside my head. There I was, a seventeen year old freshman, my name not even on the program, and I was going to start for Carolina on Big Thursday. I was hoping that Coach Enright would maybe laugh and say that he'd made a slip of the tongue, that he really wanted Mike Caskey to run back the kickoff. But he didn't. I just sat there and thought, Oh, Lord, please don't let us

win the coin toss. But we did, and I ran it back. It was nothing great, but at least I didn't faint when I caught the ball."

The following year, Brazell became a starter for the Gamecocks and played in USC's first ACC game ever, a 20-7 loss to Duke on September 22, 1953. In that contest he ran back a punt 70 yards for the Gamecock's only touchdown of the afternoon.

But his best years were still ahead of him. As a senior in 1955, he ran a punt back 95 yards for a touchdown against Virginia, still USC's third longest punt return. He also led the ACC in pass receptions that year (he was ranked 4th in the nation). Also in '55 he averaged 6.7 yards per carry, still third best in the USC record book.

More impressively, for his entire career at Carolina Carl Brazell averaged 5.7 yards per carry, still number-one in the USC record book.

For the past forty years now he has been extremely active in civic affairs in the Columbia area, where he and his family make their home. He recently retired from the banking industry.

★

Lee Collins

Meet USC'S All-Time Mr. Rebound

Life proved rather tough sledding for young Lee Collins growing up in Lancaster, S. C. during the Great Depression. His father had a job with Mullis Lumber Co., and so the Collins family had it better than most, but still times weren't flush by any means.

Yet Lee, who was born in 1932, managed to survive. He remembers that one of the first great thrills of his life came not when his parents bought him a new car or sent him to Daytona Beach for Easter vacation (he laughs at the absurdity of such an idea), but when he made the Lancaster High School basketball team in 1950, his junior year in high school.

He had always been a big kid, and he truly looked forward to playing center for the Hurricanes. They had a great team that year and went on to defeat Camden by a score of 18-15 for the state championship. Collins himself would be named to the All-State team, the only junior so honored that year.

There then arose one of those unforeseen events that can drastically change the course of our lives. It seems that Wingate Junior College back then offered junior and senior high school classes, and so Coach Danny Miller offered Collins a scholarship to Wingate. He could then complete high school while playing college basketball. To Collins, it seemed an ideal situation, and he jumped at the chance.

That year, in fact, in 1950, led by Nield Gordon and Darrell Floyd, both of whom would later be named All-American at Furman, Wingate won the Junior College National Championship. So Collins would get a chance to play with the best. Gordon graduated that year, but everyone else was back for the '51 campaign. Despite some healthy competition, Collins cracked Wingate's starting lineup. By now he stood 6-6 and weighed in at 220, a center not easily pushed around.

Thanks to Floyd's hotshot shooting and Collins' rebounding ability, Wingate went 40-3 on the season and a number-three national ranking.

The following year, in 1952, now a bona fide high school graduate, he accepted a scholarship to the University of South Carolina. But why Carolina? Because of their great athletic programs? Or maybe because of their academic excellence?

"Nah," laughs Collins. "In fact, I was dating a coed at Carolina at that time. And that, in all honesty, is the big reason I decided to go there. I know it'd make a great story to say that we got married and lived happily ever after. But in fact we broke up not long after I arrived on campus. I've often wondered what ever happened to that little girl."

Collins became a starter for the Gamecocks in '53 and immediately made his presence known. In addition to his many other accolades, he would soon establish himself throughout the ACC as Mr. Rebound.

His junior year, in 1955, he grabbed off an incredible 434 rebounds. This remains a single-season record at USC.

The next year, in 1956, he would take down 404 rebounds, an average of 17.6 per contest. This remains still another first in the USC record book.

Against The Citadel in '56, a game in which the Gamecocks scored a record 121 points, Collins claimed 33 rebounds, still second in the USC record book for single game rebounds.

Nor was he any slouch on offense. He scored 382 free throws during his career (still fourth in the USC record book), and 1,250 total points for his career.

More importantly, Collins made off with 1,159 rebounds during his career with the Gamecocks, a record that no one, not even the great Tom Owens or Alex English, have come close to breaking, despite the fact that they played many more games than Collins.

A quick check of the USC record book indicates that Collins is a member of a very select group of Gamecock players. He is a charter member of USC's Double 1,000 Club. That is, he scored more than 1,000 points and pulled down more than 1,000 rebounds during his playing career.

The other members of this exalted quintet are:

Lee Collins (#35) and his Carolina teammates of 1954. After forty years, Collins still holds almost every conceivable rebounding record for the Gamecocks.

Tom Owens, Joe Smith, Alex English, and Jimmy Foster.

His most memorable experience, he says, came at the expense of Furman University in 1956. "We played them up at Textile Hall in Greenville, and my old friend Darrell Floyd was going wild for them that year, led the nation in scoring among other things. But we upset them by a score of 89-84. My parents were able to attend that game, and I've never forgotten it."

Collins, by the way, in addition to scoring 22 points that evening, made off with a phenomenal 27 rebounds.

After completing his collegiate career in '56, Collins spent the next two years in the army. That's when, he says, he decided to realize another lifelong ambition. He became a resident of Myrtle Beach.

"That's what I did. I came down here in 1959 and established a retail mobile home business, and I've been here ever since. I retired three years ago, and now I devote all my time to enjoying the beach, which I truly love, and to reading. A lot of people who knew me in college might be surprised to hear that I now read books, but reading is now one of my main hobbies."

★
Bob Fulton

He's the Only Non-Athlete, Non-Coach Ever Inducted
Into the S. C. Athletic Hall of Fame

Bob Fulton retired as Voice of the Gamecocks following Carolina's big win over West Virginia in the Carquest Bowl on January 2, 1995. Yep, after 43 years he finally hung it up.

But prior to that time Bob Fulton had called many a game for the Gamecocks. In fact, when he first arrived at Carolina, Rex Enright was head football coach, *High Noon* was playing at your local theater, Elvis Presley was a kid truck driver in Memphis, the Beetles were enrolled in Liverpool Elementary School, and your favorite songs on the radio were *Glow Little Glow Worm* and *Shrimp Boats Are A-Coming*.

That was in August of 1952. Today, some forty-five years later, Fulton is as much a fixture with Gamecock fans as Cocky, or George Rogers, or the famous Fire Ant defense.

His rise to the top has been continuous, but not easy.

Born in 1920 in Ridley Park, Pa., he longed to become a sports announcer even as a child. "I remember when I was about six, my dream was to become a broadcaster," he says. "I would stand in our front yard all afternoon bouncing a tennis ball on our front steps and pretending it was a baseball game. I would keep a running commentary of the game going, and do it for the whole nine innings.

"In fact, in my high school yearbook, it was predicted that I would one day be a major league broadcaster and in 1950 I became one."

Following his graduation from College of the Ozarks in 1942, Fulton took his first professional broadcasting job. It was in Camden, N. J., at station WCAM, and he was paid the princely sum of $25 per week.

A year later he broke into college broadcasting as the football play-by-play man for the University of Arkansas, He remembers that he began doing baseball broadcasts in 1950. That was in Pueblo, Colorado of the Western League.

"I had never broadcast a baseball game in my life, but they wanted someone who could recreate games through the Western Union telegraph. Recreations were big back in those days. You know, I'd be

The "Voice of the Gamecocks" for 43 years, Bob Fulton defined Carolina athletics.

sitting there by the telegraph, a thousand miles away from the actual game, and I'd have to recreate it, blow-by-blow, just as though I were watching the game at Wrigley Field."

Fulton smiles at the recollection. "We even had crowd noise we'd play in the background, and we'd thump the table so the listener could hear the crack of the bat when the batter got a hit."

After a season in Cornell, N. Y. with the Pony League (Don Zimmer and Maury Wills were rookies on the team that year), Fulton arrived in Columbia, where he had been hired to broadcast games for the Columbia Reds of the South Atlantic League.

"My wife and I loved Columbia, and the station I was working for asked me if I would stay on and do Carolina football. Of course I said I would, and I've been here ever since."

In 1954 he finally made the big time. He, along with Al Helfner and Dizzy Dean, was hired to do

Hi Everybody! This is Bob Fulton

The Voice of the Gamecocks Relives a Half Century of Sportscasting

By Bob Fulton

With Don Barton

Bob, along with fellow author Don Barton, penned his memoirs in a 1997 best-selling book that gave an honest and often funny appraisal of Carolina's athletic program. Fulton and Barton also teamed up in 1996 to write the biography of the legendary Gamecock basketball coach, Frank McGuire.

Mutual Broadcasting's Game of the Day in the major leagues.

"Dizzy was just a big kid," Fulton recalls. "The funny thing is, he didn't know how to keep score. He didn't even carry a pencil. But after the game, if you mentioned that so-and-so struck out in the third inning, Diz would pipe up and say, 'Yeah, he took a low slider that just caught the outside corner.' He carried every detail of the game in his head."

Carolina fans who carry portable radios into Williams-Brice Stadium sometimes claim Fulton made the games sound more exciting on the radio than they actually appeared down on the playing field.

Fulton explains: "I'm not only in the reporting business, I'm also in the entertainment business. About ninety percent of my listeners are Carolina fans, and they want something good to happen. So there were times when I tried to make caviar out of hash. I tried to keep things upbeat and interesting. For example, if the Gamecocks were down by thirty points, I just neglected to mention the score very often.

"But you must have a sense of humor, and you have to take it simply as a game. If my happiness was predicated on what Carolina did in football, I'd have been in the hospital years ago."

He and sidekick Tommy Suggs, the former Gamecock quarterback great, were together for twenty-two years. "Tommy has a great sense of humor, which is an asset in this game, and he's very intelligent and great to work with," Fulton said. "And the same is true of Don Williams, one of the most knowledgeable people in this business."

Fulton says he enjoys the distinction of being the only non-athlete, non-coach ever inducted into the S.C. Athletic Hall of Fame.

In the fall of 1995 he was congratulated for having served for fifty years in broadcasting. Exercising his wry sense of humor, he replied: "I don't know whether I deserve congratulations or whether I should have my head examined."

Since his retirement, Fulton has co-authored two books with his longtime friend and former USC Sports Information Director, Don Barton. The first was a biography of Frank McGuire, the legendary USC basketball coach. And in 1996, Fulton published his memoir called *Hi Everybody! This is Bob Fulton*, which was his signature sign-on for each broadcast. More than an autobiography, the book gives a candid overview of the athletic program at USC during Fulton's tenure.

If there's a voice in South Carolina more recognizable than that of Bob Fulton, we'd like to know about it. Even Clemson fans perk up when they hear it. And that's saying a lot. We all miss you, Bob.

Sandy Gilliams

As For Sports, Business, And Academics, He's A Pro

Roosevelt "Sandy" Gilliam seems to have led one of those charmed lives most of us only dream about. Yes, he's done it all, everything from sports to business to academics, and every career move seems to have been another positive step in the right direction.

Although his life story reads like one of those how-to-succeed-without-really-trying books that were so popular a few years ago, Gilliam says that's not exactly how it was:

"Oh, don't worry," he laughs. "I've tried all right, tried hard. Of course luck plays a role in any man's life, but for the most part success is contingent upon three things: preparation, hard work and a good attitude.

"We used to try to instill that philosophy in the boys in football, but the same is true in the real world as well."

Gilliam is also convinced that another important aspect of success is early parental support. Born in Union in 1932, he says the thing he remembers most about his childhood is his parents' kindness and support.

"It didn't matter whether it was a football game or a play I was in at church, my parents were always there encouraging me and giving me the confidence I needed to do a good job. We were really a closeknit family."

Still, he always felt totally free to do as he chose, he says, as long as his choices fell within the framework established by his parents. Except when it came to selecting a college to attend.

"I had no choice in that matter. My parents determined the day I was born that I would have a college education, and they always guided me in that direction, and towards a particular type of college."

At Sims High School in Union, Gilliam played quarterback for Coach James Moore, who finished his coaching career with a phenomenal 135-3-5 record. In fact, Gilliam played during Sims' incredible 96-game winning streak, one that lasted from 1945 until 1954, and may be a national record.

As for college, in 1950, Gilliam had a few scholarship offers, but then—"My mother met with Coach William Lawson of Allen University, and he told her that not only was Allen a power in football, but it was also a church school, a Methodist school, and that the boys received religious instruction there. Of course, my mother decided that was the place for me."

Following his senior season in '54, Gilliam was named All-State, All-Conference and made the Pittsburgh Courier's All-American Team.

He was then offered a pro contract by the Cleveland Browns, who had scouted him during his senior year.

"But they already had Otto Graham up there, so the future didn't look too bright for a rookie quarterback in Cleveland. So I decided to go out and get a job."

He returned to Union to coach at Sims High. In 1955, now armed with both a degree and a steady job, he married his high school sweetheart, Betty Davis.

Then, following a successful tenure as head coach at Barr Street High in Lancaster, Gilliam moved onward (and upward) to Maryland Eastern Shore University as head coach. His coaching record there was outstanding, and he produced a list of pro players that reads like a Who's Who of professional football: Art Shell, Bill Belk, Jimmy Duncan, and Emerson Boozer, to name a few.

He was so successful, in fact, that in 1968 Lou Saban enticed him to become a pro scout with the Denver Broncos, a position Gilliam readily accepted. Today, looking back, he remembers that working with the Broncos was a delightful experience for his entire family.

"Truly, working with pro athletes is a great experience. My two sons, Rosie and Wayne, loved to visit the practice field in the afternoons and interact with the guys. They'd run after the footballs, help the trainers and whatnot. But just going to Denver and being a part of the pro draft and the games was a tremendous experience for the whole family."

It was a great life, he says, but he would let nothing, not even a lucrative career in pro football, stand in the way of his maintaining the close family ties begun in his own boyhood. "With the Broncos I'd come home on Sunday mornings to take the family to church. Other than that, I was always on the road. And my boys were reaching the age where I felt I should be home more. So I knew my days in athletics were numbered."

Thus in 1973 Gilliam returned to Lancaster and became Director of Special Project with Springs Industries, a position he held until 1987. He describes it as a perfect job for a man concerned with raising a family.

And apparently, if their children are any indi-cation, Sandy and Betty did a fine job. Today Rosie is Dr. Rosie Gilliam a Richmond cardiologist; Wayne is Dr. Wayne Gilliam, a Lancaster dentist; and their daughter, Patrice, is a professor at Winthrop University.

In 1988 Gilliam was named Executive Assis-tant to the Commissioner of the S. C. Department of Social Services. That same year, based on both his playing career and his impressive 113-27 record as a coach, he was named to the South Carolina Athletic Hall of Fame.

Then in '89 he was named Vice President of South Carolina State College, a position he holds today.

And he credits his success to his parents, family, friends and to his community. "You don't accomplish anything alone," he explains.

★
John Popson

After Forty Years He Is Still Furman's All-Time Kickoff Return Leader

John Popson is remembered today as perhaps the finest broken field runner ever to wear the purple and white of Furman University.

As a student at Swoyersville (Pa.) High School he excelled in all three major sports and was named to the All-Conference team in football in 1950. Then, wanting another year to mature before facing the rigors of college ball, he enrolled at Staunton Academy in Virginia.

There his speed and long slashing runs caught the attention of coaches from throughout the South. But Popson particularly liked Coach Bill Young and Furman University. Thus in 1952 he became the starting fullback for the Purple Hurricanes.

"That was back in the old days," he laughs now, "back when the Furman campus was in downtown Greenville. The men were housed on one end of the campus, while the women were safely locked away at the other."

He remembers basketball great Frank Selvy as a special friend, and describes him as "just a regular fellow and a real leader in student activities."

He had outstanding teammates, like Vince Perone, Sr., Roland Barefoot, Jackie Harris, Bo Berry, Bobby Jennings, L. G. Hightower and Jim Boyle.

Also, Popson points out, Furman has never shied away from playing, and frequently defeating, the biggies in college football. He remembers playing such major powers as USC, Clemson, Alabama, Auburn, Florida State, Georgia, West Virginia and Army.

During his freshman year, in 1952, the Hurricanes defeated West Virginia 22-14 one week, then walloped Florida State 9-0 the next—a feat to be envied by most Division I schools. They defeated Florida State again in '53 by a score of 14-7.

But the game that Popson remembers most, he says, came in '54 against NC State. "We suffered so many injuries that year that by the time we played State there were seven of us who had to play both offense and defense. In other words, seven of us were forced to play sixty minutes that afternoon.

John Popson, Furman's ace return man during the mid-fifties, was named to the All Southern team both his junior and senior seasons.

"But we finally beat them by a score of 7-6. I remember that particular game because we had to work so hard to win it."

Popson was rated as one of the best return men in the nation, and in 1954 he established a new Southern Conference record when he returned a Citadel kickoff 103 yards for a touchdown. Oddly enough, this record was tied twenty years later when Vince Perone, Jr., son of Popson's teammate, Vince Perone, Sr., raced 103 yards with a kickoff versus Wofford.

Today Popson remains Furman's all-time career kickoff return leader, averaging an incredible 37 yards per return. He also set the season record for punt returns when he averaged 24.2 yards per return in 1954.

These records become even more impressive

No, this isn't a staged shot for a Hollywood movie. It is, in fact, John Popson returning a kickoff 103 yards for a TD against The Citadel in 1954.

when it's remembered that Furman has fielded football teams since 1889. Yet, despite all the great runningbacks who've played for the Hurricanes over the years, John Popson remains without peer when it comes to broken field running.

He would have taken more post-season honors had Furman enjoyed a better won-loss record during his career. But between 1954-55, despite some sterling individual performances from Popson, Perone and others, Furman suffered 11 consecutive defeats (an all-time record that Furman doesn't often mention).

Still, Popson was named to the All-State Team for three consecutive years, and to the All-Southern Team in '54 and '55.

In 1956 he was drafted twice, once by Green Bay and once by Uncle Sam. You can imagine whose bid took precedence.

Upon his discharge from the Army in '58, he was delighted to learn that the Packers had sold his contract to the Washington Redskins. He reported to the team and immediately established himself as a potentially great pro fullback. But in the final game of the exhibition season, he suffered a career-ending knee injury.

He and his wife, the former Sybil Humphries of Gaffney, another Furman graduate, wished to return to the South, so John accepted a coaching position at Southern High School in Durham, where he remained for the next two years.

In '61 he was named head coach and athletic director at Jordan High School, a 4A school in Durham, where he would remain until his retirement thirty years later.

John, Sybil, and their three children still live in Durham, where their neighbors are totally unaware that the nice man who lives so quietly next door was once one of the most feared return men in all of college football.

Bruce & Dave Thompson

They Remain Two of the Finest Athletes Ever to Play Blue Hose Basketball

The illustrious Norman Sloan coached basketball at Presbyterian College for six years (1950-55), compiling an admirable 89-41 record and recruiting some of the finest young athletes in the history of Blue Hose basketball.

In 1952, for example, he landed the somewhat reluctant Dave Thompson, and in '53 he brought in the wildly enthusiastic Bruce Thompson. In time sports writers would call them everything from the gold dust twins to the Thompson duo. Many fans assumed that they must be brothers. After all, they had the same last name and both hailed from Indiana. But in fact neither had ever even heard of the other before they arrived at PC.

Dave had garnered All-State honors at Frankfort High School his senior year and received more than a hundred scholarship offers from major colleges across the country. But he really wasn't interested in any of them. His real ambition, oddly enough, was to start his own roofing business.

But as fate would have it, Frankfort also just happened to be the home of coaching legend Everette Case. In addition to winning national championships at NC State, Case also owned a Frankfort restaurant. Young Dave Thompson had been working there for several years, washing dishes and peeling potatoes back in the kitchen. Once Case heard that his young potato peeler was also an All-State basketball player, he did everything possible to entice him to accept a scholarship to NC State.

But Dave told Case that he simply wasn't interested. He wanted only to start a roofing business.

"In fact," laughs Dave today, "I wasn't interested in NC State or PC. To tell the truth, I'd never even heard of PC. But one day I got a call from Coach Sloan. He invited me down for a workout at PC, no strings attached. So I said, What the heck, and went down. Just for the ride, you might say. But Sloan was a straight shooter, one of the most honest men I've ever known, so I decided to give PC a try. I could always leave if I didn't like it, come home and start my roofing business."

As for Bruce Thompson, meanwhile, a native of nearby Plymouth, Indiana, he was most eager to attend PC and says that he began drooling at the lips when they offered him a scholarship. He was, he says, recruited as a center "because I was tall and had sharp elbows."

Both Thompsons say that Sloan believed in togetherness but frowned on star treatment. Bruce laughs, "We lived in small, dark, bug-infested cubicles in a big musty room above the gym. We used to call it the world's only upstairs dungeon."

Other team members during that era include Ron Ragan, Chuck Sloan (brother of Coach Sloan), Bob Burgess, Clyde Beaumont, Bill Toole, Bill Sullivan, Eddie Wile and Bob Stratton. In 1955 these guys would average 93.6 points per game, still a PC team record.

For many years now the Thompson boys have been friendly competitors who disagree on as much as possible, but they do agree that Sloan was a great coach and a terrific individual. "Whatever he said, you could take it to the bank," says Dave. "We always played hard out of respect for ourselves and Coach Sloan."

"Plus there was always an element of fear involved," adds Bruce. "Coach Sloan was a stern disciplinarian and always instilled just a little fear in his teams. And there's one thing about fear. Fear always makes you run a little faster, jump a little higher."

"Yeah, that's right," adds Dave. "We were afraid to go out there and loaf around. We'd rather hustle than to have to face Coach Sloan."

"I remember one night in '55," grins Bruce, "we were playing Furman at home, and at halftime we were down by twenty points. Back in the locker room Coach Sloan was seething. He ordered us not to go back on the court unless we were ready to turn the game around. That was all he said, Then he whirled around and slammed his fist through the door of a metal wall locker and walked out."

"That's the truth," says Dave. "And it made

Dave Thompson became a record-setting forward for the Blue Hose. He still holds almost all single-game scoring records for the Blue Hose, hitting 51 points against both Newberry and The Citadel in 1956.

Bruce Thompson, who couldn't wait to enroll at PC, once hit on 36 consecutive free throws, and still holds all the Presbyterian College rebound records.

quite an impression on us. At any rate, we did come back from that 20-point deficit, and we did upset a great Furman team that night. Coach Sloan definitely knew how to get your attention."

During his junior year, in 1956, Bruce would score 24 free throws against Furman one evening (still a single-game record at PC), and during another stretch that year he would hit an incredible 36 consecutive free throws (another all-time PC record).

But his real strength lay in rebounding. He grabbed a total of 1,199 rebounds during his career with the Blue Hose (still a record), for an average of 17.8 rebounds per game (yet another all-time PC record).

Asked the secret of his success, Bruce flashes a grin and jokes, "Heck, it was the only time I ever got to touch the ball. I'd take it out of bounds and pass it in to Dave. Then he'd dribble the length of the court and take a shot. Then I'd have to scramble to get the rebound. That's the only way I ever got my hands on the ball."

Dave winks at the author. "He's still just jealous that I was such a superior athlete."

Both laugh good naturedly.

As for Dave, he was a sharpshooting guard and twice scored 51 points in single games, once against Newberry and again against The Citadel. Both remain single-game scoring records at PC.

Bruce needles, "You can give me credit for that, too. I'd scored 50 points the week before against Furman and Dave couldn't stand it. That's why he went out and beat up on Newberry and The Citadel that way."

Today Bruce is Personnel Director for the City of Spartanburg, where he lives with his family. His daughter, Tami, once served as Head Rally Cat for the Clemson Tigers, while his son, Bruce, attended Newberry College on a basketball scholarship.

Dave is a Parole Examiner for the S. C. Department of Corrections. "It's a tough yet rewarding job," he says. "You must be realistic on the one hand, yet compassionate on the other." He and his family live in Columbia, and Dave has never had any desire whatsoever to return to Indiana to start that roofing business.

But Bruce and Dave Thompson still make up a fearsome duo, only now it's in the various golf tournaments they attend together as partners.

★
Frank Selvy

One of America's All-Time Greatest Basketball Players

There are just too many facets of the game, too many different angles to consider, to even attempt to name the greatest collegiate basketball player of all time in South Carolina. But if numbers and statistics mean anything, then we'd have to cast our vote for Furman's University's All-Time Mr. Everything, Frank Selvy.

Just consider: in 1954 alone he scored 1,209 points, an average of 42 points per game, still an all-time NCAA record surpassed only by Pete Maravich. That same year Selvy hit 355 of 444 free throws, an .800 percentage, which remains number-one in the Furman Record Book.

That same year, incredibly enough, the 6-3 Selvy demonstrated his great defensive play by snatching down 400 rebounds, an average of 14 per contest.

For his three-year career with the Hurricanes he scored a total of 2,538 points, an average of 32.5 per game. Indeed, few would argue that, as a backcourt sharp shooter, Selvy was without peer.

(It must be remembered that Selvy played back in the days before the 3-pointer became a part of the game. We can only imagine how many points he'd have gotten were he playing today.)

He was born and raised in Corbin, Ky., a small town noted mainly for its coal mines and poverty, where his primary pastime was playing around with a basketball. Indeed, back in Corbin they played basketball twelve months out of the year. "There was no place flat enough to hold a football field," he laughs. "And besides, Corbin was so small that we couldn't have gotten eleven fellows together to form a football team if we'd had a place to play."

His senior season in high school, in 1950, he was named to the Kentucky All-State Basketball Team, along with other such future greats as Cliff Hagan and Frank Ramsey.

To say that he was swamped with scholarship offers would be an understatement. But then one day he received a phone call from Furman's Coach Lyles Alley inviting him down for a tryout. It was a proposition that Selvy at first found amusing. Both UCLA and UNC, two of the greatest basketball powers in the nation, had just offered him their college libraries if he'd even consider accepting a

Frank Selvy, who must be remembered as the most incredible basketball player ever from the state of South Carolina. He also served as President of the Student Body.

scholarship to their respective institutions, and here was little Furman asking him if he'd like to come down for a tryout. But, since he had nothing better to do at the moment, he thought he'd give Furman a look.

"My family was very poor," he says, "and I'd never been anywhere. And since Furman was paying my expenses, I thought I'd just jump on a bus and take a free trip to Greenville. It was just a lark, really. But as it turned out, I liked Furman, and I thought Coach Alley was one of the finest men I'd ever met."

And the rest, as they say, is history.

By the end of his sophomore season with the Hurricanes (1952) Selvy had established himself as a force to be reckoned with. He averaged 20 points per game that season and was named to the All-Southern Team.

He was also named All-Southern in '53 and

Coach Lyles Alley, who directed Furman to 249 wins during his coaching career, and Frank Selvy who led the country in scoring in both 1954 and 1955.

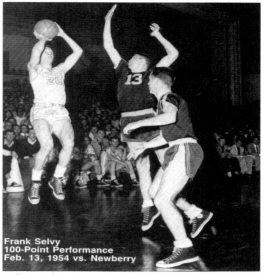

Frank Selvy
100-Point Performance
Feb. 13, 1954 vs. Newberry

Selvy sinks a jumper with only seconds left to give him 100 points on the evening versus Newberry College on February 13, 1954. This remains an all-time NCAA record performance.

'54, one of the few players in history to be named all-conference for three consecutive years.

But of all Selvy's great performances, the one that no one will ever forget, occurred on the evening of February 13, 1954, versus Newberry College at Textile Hall in Greenville.

Two weeks earlier, by the way, he had amazed fans by hitting 25 of 27 free throws against The Citadel, but that performance paled in comparison with what he did this night.

Selvy's former teammate, A. D. Bennett, describes the setting for that performance, the whole situation sounding like a plot for a *Rocky* movie:

"First, it was one of the last games he'd ever play for Furman," Bennett says. "Plus, it was played right there in Greenville before about 5,000 home folks at Textile Hall. But the big thing was the presence of Frank's mom and dad for the game. The mayor of Corbin knew that the Selvys had never had a chance to see Frank play, so he organized a party of people from Corbin to drive down for this game and spend the weekend in Greenville, with Frank's parents as the guests of honor. So if Frank ever wanted to shine, that was the night."

At the end of the first quarter of that historic contest, Furman led Newberry by a score of 38-19. At that point, with such a demanding lead, Lyles Alley pulled all his starters out of the game—except for Selvy. "He left Frank in," says Bennett, "because he knew of all the people from Corbin who had driven so far to see him play."

Selvy disappointed no one. Bennett, who scored 1 point, smiles as he recalls the finale of that encounter.

"There were about 30 seconds left in the game, and Frank had 98 points. One of our forwards was

dribbling around with the ball, like he was trying to run out the clock, and all the fans started yelling for him to pass the ball to Selvy. Well, with about 5 seconds on the clock, he finally tossed it across court to Selvy. Frank then took a 20-foot jumper and the ball swished the net just as the buzzer went off. Man, talk about exploding! Textile Hall went up in smoke!"

Today, some forty-two years later, Selvy's 100 point performance versus Newberry still remains an all-time single-game NCAA scoring record.

He was named to the Associated Press All-American Team in both '53 and '54. But just as important to him, says Selvy, he was also named to Who's-Who and elected President of the Student Body.

He played several years of pro ball with the Lakers before replacing Lyles Alley as coach of the Furman Hurricanes.

Today he is employed by the St. Joe Paper Co., and he and his wife Barbara make their home in Greenville.

Still, after all this time, the very modest Selvy downplays his record-setting performance that evening against Newberry. "Actually," he says, "Darrell Floyd had more points than I did that night when Coach Alley took him out of the game. If my parents hadn't been there, Darrell would probably have gotten the 100 points."

Selvy is a member of the South Carolina Athletic Hall of Fame.

★

J. C. Caroline

"Prayer and humility have lit my path throughout life."

Back in 1953 he became the most spectacular running back in the history of football at the University of Illinois. He amassed 1,470 all-purpose yards that season, the best in the nation, and broke the all-time records of such Illini greats as Buddy Young and Red Grange.

He was everybody's All-American and the subject of articles in *Life, Sports Illustrated, Colliers,* and *Newsweek.* His life story, they all liked to say, was truly inspirational.

Indeed, the story of Columbia native J. C. Caroline is inspirational, truly inspirational. It is a simple story that teaches that sacrifice and struggle lead almost inevitably to the promised land.

His father was named Ben Gordon, but J. C. spent his childhood in the home of his maternal grandparents, the Carolines, and assumed their name. "My grandfather gave me my name," he says, "and I've used it ever since. I like it. It has a more musical ring to it than Gordon."

J. C., by the way, are not initials. That's his first name.

As a black youth growing up in the South in the late-forties, Caroline struggled to help his family make ends meet. He remembers loading produce trucks from 5 AM until noon before attending classes in the afternoons at Lewis Junior High.

Later, at Booker T. Washington High (1949-51), he played quarterback and scored 50 career touchdowns. In track, he ran the 100-yard dash in 9.9 seconds. In '51 he made the Negro All-American High School squad.

Today, looking back, he says, "Making All-American at Booker T. Washington meant more to me than doing it at Illinois. That was my ticket to success. Otherwise, I could still be loading produce trucks."

His high school coach, John McHugh, collaborated with Columbia sports editors Jake Penland of *The State* and Van Newman of *The Record* to write letters of recommendation on Caroline's behalf to Coach Ray Eliot at Illinois.

Eliot's reply was something of a disappoint-

He was just a poor boy from Columbia, but in 1953 J. C. Caroline led the nation in rushing yardage and was named to the AP All-American Team.

ment. Caroline should enroll at Illinois at his own expense and go out for football. If he made the team, a scholarship would be forthcoming.

For the next year, Caroline remembers, he earned expense money digging ditches, painting the football stadium and checking skates at a skating rink. He skipped breakfast, earned his lunch working in a hotel kitchen, and ate free dinners at the football training table.

"I also ate about a million bananas," he grins. "They were cheap and filling. Gosh, I ate a lot of bananas my freshman year at Illinois."

As a sophomore in '53 he earned a starting role in the Illini's opening game with highly favored Nebraska. He remembers his first game this way:

It was the fourth quarter and we were behind 21-14. Then I took a pitchout and ran 73 yards for a touchdown. The game ended in a 21-21 tie, a real upset."

But his most memorable game came two weeks later against Ohio State. "As usual, they were highly ranked," Caroline says. "But we went to Columbus and upset them 41-20. That game gave me a tremendous amount of confidence that I could play in the Big Ten."

It should have. He finished the game with 204 yards rushing, not counting a 39-yard TD run that was called back because of a penalty.

By season's end he led the nation in rushing with 1,256 yards and earned consensus All-American honors.

When he arrived back in Columbia for Christmas vacation, he stepped off the train to find a huge crowd of well-wishers awaiting him. He was then driven to the Township Auditorium where he was showered with gifts. Testimonials were read by Mayor Clarence Dreher and Judge J. C. DuPre.

Called on to say a few words, Caroline stepped to the podium. Typically, he said simply, "Thank you," then turned away to thunderous applause.

Today he smiles when remembering how shy he had been in his youth. "But my grandmother Caroline always taught me that there is power in prayer and dignity in humility," he says. "Prayer and humility have lit my path throughout life."

Following successful seasons at Illinois in both '54 and '55, Caroline then spent the next 11 years at a defensive back with the Chicago Bears. Then he returned to his alma mater as a defensive backfield coach, a position he held for the next 10 years. Today, he teaches physical education at Urbana Junior High in Illinois. It gives him a chance, he says, to try to guide young lives in the right direction.

Following a successful career with the Fighting Illini, Caroline became a star defensive back with the Chicago Bears for the next eleven years.

★
Allen Morris

This PC Great Played At Wimbledon

Fate does indeed deal some funny hands. Just ask Presbyterian College's all-time great tennis champion, Allen Morris.

Twice he was named to the U. S. Davis Cup Team, and in 1956 he received the greatest honor accorded a college tennis player—an invitation to play at Wimbledon.

Yet he was no tennis player. Football was his game. Indeed, in 1949, his senior year at Atlanta's Marist High School, he was considered one of the top quarterback prospects in the state of Georgia and received scholarship offers from all over. But young Allen chose to stay home and play for the legendary Bobby Dodd and his highly vaunted Georgia Tech Yellow Jackets, one of the top teams in the nation.

Allen was a starter on Tech's undefeated freshman team of 1950, which featured such future standouts as Pepper Rodgers, Bulldog Carothers, Leon Hardeman, and Henry Hair. Allen's biggest contribution to this team was his phenomenal 44.4 punting average.

But that's when Fate stepped in. In the final game of the '50 season he suffered a severe eye injury. The team doctor told him he could never play again.

It was the most depressing day of young Allen's life. He withdrew from Tech. For weeks then he just sat around, quietly pondering what he should do with his life.

Again Fate put in an appearance. This time in the person of an old friend Allen had known back at Marist High. His name was Sonny Mullis, and he had been invited to visit Presbyterian College to try out for Coach Jim Leighton's tennis team. He invited Allen to go along, telling him to be down at the Greyhound Bus Station at eight the next morning if he wanted to enjoy a free weekend in Clinton.

Actually Allen himself was no babe in the woods when it came to tennis. He had won the Georgia State High School Championship in 1949 and had been ranked among the top five juniors in the South. Yet he still considered football to be his

Allen Morris began his college athletic career as a punter for Georgia Tech. Strangely enough, he would wind up his career at Presbyterian College as one of America's most outstanding tennis players.

major sport, and says that he had not even handled a tennis racket for over a year when he made that fateful trip to Clinton. But a scholarship was a scholarship, and he would take one in tennis if it were offered.

"Boy, I still remember that bus ride to Clinton that morning. I was hoping for a tennis scholarship, so I could continue my education, but I didn't want to get my hopes up. So I just kept telling myself that if things didn't work out, and I really didn't think they would, that at least I could enjoy a weekend out of town."

To make a long story short, Allen was given a scholarship, did make the team, and he remembers meeting with Coach Leighton in the fall of '51.

"Allen," Leighton said, "you can be more than just a good college tennis player. You can be as good as you want to be. It all depends on how hard you're willing to work. Now, how good do you want to be?"

"I was surprised to say the least," Morris says, "and very excited. I told Coach Leighton that I was eager to do whatever he suggested."

"Even when there was snow on the ground, Coach Leighton would have me on the court hitting backhands. When it was raining heavily we'd go in the gym and hit backhands. At night we'd go to his home and spend hours watching films of Don Budge and his famous backhand, and talk more about my backhand."

Back in those days PC's tennis program ranked among the nation's best. Leighton recruited on a national basis and scheduled games with the finest teams in the country. Morris remembers Miami, the number one team in the nation, coming in and falling victim to the Blue Hose (this loss snapped Miami's 72-game winning streak). Then Morris and the team went on a tour of Texas, beating everybody in the Lone Star State, including the number-five Long Horns.

Morris was chosen for the U. S. Davis Cup team in both '55 and '56, and played at Wimbledon in '56, the greatest honor an American tennis player can know. Still, being a totally down to earth sort of fellow, he never considered himself a celebrity. "At PC I was just another student," he says with a smile, "and I still remember rooming upstairs at the old YMCA house on campus. I attended ROTC drills at eight o'clock every morning, then I sat and snoozed through chapel every morning. At PC I was a student who just happened to play tennis."

Following his graduation in '56 he spent two years in service, then launched a successful business career, first with an investment firm, then later as a vice president in industry.

But he still found time for tennis and in 1978 he

Coach Jim Leighton, one of the nation's most outstanding tennis coaches. Morris gives Coach Leighton credit for developing him into a Wimbledon-class tennis player.

won the National 45 Tournament. He is a member of both the North Carolina Sports Hall of Fame and the Southern Tennis Hall of Fame.

He became head tennis coach at the University of North Carolina in 1980, a position he still holds. He was chosen ACC Tennis Coach of the Year in 1983.

Still, he remembers that morning forty-five years ago when he just happened to bump into Sonny Mullis, and he cannot help but wonder what he'd be doing today had it not been for that very fateful meeting.

★
Billy O'Dell

For Thirteen Years He Was One of the Best Pitchers in the Major Leagues

Billy O'Dell
Major League All-Star Game MVP, 1958
Clemson Tigers, 1952-54

Billy O'Dell, a former pitching great with the Clemson Tigers, was the first player signed by the Baltimore Orioles. Over the next thirteen years he would prove that those Oriole scouts knew what they were doing.

For years Billy O'Dell had dreamed of his first major league appearance. He would be pitching at a packed Yankee Stadium in the final game of the season, the one that would determine who would face the Dodgers in the World Series. With O'Dell holding a one run lead, the bases were loaded and Mickey Mantle was at the plate. The count was three balls, two strikes. O'Dell very coolly looked Mantle in the eye, then wound up and uncorked his famous fastball right down the middle. STRIKE THREE. . .HE CAUGHT THE MIGHTY MANTLE LOOKING. THE BALL GAME IS OVER. O'DELL IS GOING TO THE SERIES. O'DELL IS EVERYBODY'S HERO.

Then the dream would fade slowly away.

In fact, O'Dell remembers his first major league appearance. Unfortunately, it didn't go exactly as he as he had always dreamed it would.

It was his first start on the mound for the Orioles, and with 40,000 Baltimore faithful in the stands and his own heart in his throat, he took the signal from the catcher. Then he wound up and threw his famous fastball. The worst thing that could possibly have happened did happen. O'Dell watched in horror as the ball hit the dirt ten feet in front of the mound, bounced once high in the air, then rolled across the plate. There was laughter from the stands.

Catcher Pete Courtney fielded the pitch, a hot ground ball, then walked slowly to the mound and put his hand on O'Dell's shoulder.

"Billy," he grinned, "in all my years in organized baseball, I've never seen anybody try to roll the ball by the hitter before. I mean this ain't rollerbat, son. Now you settle down and throw that ball the way you know how."

And for the next thirteen years, O'Dell did just that. With a fastball clocked at 94 mph, he became a solid major league pitcher. During that long career he posted a 105-100 record, with a 3.29 earned run average. He was also credited with 48 saves.

Today, looking back, O'Dell says, "We didn't play much ball out in the country where I was born in Newberry County. But we moved to town when I was eleven, and I started pitching in a summer league run by our high school coach, Harry Hedgepath. Coach Hedgepath recognized early that I had talent, and he really did a lot for me.

"In fact, I don't believe anybody, either in college or the pros, ever told me anything about the basic fundamentals that Coach Hedgepath hadn't already drilled in me in high school. He was truly a great coach."

In 1952 O'Dell was rated the best high school pitcher in the state, and accepted a scholarship to pitch for the Clemson Tigers.

"I really liked Clemson. It was close to home. Plus I'd played summer textile ball up in the old Greenville Textile League where I met some of the Clemson players. I was playing for Liberty Mills. Of course you had to actually work in the mill to play for them."

O'Dell played for Clemson's Coach Bob Smith for three years. He was named to the All-Southern team his freshman year, then he made the All-ACC and All-American teams his next two years. In 1954, following his junior season, he signed a contract with the Baltimore Orioles.

"Contracts back then were nothing like to-day," he says. "I didn't make that much measured by today's standards. Certainly not as much as the newspapers said I was making. Back then, $100,000 a year was top money. I think Ted Williams was making $125,000 or thereabouts."

Prior to 1954 the Orioles had existed as the hapless St. Louis Browns. "I was the first bonus player the Orioles signed. So I was sort of their boy. The organization looked after me, and the fans were great."

And who was the greatest hitter he ever saw in the majors? "You have to talk about Ted Williams, then you can talk about everybody else. He was just head and shoulders above everybody. You can't believe it if you didn't see him play, but it's inconceivable that he could hit the ball as hard as he did, as consistently as he did. Of course he spent five of his best years in the military."

During his thirteen years in the majors, with Baltimore, Milwaukee, San Francisco, Atlanta, and Pittsburgh, O'Dell was always considered a power pitcher who simply blew it by the hitters.

"In those days everybody threw hard," he laughs. "I believe that's the biggest difference in pitchers today as compared when I was coming along."

He played in the '58 and '59 All-Star games, and was voted the MVP Award in the '58 game. In 1962 he won the first game of the World Series for the Giants.

He retired in 1967 and returned to Newberry where he and his family still make their home. He says he helps coach the Newberry College baseball team in his spare time, "when I'm not hunting or fishing."

O'Dell is a member of the Clemson Athletic Hall of Fame.

★
Joel Wells

This Great Clemson Runningback Went On To Star For One of the Greatest Pro Teams of All Time

Tall, handsome and one of the best running backs in America, he became the living dream of every PR man in Clemson's sports information office during the mid-1950s. Their press releases called him by such illustrious names as The Blond Bomber and The Columbia Clipper.

But he was simply Joel Wells, a product of Columbia's Dreher High School, which fielded some of the strongest prep football teams in the South during that era. Indeed, Wells remembers such teammates as Carl Brazell, Crosby Lewis, Steve Coleman, and B. C. Inabinet, all of whom would become great collegiate stars.

"Heck, " he says, "It was my senior year before I made Dreher's starting backfield. There were just too many great running backs there for me to break in with 'em."

During Wells' senior season in high school, 1952, Dreher easily won the state championship, while he became a unanimous All-State selection at halfback. Scholarship offers poured in from schools all over America. But he opted for Clemson.

"While I was in high school," he says, "my older brother, Jimmy, had been a starting halfback for Clemson, and I'd really gotten caught up in that Clemson mystique. To me, there was something really unique about Clemson, and even today I wouldn't take a million dollars for the time I spent up there.

"Plus," he continues, "and this is nothing against Carolina, but USC was right there in Columbia, and I just wanted to feel that I was getting away from home."

At 6-0 and 190 pounds, Wells was considered big for a runningback in 1952. Yet he was amazingly light on his feet and ran with the speed and quickness of a gazelle. He broke into the Tigers' starting lineup at left half his sophomore season, 1954, picking up where brother Jimmy had left off the year before.

Joining him in the backfield that year were Don King at quarterback, Billy O'Dell at right half, and

Joel Wells was named to the AP All American Team in 1955.

Joe Pagliei at fullback, while in the line were such stalwarts as Dalton Rivers, Earl Green, Dick Marazza, Don Bunton, John Grdijan, Bill Hudson, Willie Smith, and his old Dreher teammate B. C. Inabinet (jokingly known to his teammates as B. C. Inadequate).

In Clemson's 13-8 loss to Carolina in '54, the versatile Wells completed an 81-yard TD strike to Joe Pagliei for the Tigers' only score. Today this toss remains the third longest pass completion in the history of Clemson football.

But Wells' fondest memory concerns Clemson's 28-14 win over Carolina in 1955: "We hadn't beaten Carolina since 1948," he says, "and the folks back in Columbia were really giving me a fit about it. So when we won in '55 that shut a lot of people up." Wells doesn't mention it, but he was Clemson's leading ground gainer that afternoon, despite the fact that Carolina had wisely stacked their defenses to stop him.

He was named All-ACC both his junior and senior seasons. Then in '55 he was named to the AP

Jolting Joel moves out behind heavy blocking in this photo that captures so well the hardnosed brand of football played by the Tigers under Coach Frank Howard during the 1950s.

All-American Team. After playing in numerous postseason bowl games, he became the 13th player selected in the pro draft that year, and the second pick of the Green Bay Packers.

But Wells skipped the NFL to play with Montreal of the Canadian Football League. "Back then," he explains, "Canadian football paid a heck of a lot more than the NFL. Plus, Coach Peahead Walker up at Montreal was a good friend of Coach Howard, and I felt comfortable playing for him."

For the next three years then, Wells started at left halfback for the Alouettes, and his pro career seemed assured. But always, he says, there was something nagging at him. He couldn't help but wonder if he was truly good enough to play in the NFL.

So in '61 he signed with the New York Giants. And how good were they? Well, just take a look. There was on the team that year such NFL greats as Joe Morrison, Alex Webster, Jim Patton, Jim Katcavage, Sam Huff, Andy Robustelli, Dick Modzelewski, Charlie Connerly, Kyle Rote, and Y. A. Tittle.

Following pre-season drills, the Giants an-nounced that starting at right half would be Alex Webster, at left half Joel Wells. He no longer had to wonder.

Indeed, the '61 Giants won their division, then went on to defeat Green Bay for the NFL champi-onship in a game most experts still remember as an all-time classic. Wells then decided, since he had nothing left to prove, to retire.

"I started for the greatest team in pro football in '61, so after that I was happy. I didn't have to prove anything to myself anymore."

Armed with a degree in industrial manage-ment from Clemson, he then went into the textile business, which soon led him to Greenville. In 1980 he started his own company, I. H. Services, Inc., which performed contract maintenance work in industrial facilities. He retired for the final time in 1992.

He is married to the former Alexandra Lee of Sumter and they have six children. They continue to make their home in Greenville.

He is a member of the Clemson Athletic Hall of Fame.

★

Bill Yarborough

He Still Remains Clemson's All-Time Number-One Hottest Shooter

For lack of a better term, Bill Yarborough and family might well be called Mr. and Mrs. Clemson Tiger Athletics. His sister is married to Dr. Tom "Black Cat" Barton, an All-American guard for the Tigers during the early-fifties, while his wife, the former Carolyn Few, is a first cousin of Bill Few, an All-ACC end with the Tigers during the mid-fifties. As for Yarborough himself, he was twice named All-ACC and remains one of Clemson's most memorable basketball players ever.

As a senior at Walhalla High School in 1952 he received the Most Valuable Player award in the North-South All-Star basketball game, and scholarship offers poured in. There was one from USC that particularly caught his eye. But then came a visit from Clemson's Coach Frank Howard.

Yarborough smiles at the recollection: "Coach Howard says, 'I guess USC's okay, son, but who's gonna drive 150 miles from up here just to watch you play for them ol' Gamecocks?' Well, that sort of put things in a different light, so I just went right down the road and enrolled at Clemson. That way Mom and Dad could see me play."

Clemson's immortal Banks McFadden was head coach during Yarborough's first three years with the Tigers. Then came Press Maravich during his senior year.

"I remember Coach Maravich's son, Pistol Pete, who would go on to become one of the greatest shooters ever to play the game. He was in about the seventh grade back then, and he'd come down to the gym and work out with us in the afternoons. He could outshoot most of the guys on the team even then. He just had that determination to be the best."

Yarborough remembers that Clemson was all military back in the '50s but he had the good fortune to become one of the few students declared exempt from ROTC drills. "The Korean War was in full swing back then, and I actually got drafted in 1952. But I flunked my physical because of a hearing impairment and was declared 4-F. So Clemson concluded that there was no good reason to go to all the expense of training me to become

In 1954 Bill Yarborough averaged 28.3 points per game for the Tigers, an all-time Clemson scoring record.

an Army officer if I couldn't serve in the Army. That made sense."

Yarborough still retains fond memories of the Clemson mess hall back during his playing days: "We absolutely could not have enjoyed better food. We ate family style, which meant you got all you wanted of everything. Of course, the food was grown right there at Clemson, and every night we'd have veal, pork chops, roasts or steak. Really, as far as the food was concerned, it was like staying in an exclusive hotel."

Following his freshman season Yarborough dropped out of school and spent the next year playing basketball for Woodside Mills in Greenville. He says that textile ball was the best thing to come along since Pepsi Cola.

"But that was back before TV began dominating our households. Back then, in small towns across the South, our big entertainment was getting out a couple of nights a week with our neighbors to watch the local mill team play baseball or basketball. In addition to giving youngsters a chance to show what they could do as athletes, it got people out of the house and gave them an opportunity to mingle with their neighbors."

He returned to Clemson in '54 and it was then that he truly came unto his own. He averaged a phenomenal 28.3 points per game that year, which remains the highest scoring average in Tiger history.

That year he scored more than 30 points in nine games and more than 40 twice. His 46 points against USC that season still remains a single-game scoring record at Clemson.

Not to change the subject, but we were curious as to how his sister came to marry Black Cat Barton. "Well, back then," he explains with a laugh, "back when I was in high school, those Clemson guys would pile into Walhalla every weekend. There was a nice restaurant on Main Street and those Clemson guys would be lined up for a block trying to get in. We Walhalla boys would drive by and yell at 'em and make fun of 'em, you know, because they'd been locked up at Clemson all week. See, the big thing was those Clemson guys would come over and try to date our high school girlfriends, so there was no love lost between us.

You can imagine how thrilled I was to learn that my own sister was dating one of 'em.

"But ol' Barton turned out to be a pretty decent sort of fellow. And after forty years I've kind of forgiven him for being a Clemson cadet."

Yarborough took his degree in Education in 1957 and spent several years in high school coaching. Then in 1962 when technical education was first being instituted in this state, he and Dr. Tom Barton were hired to help get Greenville Technical College off to a good start.

Indeed, Dr. Barton has for many years now served as President of Greenville Tech. As for Yarborough, he went on to become President of Tri-County Technical College in the Clemson area, a position he held for many years.

For the past few years he has devoted his time to land development, designing and constructing golf courses for Fairway Development, headquartered in Pineville, N.C.

He and Carolyn have four children (two of them USC grads) and make their home in Columbia. He is a member of the Clemson Athletic Hall of Fame.

Yarborough demonstrates his leaping ability as he goes way up to block this shot versus Furman in '54.

★
Tommy Brewer

His Arm Was His One-Way Ticket To Fenway Park

It was 1954, back when nobody had ever heard of Sputnik, the Warren Commission, or Vietnam. Dwight Eisenhower was president, "On the Waterfront" was the best movie of the year, and the Chordettes' "Mr. Sandman" was the big hit on every jukebox.

That was also the year Tommy Brewer, a young pitcher from Cheraw, realized a lifelong dream by breaking in with the Boston Red Sox.

I recently talked with Brewer in the cab of his pickup truck in the parking lot of a Cheraw fast food restaurant. A friendly, soft-spoken fellow, he is now 65 but still trim at 6-2 and 200 pounds. In fact, if appearances mean anything, he could still go a few good innings for the Red Sox.

But he pooh-poohed such wistful thinking.

"Nah, I tore the rotator cuff in my shoulder in '62, and that was the end of the road for me. Still, I'll admit there's something about the month of April that stirs something inside me. I walk around with the feeling that there's something I'm supposed to be doing and not doing it. I start reminiscing too much. Sure, I miss playing ball and always have. But when it's over, it's over.

I don't even let myself watch the games on TV in the early spring. Too painful."

Brewer was born in 1931 in Cheraw, an area of small farms and cotton mills, where there was really little for a boy to do except play baseball.

"As far back as I can remember, my dad would come home in the afternoons, and we'd go out in the back yard and play catch. But my dad finally quit one day, said that when I got to where I could throw it harder than he could, he wasn't going to play anymore."

At Cheraw High School he was considered an ace infielder for the Braves. "But I wasn't just playing high school ball," he says. "I played for anybody who had a team. My senior year, in addition to playing in school, I played in the textile league for Bonnette Mills in Rockingham two nights a week and for Sunoco in Hartsville two nights a week. If they had a team and I could get there, I

A pitching ace with the Boston Red Sox, Tommy Brewer won 19 games and pitched the American League All-Stars to a big win over the Nationals in 1956.

wanted to play. It's all I thought about."

In 1950 Brewer entered Elon College on a baseball scholarship. "The coach up there liked the way I could whip that ball from shortstop to first and decided I should become a pitcher. That's when I found myself."

In 1951, with the Korean Conflict in full swing, Brewer was drafted and stationed at Camp Attenbury, Indiana. The next year, as a pitcher for the post team, he was named to the All-Army team. Upon his discharge, the Red Sox were waiting with a lucrative contract.

After a year with the Class D High Point High

Tops, where he won 23 games in '53, it was on to Fenway Park and the big time in '54. Those were the glory years of Red Sox baseball. Lou Boudreau was the manager, and the team was blessed with such legends as Ted Williams, Jackie Jensen and Jimmy Piersall. Brewer remembers with a laugh his initiation into major league action.

"I'd just arrived in Boston a couple of days before, so I hardly had time to unpack my bags when we took off for a series with the Yankees. So there I was, sitting in the bullpen at a packed Yankee Stadium, just sort of sitting back enjoying watching the first major league game I'd ever seen. We were doing pretty well, but then the Yankees suddenly had the bases loaded, only one out, and Yogi Berra, Mickey Mantle, and Moose Skowron on deck. I didn't envy our pitcher at that point.

"It was then that our pitching coach answered the phone in the bullpen. Then he looked at me and said, 'Okay, Brewer, let's go.' I just sat there looking at him. I thought he must be mistaken, or at least I hoped he was. But then he said a little louder, 'Hey, Brewer, let's get it. Boudreau's not gonna wait forever.'

"Boy! That was one more long walk from the bullpen to the mound. Was I nervous? I couldn't have told you my name if my life had depended on it.

"To this day I only remember the fellows slapping me on the back and congratulating me for pitching us out of a jam. I still have no recollection of what happened in that inning."

The base salary for a rookie in '54, says Brewer, was $7,500 per year. "But that really wasn't bad money back then. The Red Sox were famous for paying their players well, and I made a little better than the minimum."

He also says that Ted Williams was the finest baseball player he ever saw. "He was truly in a league by himself. But you'd never know it. He was a real down to earth sort of fellow and wouldn't tolerate star treatment. He was the most popular guy on the team."

Brewer's best year with the Red Sox came in 1956. He won 19 games that season and pitched the American League to a win over the Nationals in the All-Star game.

Then in '62, after establishing himself as a fierce competitor over the past eight seasons, he tore his shoulder. And that was it for Tommy Brewer. He was only 31, an age when most pitchers are just beginning to hit their stride.

He then returned to Cheraw and spent the next thirty years working with the state Pardons and Parole Board. Retired now, his only connection with baseball, he says, consists of occasionally helping with Little Leaguers and informally coaching kids in his neighborhood. "I like to catch 'em young," he laughs, "before they develop all those bad habits."

He is married to the former Barbara Wilkins of Cheraw, and they continue to make their home there. His spare time is spent "gardening, golfing, and doing whatever else I darned well please."

After the interview, as I stood alone in the parking lot watching Brewer's tail lights disappear in the darkness, I couldn't help but wonder what scenes of former glory must have been passing through his mind at that moment. There were so many of them.

★
Darrell Floyd

He May Be The Only Athlete In History To Be Named All-American For Four Consecutive Years

We aren't quite sure how the NCAA Record Book handles this, but in our book Darrell Floyd will go down in history as one of the few college athletes in history, in any sport, to be named All-American for four consecutive seasons. Admittedly, this phenomenal record came about in sort of an odd way: his first year he was named to the Junior College All-American team, his last three he was a bona fied All-American at Furman University. But since one plus three equal four, then...

Another distinction enjoyed by Floyd is that in 1954 he was a teammate of the great Frank Selvy, he at one guard position, Selvy at the other. Together they formed a scoring threat that has never been equalled before or since. Still, those who played with them and thus knew them best, say there has probably never been a more unlikely duo than Floyd and Selvy. Whereas Selvy was quiet, serious and intense, Floyd was jovial, outgoing and totally outspoken, a young man with a fine sense of humor who seemed to always enjoy himself, regardless of the circumstances.

Also, whereas Selvy was one of the most heavily recruited athletes in America upon his graduaton from Corbin (Ky.) High School in 1951, Floyd laughingly describes himself as probably "the most unrecruited basketball player in the history of the game."

He is a native of Thomasville, N. C., where he attended tiny Fair Grove High School. He remembers that it was always a struggle just to find enough players to form a team at Fair Grove. "Heck," he says, "we did well just to get enough fellows together to shoot marbles."

He swears that he did not receive a single college scholarship his senior year in 1952. But he was a young man with talent for stripping that net from way outside, and he wanted to play. Thus he became a walkon for Coach Danny Miller's team at Wingate Junior College. Also a member of that team, remember, was the great Nield Gordon, who would go on to fame at Furman University. To say the least, Floyd was sensational. Behind the scoring of Floyd and Gordon, Wingate won the National Junior College Championship, and Floyd and Gordon were both named to the Junior Col-

Furman's ace guard, Darrell Floyd, led the nation in scoring both his junior and senior seasons, was named All American for four consecutive years, then, in his spare time, was elected President of the Student Body.

lege All-American Team.

Ignored earlier, Floyd now could hardly walk for all those big time college coaches trying to entice him to sign a scholarship. But of them all, he liked Furman best. Knowing that Frank Selvy, the nation's leading scorer, was playing for the Hurricanes deeply influenced his decision. Plus his old scoring buddy Nield Gordon had enrolled there. Or, as Floyd put it at the time: "If Furman's good enough for Nield Gordon, it's good enough for me."

Thus Floyd, as a sophomore, joined Selvy and the Hurricanes in 1954. He immediately showed that this was no longer a one-man team as he began to bomb the nets in contest after contest. He scored 56 points against Clemson that year, which was just a warmup for the 67 he hit against Morehead State.

The Harlem Globe Trotters could have taken a few lessons from Floyd in ball handling. Here he leaves a bevy of befuddled Wildcats in his wake as Furman upends Davidson in '54.

But the game that Floyd remembers most is Furman's historic game against Newberry College that year, the night that Frank Selvy scored exactly 100 points, still an all-time NCAA single game scoring record.

Sports writers over the years have tried, it seems, to create controversy between Selvy and Floyd concerning that record-setting evening. But both men deny that any such controversy ever existed. It is true that Floyd and the other first stringers were taken out of the game after the first quarter, while Selvy was left in for the entire game. And it is true that at the end of that first quarter Floyd had 27 points while Selvy had only 25.

The modest Selvy says: "Darrell had 27 points in the first quarter. Coach Alley took him out and let some of the younger fellows play. I think if Darrell had stayed in, he would have scored the hundred points."

Floyd, on the other hand, very graciously says: "Sure, I had a couple of more points than Frank in the first quarter. But if I'd stayed in I might still have wound up with 27 points for the whole evening. I think Coach Alley made the right decision."

Whereas Selvy led the nation in scoring in '53 and '54, Floyd stepped right in and led the nation in scoring in '55, averaging 35.9 points per game, and again in '56, averaging 33.8 points per game. And them ain't bad averages!

Floyd, a very popular young man on campus, was elected President of the Student Body his senior year and was also named to Who's Who.

Today Floyd is Area Manager for the L. B. Smith Company in Greenville, where he and his wife Kay make their home. He describes himself as "very family oriented. Most of my goals at this point center around my children and grandchildren."

Grandchildren! Darrell Floyd? Gee, how the time flies.

★

Buddy Sasser

This Talented Conway Quarterback Became
One of the Best Known Sports Leaders in the South

Buddy Sasser has come a long way since his high school days in Conway, even though he's still called "Buddy," and he still calls Conway home.

Professionally, he began his athletic career as a gangly high school quarterback in 1950 and now winding up, some forty-eight years later, he is athletic director at Coastal Carolina.

Sasser's success in athletics obviously didn't happen overnight, but followed a sure and steady progression as time went by.

He made All-State in high school and quarterbacked the Sandlapper team in the 1953 Shrine Bowl. He was one of the most sought after high school football players in the state.

Clemson and Carolina wanted him, of course. But Sasser fell in love with the beautiful campus at UNC and enrolled there in the fall of 1954.

His head coach was George Barkley, though the legendary Jim Tatum would arrive before Sasser's playing days had ended. Among his outstanding memories of his gridiron days concerns the UNC-USC game of 1955. Sasser scored three touchdowns as the Tarheels won by a score of 34-14 in a game played in the Oyster Bowl in Norfolk.

He also remembers playing against the number-one team in the nation in '55: "We opened the '55 season against Oklahoma, then coached by Bud Wilkerson. They had a 45-game winning streak going when they came to Chapel Hill that day and they were really a terrific football team. They finally beat us 13-7, but it was a close game, and we came very close to ending their win streak."

He also has vivid memories of traveling to South Bend, Ind. to play Paul Hornung and the Fighting Irish of Notre Dame, and later going up against Tennessee before 100,000 fans at Neyland Stadium in Knoxville.

"Those games were typical of the out-of-conference schedule we played back then. It was really a killer schedule, but we did okay."

Following his graduation in 1958 Sasser became a high school coach at both Eau Claire and Conway. Later, after having served as an assistant coach on the college level, he became head coach at Wofford, a position he held for six years.

Then it was back home to Conway again,

Buddy Sasser, once one of the most highly sought after quarterbacks in the state, still devotes his life to athletics.

where he became athletic director at Coastal Carolina University in 1986. Then in '89 he was appointed Commissioner of the Big South Conference.

"These schools (Winthrop, Charleston Southern and Coastal Carolina in South Carolina; Davidson, Campbell, and UNC-Asheville in North Carolina; and Radford and Liberty in Virginia) offer scholarships on a per need basis," he says. "And athletes can qualify for a scholarship just like any other students. But they aren't singled out for scholarships just because they're athletes.

"We feel this is an ideal way for college athletics to go, and it's an idea that's gaining popularity across the country. In other words, we feel that our program offers an ideal balance between academics and athletics."

Sasser again became athletic director at Coastal Carolina two years ago.

He married his high school sweetheart, the former Sara Jean Long of Conway, and they have three children. They make their home in Conway.

★

Ray Masneri

He Led Clemson to Three ACC Titles and Trips to Both The Orange and Sugar Bowls

Ray Masneri was a classic Jekyll-Hyde personality. Those who knew him best swore that for six days a week he wouldn't harm a fly. They describe him as a guy with a heart of gold, a champion of those who could not defend themselves, a gentleman who went around opening doors for elderly ladies.

But on Saturday afternoons something seemed to snap in Masneri's personality.

There was just something about bright Saturday afternoons that seemed to trigger murderous impulses in this mild mannered gentleman. He would become a raging maniac. Then, aided and abetted by his ten ruffian accomplices, he would go out and commit absolute mayhem.

Simply put, Ray Masneri was one of the finest ends ever to snare a pass or nail an opposing ball carrier for the Clemson Tigers. Born in 1937 in California, Pa., a Pittsburgh suburb, Masneri's primary interest in high school was football. He was highly recruited his senior year, but he particularly liked Clemson College and Coach Don Wade who recruited him for the Tigers.

Following his enrollment in the fall of '55 he found himself hundreds of miles away from home. Was this Pittsburgher lonely down in the foothills of South Carolina?

"Hardly," he laughs. "By that time Coach Frank Howard had discovered that there was gold up in them thar hills, kids raised up in the shadows of the smokestacks of the steel mills of Pittsburgh. In fact, there were twenty-six boys from the Pittsburgh area on Clemson's roster my freshman year. It was pretty much like being at Penn State."

Masneri played both offense and defense for Clemson, but says that he preferred defense. "I would rather hit than get hit," he says. "It's that simple."

During his three years as a starter for the Tigers ('56-'58), Clemson won twenty-two games while losing only eight. More impressive, they won the ACC championship all three of those years, and played in the Orange Bowl in '56 and in the Sugar Bowl in '58.

Ray Masneri, a product of Pittsburgh, Pa., saw Clemson win 22 games during his three years as a starter ('56-'58) for the Tigers. More impressive, Clemson won the ACC championship all three of those years and played in both the Orange and Sugar Bowls.

And little wonder. A list of his teammates reads like a Who's-Who of Clemson football, guys like Harvey White, Dalton Rivers, Harold Olson, Lou Cordileone, John Grdijan, Bill Hudson, Charlie Bussey, Joel Wells, Rudy Hayes, Dick Marazza, Bill Thomas and Bill Mathis.

Masneri remembers playing Colorado in the '56 Orange Bowl and trying to stop the great All-American fullback John "The Beast" Bayuk.

"Bayuk was truly incredible," he says. "He'd been chewing us up all afternoon, just like he'd done everybody else all year. I remember one play Bill Thomas and I brought him down, and as we were getting up, Thomas kind of shoved down on Bayuk's helmet, looked him straight in the eye, and said, 'No wonder they call you The Beast—you're the ugliest guy I've ever seen.'

"I grabbed Thomas' arm and said, 'For God's sake, man, don't make him mad. He's bad enough as it is.'"

As for the '58 Sugar Bowl, when Clemson lost

Here Masneri gathers in a Harvey White pass as Clemson beat Virginia 20-7 in '57. Masneri was named to the All ACC Team in '58.

7-0 to national champion LSU, Masneri says his most vivid memories are not of the game itself but of the night before the game. "Yes, unfortunately, some of the fellows decided they'd slip out late that night and taste some of that New Orleans night life. And I can still picture Coach Howard sneaking around the motel parking lot in the wee hours, nabbing those guys coming back to the motel. He threatened to put 'em all on the bus the next morning and ship 'em back to Clemson, but he didn't. And they played pretty well the next day."

Masneri also has fond memories of Horace Turbeville, quarterback on their freshman team who later transferred to Newberry College and still later served as baseball coach at Winthrop University. But he says that Turbeville would keep the team in stitches with his imitation of Clemson's legendary freshman coach Goat McMillan.

"He could do Goat perfectly," laughs Masneri. "He could walk like him, talk like him, and he even wore his hat on the back of his head the way Goat did. I remember before a game we'd always walk out onto the field just to look things over. And there would be Goat walking down the sidelines, with Horace a step behind him, mimicking his every move, as though he were Goat's shadow."

It was during his senior year at Clemson that

Masneri met the girl of his dreams. "Her name was June Fox. She was a native of York, but she was then a student at Anderson College. I was at Cowen's Drive-In in Anderson one night and I saw June and some of her friends sitting in their car. So, being a friendly guy, I just walked over and jumped in the car with them. June was pretty outraged. She called me a typical fresh Yankee, and wouldn't speak to me."

A year later, however, Ray and June were married.

June, by the way, was voted Mrs. Taps, queen of the Clemson Yearbook, in 1960.

Following graduation, Masneri joined the Clemson coaching staff for a year. But he had a sincere concern for the welfare of people less fortunate than himself, and thus he decided to pursue a health care career.

He spent several years with Blue Cross-Blue Shield, then moved into the area of nursing for the elderly. Today he is regional director for the Brian Center and stationed in Rock Hill, where he and his family make their home.

He and June have a son, Joey, who is a Charlotte pharmacist. They also have two daughters, Terri and Julie. Soon Ray and June will celebrate their thirty-eighth wedding anniversary.

★
Jimmy Orr

He Was Named The Colts All-Time Greatest Receiver

Jimmy Orr was one of those individuals who always had to prove himself at every stage of his athletic career. He was inevitably regarded as too small, or too slow, or simply not good enough to make whatever team he was trying out for. Yet he proved in the end that he was one of the greatest football players ever to hail from South Carolina.

At Seneca High, under Coach Red Lynch, Orr was an excellent basketball player, and was named to the All-State team both his junior and senior seasons. But in football, as one former teammate says, "he was considered just sort of okay."

Following his graduation in 1954 he enrolled first at Wake Forest in hopes of landing a basketball scholarship. Unfortunately, he says, a scholarship failed to materialize. Thus he transferred to Clemson. In fact, his chances of landing a hot basketball scholarship seemed to be growing dim.

At that point he was approached by Coach Frank Howard who offered him a football scholarship. Orr turned him down. "I was a restless kid," he remembers today, "and Clemson really was just too close to home. I wanted to see the world. So I traveled all the way down to Athens, Georgia, a whole hundred miles from Seneca, and enrolled there."

At Georgia, Orr says he received little encouragement from Coach Wally Butts, and eventually became a member of the scout team, which Orr describes as "legalized murder."

Then came his big break. In the first game of the '55 season, against SEC power Old Miss, Orr was listed as a fourth-string wide receiver. But as the game progressed, injuries mounted for the Bulldogs. "Our sideline looked like that famous hospital scene in Gone With The Wind," Orr commented with a laugh. Finally, another wide receiver went down. Coach Butts looked to his bench and saw no one sitting there but Jimmy Orr. Butts reluctantly gave him the sign and in he went. By game's end Orr had three catches for 105 yards, including a game-winning TD catch of 45 yards. From then on, Orr could do no wrong in Butts' opinion.

Aways consided too small and too slow, Jimmy Orr is still remembered as one of greatest college and pro players ever.

At season's end not only had he made the Bulldogs' starting lineup, he was voted Rookie of the Year in the SEC.

He later led the SEC in receiving in both '56 and '57 and was voted All-SEC both seasons. In '58 he as named to the All-SEC Academic team and was selected to play in the Blue-Gray Game.

Still, predictably enough, he was almost overlooked in the '58 pro draft, going in the 22nd round to the Los Angeles Rams. The Rams immediately traded him to the Steelers.

"But I was used to the underdog role," Orr shrugs. "All I wanted was chance, even a small chance."

Not only did he survive the pre-season cuts, he

also became the favorite target of Bobby Layne, finishing the season with 33 catches for 910 yards and 7 touchdowns. More incredibly, he was voted NFL Rookie of the Year. Not a bad start for a little slow boy from Seneca, S. C.

As though that were not enough, in 1959 he was named to the All-NFL Team.

In 1961 Baltimore needed an ace receiver to complement the passing talents of NFL great Johnny Unitas. Thus they traded All-Pro tackle Big Daddy Lipscomb and a high draft pick to Pittsburgh for Jimmy Orr. He was delighted to join such Colts as Unitas, Lenny Moore, Raymond Barry, Jim Parker and Alex Hawkins.

"There were three secrets of our success," says Orr. "The first was Johnny Unitas, one of the finest quarterbacks ever to play the game. The second was timing, and the third was our big offensive line. We ran the fanciest pass patterns in the league, thanks to our big offensive line. Other teams simply couldn't give their quarterbacks the time needed to run those patterns. And Unitas was always right on the money because we practiced timing so much. He always knew where we all would be on any given pattern, and we always knew exactly where the ball would be and when it would be there. And it always was. That was the secret of our success."

During his ten years with the Colts Orr caught three-hundred passes. He also scored fifty touchdowns, sixth in all-time scoring.

But of all those catches, there is one that still stands out in Orr's memory. He remembers it was early in the third quarter against the Philadelphia Eagles and he went down with a dislocated shoulder.

"They put me in the ambulance and took me to the hospital. But when I got to the emergency room there were about twenty people already ahead of me, and they were all watching the game on TV. Luckily, when they heard who I was they motioned for me to go to the head of the line. Then a doctor came out, snapped my shoulder back in place, and that put me back on my feet."

Orr then insisted that he be driven back to the stadium, putting his uniform back on as the ambulance flew down the street.

"Well, when I arrived back at the stadium there was about a minute left in the game and the Eagles were on top 31-27. Coach Shula saw me running up, so he motioned for me to join the team. They were huddling at the fifty-yard line. So of course the fans saw me jogging down the field and everyone began cheering. It was really an electric moment for me.

"On first down Unitas hit Lenny Moore on a long pattern down to the Eagles' twenty. Then on the next play I did a little wideout, and John hit me in the corner of the end zone for a touchdown, and we won 34-31. But that's the catch I remember the most, the one I got out of the hospital to make."

His greatest thrill, he says, in addition to being a teammate of Johnny Unitas, was playing in Super Bowls III and V.

"The last game I ever played in was Super Bowl V against the Dallas Cowboys, which we won 16-13. I've worn that Super Bowl ring ever since."

He is a member of the University of Georgia Athletic Hall of Fame, and he was recently named to the All-Time Baltimore Colts squad.

Today he is involved in resort real estate sales in Greensboro, Ga.

★

Bobby Richardson

Sumter's All-Time Yankee Great

Talk about a child prodigy, get this: at the age of fourteen, already a star second baseman on the Sumter High School baseball team, Bobby Richardson was approached after a game by Mayo Smith, the chief scout for the New York Yankees. Mayo said, "Bobby, we've had our eye on you for some time now. As soon as you finish high school, the Yankees want to sign you to a contract."

Pretty heady news for a fourteen year old kid.

But sure enough, says Richardson, the day he received his diploma Smith drove him to New York, where he spent four days working out with probably the greatest team in baseball, the '53 Yankees. Casey Stengel watched him closely, nodded his head, and the Yankees signed him to that lucrative contract Smith had mentioned.

Bobby had just turned seventeen.

At 5-9 and 165 pounds, he was rather on the small side for a professional athlete, but he credits his father, a Sumter tombstone maker, with encouraging him to develop his athletic talents. "Dad especially encouraged me to play baseball and basketball," he says. "Oddly enough, I twice made the All-State Team in basketball and was offered several scholarships. But in baseball, I received no post-season honors whatsoever."

"This might sound corny," he grins, "but I saw that old movie _Pride of the Yankees,_ all about the life of Lou Gehrig, and I decided then that I wanted to be part of their team.."

In 1953, he played for Class A Binghamton, N. Y., where he finished the season with a .310 batting average. The next year, he was jumped to Class AAA Denver, where he hit an amazing .328.

It was in '55 that he began his long career in the Yankees pinstripes. Yet neither the big money nor the glare of the spotlight turned his head. "I have my parents to thank for always helping me to see things in their proper perspective," he says. "They always tried to instill spiritual values in me, so by the time I was nineteen, material things really didn't mean that much. They still don't."

The Yankees of the '55-'56 era are arguably

Bobby Richardson is remembered today as one of the finest players ever to wear the pinstripes of the New York Yankees. He still holds numerous major league records.

the finest collection of players ever assembled by any team in the history of major league baseball. Remember their starting lineup of that era: Mickey Mantle, Roger Maris, Phil Rizzuto, Gil McDougal, Billy Martin, Moose Skowron, Hank Bauer, Yogi Berra, Tony Kubek, Clete Boyer, Elston Howard, and Whitey Ford.

As for Manager Casy Stengel, what can we say? It was truly the Golden Age of Yankee baseball.

Incredibly, during Richardson's eleven years with the Yankees, they would play in the World Series nine times. Richardson was named to the American League All-Star Team seven times, and won the Golden Glove Award, as the league's best defensive infielder, five times.

Today, thirty years after his retirement, he still holds numerous major league records: for example, he played in thirty consecutive World Series games. In the 1960 World Series, versus Pittsburgh, he was credited with twelve RBIs (six of those came in one game, still another all-time record). And in the '64 Series, versus the Cardinals, he collected a total of thirteen hits.

Typically enough, the modest Richardson's most memorable experience concerns not himself, but teammate Mickey Mantle. "I recall Mantle was put in a game as a pinch hitter after being sidelined for over a month with a severe back injury, and the fans at Yankee Stadium gave him a tremendous ovation as he walked to the plate. It was the ninth inning, and we were down by two runs but had a couple of guys on base. So we needed a hit badly. It was a real pressure situation, but Mantle very coolly whacked the first pitch. That ball finally came down on top of the roof over the bleachers in center field. But I've always remembered that moment as typical of Mantle's character and courage, his greatness as a clutch player."

Well, yeah, okay, but how about Yogi Berra? Was he really the zany character we always read about?

Richardson laughs, shakes his head and says, "When I first went up to the Yankees, I was nineteen and just married. But my wife hadn't arrived in New York yet, so Yogi invited me to stay with him and Mrs. Berra at their apartment until Betsy came up. I didn't want to be an imposition, so I asked him how many bedrooms they had. Yogi shrugged and said, 'Gee, I dunno. My wife takes care of things like that.' But that was typical of Yogi. He'd make a statement, then leave you to ponder what it meant.

"But sitting in the dugout between Yogi and Casey Stengel was a real experience—especially if you spoke English."

In 1968, at an age when most fellows are just getting started in their careers, Richardson decided to hang it up.

"It had nothing to do with money or any sort of discontent with the Yankees," he says. "It was just that by then Betsy and I had five children, and I felt I needed to be in an occupation where I could spend more time with my family."

Still, he has never really gotten out of baseball. He worked part time for the Yankees for several years as a scout and with their young players during spring training. From 1970 til '76 he enjoyed an excellent tenure as coach of the Carolina Gamecocks. Then he would serve in a dual capacity as coach and athletic director at Coastal Carolina College and later at Liberty University.

Since 1990 he has served as President of an organization known as Baseball Chapel. "We have a church service in the locker room of every major and minor league team in the country on Sunday mornings. We generally have about forty players participate, and it's all voluntary, of course."

He finished his career with the Yankees, by the way, with a highly respectable .266 batting average, which leads Art Baker, another Sumter native and currently special advisor to Coach Brad Scott at Carolina, to boast to audiences that he once struck out Bobby Richardson twice in one game.

"Of course," concludes Baker with a grin, "that was back in our Little League days when I was twelve and he was eight."

Richardson is married to the former Betsy Dobson of Sumter and they have five children and ten grandchildren. They make their home in Sumter.

★

Paul Maguire

This Bulldog Receiver Became One of the Nation's Greatest Pro Football Sportscasters

Although courted by such football powers as Ohio State, Michigan, Notre Dame and Southern Cal, Paul Maguire chose to attend The Citadel, which seems odd when one remembers that The Citadel is not exactly considered a country club for college athletes.

"There's nothing odd about it," Maguire says, shaking his head. "I visited down there, and I loved both The Citadel and Charleston. Plus I thought Coach Eddie Teague was the greatest guy in the world."

Maguire pauses, then chuckles. "Well, to be perfectly honest, the real reason I chose The Citadel was Coach Al Davis. He was Teague's assistant, and he's the one who recruited me. So, what can I say about him now that hasn't already been said a million times? He was great, and that about says it all. Later I played pro ball under him with the San Diego Chargers. He's been an influence in my life now since 1955."

Maguire had distinguished himself as a promising young athlete as a receiver at Ursuline High School in Youngstown, Ohio. His senior season he was inducted into one of the most exclusive clubs in America—the Ohio All-State Football Team.

After entering The Citadel in 1956 he says he adapted easily to military life.

"Well, yeah, the military's different," he says, "but as an athlete I'd been subject to a great deal of self-discipline for years. To me, the corps of cadets was just another team I very badly wanted to become a part of. So for me it wasn't a chore but more like a challenge."

He started at end for the Bulldogs his freshman year and did well. In fact, he was chosen Southern Conference Freshman of the Year.

His best season came his senior year in 1959. The Citadel went 7-2 on the year, losing only to Florida State and VMI, as they headed into their season finale against the mighty Mountaineers of West Virginia. By game's end Maguire and Company had pulled off a 20-14 shocker.

In that game Maguire caught two TD passes

Paul Maguire as a member of the corp of cadets at The Citadel in 1959. A native of Ohio, he says that the corp of cadets was just another team he wanted to make.

from Bobby Schwartz. More importantly, he kept the Mounties bottled up all afternoon with his booming punts, one an 83-yarder, which still remains the longest punt in The Citadel Record Book.

For the season Maguire caught ten touchdown passes and was named Southern Conference Player of the Year. Today he still remains second in The Citadel Record Book in punting and fourth in receiving.

His old coach, Al Davis, wasn't shy about drafting him in the early rounds for the San Diego Chargers. To Maguire's surprise, he was switched from receiver to a linebacker position.

"Actually," he says, "I was drafted as a receiver. But the Chargers were desperate for another linebacker, and I fit the bill physically. So I got the job and that's where I played for the next eleven years, four with the Chargers and seven with

Maguire's most vivid memory concerns The Citadel's 20-14 upset win over mighty West Virginia in 1959. He caught two TD passes in that contest and had an 83-yard punt (still a record at The Citadel). For the '59 season he caught ten TD passes and was named Southern Conference Player of the Year.

the Bills."

Pro football then opened the door for Maguire to become a sports broadcaster. Today he laughs that he'd never been inside a TV station when he accepted a job with NBC Sports as their prized new sportscaster.

"Nah, I wasn't nervous about it," he says. "Broadcasting was just another job as far as I was concerned. Frankly, I'd never even thought about doing a sportscast, but Curt Gowdy recommended me, and NBC gave me a shot. They liked what they saw, gave me a contract, and I've been doing it ever since. Actually, it's a pretty easy way to make a living."

Working primarily as a color analyst, Maguire was with NBC for nine years, then joined ESPN in '85,

then went back again to NBC the same year.

"The people I've worked with have made it a real pleasure," he says. "People like Dick Enberg, Jim Simpson, Jay Randolph and others. Those guys are such great professionals that they make it easy for everybody else."

Looking back over his life today, he says, "From the moment I entered The Citadel, life has been great. I've been associated with pro football for over thirty years now and that's worked out real well. Right now I think I'll give it another five years or so, then I'll start concentrating on my golf game."

Maguire and his family make their home in Eden, N. Y.

★
Grady Wallace

USC'S All-Time Mr. Hardwood

Carolina's Grady Wallace, a native of Mare Creek, Ky., led the nation in scoring in 1957 with a 31.2 average and was named to the All American Team. Here he is carried off the court by jubilant fans following USC's 94-79 win over Clemson in '56.

After all these years, and despite the appearance of more Carolina basketball greats than we'd care to mention, good old Grady Wallace (1956-57) is still the man to beat.

For starters, Wallace led the entire nation in scoring in '57 with a 31.2 points per game average. He scored a total of 906 points that season, still another USC record. For his two-year career at Carolina he averaged a phenomenal 28.1 points per game. As for free throws, he once scored 21 in a single game (versus Duke in '57), while sinking 234 for the season, yet another USC all-time record. In his spare time, he also took down 12.8 rebounds per game during his career, trailing only Tom Owens and Lee Collins in this category.

But Wallace strikes one as a most unlikely hero. At 6-4, he is easygoing, soft-spoken and modest to a fault. There is still much in his manner that reflects his rural upbringing in the mountains of Kentucky (he's from Mare Creek, to be exact) where his folks were your proverbial poor-but-honest coal miners who raised their kids to go to church on Sundays and to respect the things we're all supposed to respect. In fact, Grady doesn't recall ever meeting a single flag-burner in Mare Creek, Kentucky.

"Well, it's sort of stretching it to call Mare Creek a town," grins Wallace. "It's what folks up in the mountains call a holler. A holler's sort of a low place surrounded by mountains."

Okay, but what about the rumor that Kentucky is about to change its nickname to the Basketball State?

"Well, they should," he laughs. "Back when I was in high school basketball was THE sport. There were nine high schools in our county and only

Wallace scored 54 points in Carolina's 96-81 win over Georgia in '57. This was the most points scored in a single game by any player in America that year.

one had a football or baseball team. We played basketball all year long. It was really our national pastime."

But Wallace was a late bloomer, and upon his graduation from Mare Creek High in 1954, he showed little evidence of the greatness he would achieve later in life. He received not a single post-season honor, and wound up with only a partial scholarship (to Eastern Kentucky University).

"I went up to Eastern and played my freshman year, but then I got really homesick and came back to Mare Creek. I then enrolled at Pikeville Junior College, about fifteen miles from home, and played there my sophomore year. I didn't have a car, so I had to thumb back and forth to class. Which got pretty old real fast."

As for his great exodus from Pikeville to USC, he says that Carolina Coach Frank Johnson (1946-58) recruited the entire Pikeville team in '55 and that all of them, including Wallace, came down to see what USC had to offer. Sort of a package deal, in other words.

But still, even at that point, Wallace had not hit his stride. In fact, Coach Johnson displayed little

more interest in Wallace than he did in several other players from Pikeville. But then, once he'd donned the garnet and black, strange things began to happen. This ugly duckling suddenly became the beautiful white swan the Gamecocks had been looking for. Overnight he became Super Shooter, the top scorer in the history of Carolina basketball. Was he surprised at his new-found brilliance?

"You bet I was! Honestly, I played basketball because I loved the game. And there was no competition anywhere like that in the ACC. It's real odd, and I can't explain it, but the tougher the competition, the better I performed. I certainly accomplished things I'd never anticipated when I came down here."

His teammates during his two years with the Gamecocks were Ray "Cookie" Pericola, Richie Hoffman, Fred Lentz and Bobby McCoy (another Mare Creek boy). They were the hottest shooting outfit in the history of Gamecock basketball and still hold team records for the most points ever scored in a single game (121 points versus The Citadel in '56), as well as the most points scored in a season (2,386 points in '57).

As for Wallace himself, not only was he the number-one rebounder in the Atlantic Coast Conference, he was also the number-one scorer in the entire nation with a 31.2 points per game average.

Indeed, Wallace's closest competitor for the national scoring title in '57 was the great Wilt Chamberlain, but the race wasn't even close. Wallace was then named to the AP All-American team. In fact, he was voted runner-up to UNC's Lennie Rosenbluth as the best collegiate basketball player in America that year. He also graduated in '57 with a degree in education.

"Actually my ambition was to become a high school coach back in Kentucky. But somehow I never did either. I never became a coach nor went back to Kentucky. I played pro ball for a couple of years with the Phillips Oilers, then I took a job with the State Board Of Pardons and Parole. I just recently retired from there after thirty-three years of service."

Today, after 88 years of intercollegiate basketball, USC has retired only four jerseys, those of John Roche, Alex English, Kevin Joyce, and, yep, good old number-42, Super Shooter himself, Grady Wallace.

A member of the South Carolina Athletic Hall of Fame, Wallace says that he is now the world's most retired retiree: "I spend all my spare time doing what I like to do most—losing golf balls."

He is married to the former Janet Boney and they make their home in Columbia.

★
Harvey White

He Was Clemson's All-ACC Quarterback
for Three Consecutive Years

Today he's a sales executive for American Can Company in Charlotte, but years ago he played under the legendary Pinky Babb at Greenwood High, and was selected the outstanding football player in South Carolina in 1955. He quarterbacked the Sandlappers in the Shrine Bowl that year and had his pick of scholarships from dozens of colleges throughout the nation.

But he chose Clemson, he says, because he had relatives who were alumni of that institution. "Plus my dad and Frank Howard both chewed tobacco and hit it off real well."

During his sophomore season Clemson went 7-3 and Harvey White became the only Clemson quarterback in history to make the All-ACC team as a sophomore. He finished the year with a 154.6 passing proficiency rating, still second only to Homer Jordan's 155.2 in 1975.

The next year he led the Tigers to an 8-2 season and the ACC championship. That was the year that Clemson traveled to New Orleans to take on LSU, the number-one team in the nation, in the Sugar Bowl. When speaking with White, I asked him the question that has been on everyone's mind now for the past forty years: Why did Clemson wear navy blue jerseys that afternoon instead of their traditional orange ones?

"Well, there's really no mystery to it," he grinned. "The TV people requested we do that. Blue and white show up better on TV than orange and purple. There was really no secret strategy involved there at all."

Though Clemson finally lost the game 7-0, they manhandled LSU and their great running back Billy Cannon, who was held to only thirty-five yards rushing during the entire game.

"Actually we weren't surprised at how well we did defensively," White says. "Because we truly had a great line that year. Guys like Ray Masneri, Harold Olson, and Lou Cordileone, guys who could have made anybody's team."

But what he remembers most about the '59 Sugar Bowl occurred late in the fourth quarter. Trailing 7-0, and with only minutes left on the

Harvey White and Paul Snyder, co-captains of the '59 Clemson Tigers. White remains the only Clemson quarterback ever named to the All ACC team for three consecutive years. In '58 and '59 he led Clemson to 18 wins and two bowl games.

clock, Clemson faced a fourth-and-five at the LSU 15 yard line. White took the snap from center, then faded back rapidly. But the entire LSU defensive line was on him.

Which was just what he wanted. As he was going down he lofted a short screen pass to a wide open George Usry. But. . .

"I was going down as I threw the ball, and Usry had to bend over to get his hands on it. Unfortunately, he turned up field before he really had possession and dropped the ball. It was a sure seven points if he'd caught it, because there wasn't

In a viciously fought contest, Clemson finally fell to national champion LSU by a score of 7-0 in the '60 Sugar Bowl. Here Harvey White appears to have the Chinese Bandits totally surrounded.

a white jersey anywhere between him and the goal. Of course George felt terrible about it.

"Well, our '58 team meets every five years for a reunion. And sure as the world somebody always brings a film of that Sugar Bowl game. Always, just before it shows George dropping that pass, all the guys start clapping their hands and yelling, 'Okay, George, here comes your big play. Catch it, George!' But George Usry was one of the great ones at Clemson, and it's too bad that one play has stuck with him all these years."

If '58 was good, then '59 was even better. The Tigers again went 8-2 on the season, again won the ACC championship, then they upset a great Texas Christian team 23-7 in the Bluebonnet Bowl.

White was named to the All-ACC team for the third consecutive year, one of the few players ever so honored.

He went high in the '59 pro draft and was given a no-cut contract by the Boston Patriots. But Boston was already deep in quarterbacks that year, and for the first time White found himself riding the bench.

"They couldn't cut me," he says, "but they did everything else with me. For a while they even had me playing tight end. Frankly, I didn't relish going head-on with those 280 pound linemen.

"So the next year I jumped to Montreal of the Canadian Football League. But really, I was always a rollout passer, while those pro teams were looking for a drop-back passer. So I decided to come home and look for a real job in the real world."

Today White and his wife live in Charlotte, as they have for many years. Their daughters both attended South Mecklenburg High, and both graduated from the University of North Carolina.

White is a member of the Clemson Athletic Hall of Fame.

★
John Saunders

"Always Make The Most Of Whatever You Have"

Norman Vincent Peale's essay on positive thinking was never on John Saunder's required reading list. He didn't need it. He could write his own such book.

"Worrying about things doesn't help," the former University of South Carolina football star says. "If life deals you a negative hand, which it does sometimes, you just have to go to work and try to turn it into something positive."

Growing up as the youngest in a family of thirteen children can give one such an attitude. He was always the last in line at mealtime, the one where all the hand-me-downs finally wound up before being tossed in the trash bin. But despite the fact that he received short shrift as a youngster, before he finished high school he was considered king of the hill.

A native of Churchland, Va., Saunders, running from his fullback position, led the state in scoring both his junior and senior seasons, and was named to the High School All-American Team. Soon he announced that he would play for the University of North Carolina in '56.

Then Fate, disguised as USC alumnus and former football great Droopy Atwell, intervened. "I got hijacked," Saunders laughs. "I mean literally hijacked. There was this guy, Droopy Atwell, living in Churchland and all he talked about was USC and how great it was.

"I told him I didn't even want to hear about USC, that I was headed for UNC. But he wore me down, and finally I agreed to accompany him down for a weekend visit. Well, we arrived in Columbia on June 10th. I didn't see Churchland again until August 25th."

Well, yeah, okay, John, but just how did that happen?

"In all honesty, I'm still not quite sure how all that happened. But somebody in the athletic department told me I'd been enrolled in a summer school course and that it was too late to drop out. So, naive as I was, I attended classes all summer there. And that's a true story. Of course by the end

John Saunders, one of the Gamecocks' finest fullbacks ever, led the ACC in rushing yardage in '58, won the ACC Jacobs Blocking Trophy, and was named to the All ACC Football Team.

of the summer I was in love with USC and best friends with everybody on the football team."

During his sophomore season, in 1957, he moved into the starting fullback position. And though the Gamecocks finished with a mediocre 5-5 record, Saunders says that season produced his most memorable game, USC's 27-21 upset win over national power Texas.

"I have this very vivid memory of King Dixon running that opening kickoff back 98 yards for a touchdown," he says. "And I remember us being down by 14 points with only five minutes remaining in the game, and how we finally fought back to win. That was a great day for USC."

A typical scene here as Saunders (#33) lowers the boom on a rash Terrapin defender as Joe Gomes breaks out for good yardage in '58.

Saunders came unto his own during the '58 season when he was named the Most Valuable Player in Carolina's 26-6 win over Clemson on Big Thursday. That was the year he led the ACC in rushing yardage, won the ACC Jacobs Blocking Trophy, was named to the All-ACC Football Team, and was named Honorable Mention All-American.

Not a real bad season. And he was only a junior.

Then again Fate stepped in. He was elected Team Captain his senior season of '59, and great things were expected of him. But then disaster struck. He suffered a severe shoulder injury during the first five minutes of the season opener against Duke. It was a blow from which he never recovered.

"I ran a few plays late in the season, and I played in the North-South Shrine Game, but I was unable to go full speed anymore. I'd hoped to play pro ball, but of course that was out of the question."

But, he says, the loss of a pro career never really bothered him. It was just another of those negative hands that we have to play as best we can.

"I try never to look back at what might have been," he shrugs. "I don't look at what I don't have. I look at what I do have. And what I had then was a degree from a great university. I built on that and always tried to do the best I could with it."

Today Saunders is President of Palmetto Wholesale in Columbia. He and his family make their home in Chapin.

★

Harold Stowe

Clemson's MVP Award Is Named In His Honor

Former Clemson baseball coach Bill Wilhem says that during his entire long career in college baseball he never saw anyone who loved to pitch more than Harold Stowe.

"He had more guts than anybody I ever saw when he was standing on that mound," Wilhelm says. "And the more he pitched, the better he got. He was really a horse."

Stowe, who now owns a seafood restaurant in Gastonia, N. C., took up the game as a kid and climbed the ladder all the way to the Big Show.

Yet the record book lists him with only one inning pitched in the major leagues. And his most vivid memory of his brief stint with the New York Yankees isn't the kind of stuff of which Baseball Encyclopedias are made.

"I can say that I did pitch batting practice to Roger Maris the night he broke Babe Ruth's home run record," laughs Stowe. "And that's the highlight of my major league career."

The route to the majors began back in his native Belmont, N. C., where he rode his bicycle as a grade schooler to nearby Cramerton to pitch Junior American Legion ball under Coach Benny Cunningham.

Then two years later he became a stalwart for Gastonia's American Legion team under Coach Larry Davis. Gastonia won the state championship in both '53 and '54. In fact, in '54 they went on to the national finals before losing 3-2 in eleven innings to San Diego.

"Cunningham and Davis were both excellent coaches," says Stowe, "and they, along with Coach Bill Wilhelm, have meant more to my life than anyone will ever know."

He had intended to play college baseball at

Harold Stowe and Coach Bill Wilhelm talking it over. Stowe twice led Clemson to the College World Series and was himself named to the College All Star Team in '59. A personality clash with Yankee manager Ralph Houk cut short his pro career.

Florida State, but when he arrived home one Sunday afternoon, there sat his mom and dad at the kitchen table with a couple of guests. It was Clemson coaches Frank Howard and Bob Smith.

"They were eating country ham and eggs, and cornbread and milk," laughs Stowe. "Before I could even say hello, my dad said, 'Son, I don't know what you want to go way down to Florida for. We just met the fellows right here who coach where you ought to go to school.' Well, five minutes later I'd signed all the papers and was on my way to Clemson."

His decision turned out to be a good one. Indeed the records he set at Clemson died hard. In 1958, for example, he had an ERA of 1.58 in the fifteen games he started for the Tigers. In fact, he won 14 of the 32 games that Clemson played that year, setting both a school and ACC record for most wins in a single season. (This record stood until broken five years ago, but of course Clemson plays twice as many games now as they did in '58.)

During his three-year career Stowe compiled a 24-13 record, with a 2.32 ERA. He set many records during that period that have since been broken by players who were allowed to play varsity ball as freshmen.

He led the Tigers to the College World Series twice, while he himself was named to the CWS All-Star Team in '59.

That same year the New York Yankees signed the 6-0, 175 pound Stowe, a southpaw, and sent him to Fargo, N. D., of the Class B Northern League for a year.

Then in 1960 he advanced to Amarillo of the Class AA Texas League. The next year, after losing the season opener, he then rattled off fifteen consecutive wins for Amarillo, which still remains a Texas League record for consecutive wins. That earned him a shot with the Yankees.

In seventeen spring training innings in '61 he allowed but three runs on four hits to earn the team's Most Outstanding Young Pitcher Award.

But Stowe says a personality conflict with Yankee manager Ralph Houk really destroyed his pro career. "Houk simply didn't like me. I hate to say that, but it's true. He kept me on the bench until July 1. He wouldn't play me, yet he wouldn't trade me. Then he called up Al Downing and sent me down to Richmond. And that was my cup of tea with the Yankees."

He came home and worked for Burlington Industries until 1968, then he purchased his father's business in Gastonia, aptly known far and wide as Stowe's Fish Camp, a frequent meeting place for his old teammates from Clemson and the Yankees.

Clemson inducted Stowe in its Athletic Hall of Fame in 1979. In 1984 the Tigers honored his accomplishments by instituting the Harold Stowe MVP Pitchers Award.

★
Horace Turbeville

At Newberry College He Became America's Youngest
Head Football Coach

Today, after some thirty-two years in athletics, Horace Turbeville is a man well known throughout the South for his expertise as a coach in both football and baseball. What many have forgotten is his past excellence as a football player.

Back in 1950, at the age of fourteen, Turbeville broke into the starting lineup of one of the most outstanding teams in the state, the Camden High Bulldogs. They ran the single-wing formation back then, and Turbeville became their starting tailback while still a student at Camden Junior High.

More incredibly, he was named All-State that year, and still remains the only high school football player in South Carolina ever to be name All-State for five consecutive years.

His senior year, in 1954, he was named Captain of the All-State team, and was chosen to play in both the Shrine Bowl and the High School All-American game in Memphis.

Obviously he became one of the most highly sought after high school athletes in the nation, and the colleges that still ran the single-wing (Clemson, UCLA, Penn and Tennessee) went after him in a big way.

But the past few years had been very successful years for Clemson, and the Tigers were almost annual participants in one great bowl game after another, which did nothing to hurt their recruiting. Thus Turbeville cast his lot with Clemson. Besides, he says, he had no desire to stray far from home and his high school sweetheart, Kate Lee of Camden.

He was well known to be a tough, rock-'em type runner and an adroit passer, the sort who would fit right in with Coach Frank Howard's no-nonsense, cram-it-down-their-throats brand of football. By his sophomore season he and Charlie Bussey had earned the starting quarterback positions in Clemson's two-platoon offense.

Supplementing them in the backfield in '56 were such Tiger greats as Joel Wells, Jim Coleman, and Rudy Hayes. Turbeville still recalls their game against Wake Forest that year when he was called on to kick a 39-yard field goal against Wake Forest.

Horace Turbeville was a great quarterback for both the Clemson Tigers and the Newberry Indians during his playing career. Later he would become head coach of both football and baseball at Newberry, as well as their recruiting coordinator, professor of physical education, and Dean of Men.

The kick was good and Clemson went on to win 17-0. (This kick also set a distant record that stood for many years at Clemson.) In fact, the Tigers went 7-2-1 on the season, won the ACC championship and a big trip to the Orange Bowl, where they lost a squeaker to Colorado 27-21.

Turbeville himself was named to the All-ACC

Sophomore Team, and we would assume that his career was set. But no. He decided to transfer to Newberry. Still, he was very happy at Clemson, he says, but he wished to pursue a career in Education that Clemson did not offer. So the next season he would don the regalia of the Newberry Indians, then coached by Harvey Kirkland.

And what is his most outstanding memory of his playing days at Newberry? Turbeville quips: "In 1959 we should have been crowned national champions. You see, that was the year we beat The Citadel, who had just beaten West Virginia. West Virginia had just beaten Purdue, and Purdue had just beat Oklahoma, the number-one team in the nation. So we claimed that we should rightfully be the national champs, based on our win over The Citadel."

In 1960, after coaching for a year in the high school ranks, Turbeville was named head coach at Newberry College. At the age of twenty-four, he was the youngest collegiate head coach in America. But from all appearances, Newberry got their money's worth. Over the next nineteen years, then, in addition to coaching both football and baseball for the Indians, he would also serve as recruiting coordinator, professor of physical education, and Dean of Men.

"My career there was certainly varied," he laughs, "and I enjoyed every minute of it. But the best part was working with the kids. The worst part, for me, would be having to practice and play in cold weather. I never liked playing football in the cold."

In 1978 he left Newberry and initiated the baseball program at Winthrop College. Their second year of competition, in 1979, the Eagles went to the NAIA World Series, where they finished second in the nation, behind only Grand Canyon College. Not a bad start.

Turbeville resigned from Winthrop following the 1991 season. Since that time he has received many inquiries concerning his becoming a college coach or a pro scout. But, he says, he is not particularly excited about either prospect at this point in his life.

"After thirty-two years of coaching, I have no definite plans at the moment. I think I just want to enjoy retirement for a while. Maybe then I'll start my career all over again."

He and Kate Lee have three daughters and three granddaughters and make their home in Rock Hill.

★

Ty Cline

He Became A Mainstay With The Cleveland Indians

In his first at-bat in the major leagues, says Ty Cline, he wanted to crawl under home plate and hide there forever. Instead, he closed his eyes, swung, and luckily rapped a single. It was a hit that began a career that would insure him a place among baseball's elite for the next twelve seasons.

Reaching the big leagues was the culmination of a dream that had begun years earlier down in the Low Country of South Carolina and would later lead him to become an All-American at Clemson and a participant in the College World Series.

A native of Hampton, he was named All-State in both baseball and basketball at Charleston's St. Andrews High School in 1957. Clemson offered him a scholarship in either sport.

Baseball won out, and Cline helped the Tigers advance to the College World Series in his junior year of 1960. He departed Clemson at that point to sign a pro contract with the Cleveland Indians.

Ty Cline was a Clemson All-American before going on to a brilliant career in professional baseball.

Major league players today are supported by a strong union and command huge salaries, thanks to television money. But back in '62 such was not the case. Management sat squarely in the driver's seat and their word was law. Cline's first encounter with Indians' general manager Gabe Paul typifies the situation as it existed back then:

"Al Luplow and I had driven all night to reach Cleveland and arrived there about 6 AM, totally exhausted. We drove straight to our hotel and collapsed in bed. But about 10 AM the phone rang. It was Gabe Paul. He said he wanted to see us immediately. So we got up and dragged ourselves down to his office. He stuck a contract under our noses to sign so that we could play that night.

In his first at-bat in the majors that night, against the Boston Red Sox, he recalls: "I was really nervous, and the last thing I wanted to do was call attention to myself or make anybody mad. I hit the first pitch off the end of the bat, and the ball went zinging straight into the Red Sox dugout. I mean I literally emptied their bench.

"I think I just closed my eyes and swung at the next pitch. I hit the ball to deep center. I think I could have stretched it into a double, but I was so scared, I didn't even round the first base bag."

Cline relaxed enough to become a fixture in the majors through the '71 season, playing the outfield for the Indians, Braves, Giants, Cubs, Expos, and Reds and compiling a career .238 batting average.

His best year came in 1964 with Milwaukee when he batted .307, and he played in the 1970 World Series with Cincinnati.

Being traded so much gave him the opportunity to play with so many great players, he says. Indeed, a list of his teammates reads like a Who's Who of major league baseball: in Milwaukee there was Hank Aaron, Warren Spahn, Joe Torre, and Eddie Mathews; in San Francisco there was Willie Mays, Willie McCovey and Gaylord Perry; and in Cincinnati guys like Pete Rose and Johnny Bench. The list goes on and on.

Still, being traded so often also made family life difficult. And following the '71 season he and wife Diane and their daughters returned to Charleston.

"Back then the money wasn't that great in baseball," he explains. "Plus we had three children and we were pulling them out of school three times a year and starting them somewhere else. It was becoming just too difficult for the family."

Upon his retirement, Cline opened three Baskins-Robbins ice cream parlors in Charleston, a business he continues to operate there.

★
Jerry Nettles

He Remains The Citadel's Quarterback Par Excellance

Jerry Nettles is still remembered as one of the finest quarterbacks in the history of football at his old alma mater, The Citadel. And for good reason.

During his career there, 1958-60, an era when the forward pass was still viewed with some suspicion, he completed 122 passes for 1,900 yards. These numbers become even more impressive when certain other characteristics of the game of that era are remembered.

Nettles explains: "Back then, before the free substitution rule went into effect, most colleges had two teams. The first team would play a quarter, on both offense and defense, then the other team would play the next quarter. So I, like most other players of that era, got to play only half the offensive plays of any game."

Which probably explains why most players who hold rushing and passing records today came along after the free substitution rule went into effect—they had the advantage of playing the entire game offensively.

"And of course," Nettles continues, "back when I was playing the game, I called all the plays. Coach Eddie Teague would go over our essential game plan with me during the week, but it was up to the quarterback to call his own plays once the game started. In fact, a team was penalized fifteen yards if the coach was caught signaling plays in from the sideline. That was strictly forbidden back in those days."

It was Coach Paul Brown, says Nettles, the innovative coach of the Cleveland Browns, who came up with the idea of running plays in from the sideline. "Coach Brown, you remember, had about a dozen guards on his squad, and he would send in plays by shuttling those guards in and out of the game. He could do that and not be penalized, and the idea eventually caught on with other coaches."

Nettles was a starter at quarterback at Summerville High, playing under legendary coach John McKissick. He was chosen for the North-South All-Star game his senior year and voted the team MVP Award following that contest. He had

Following an illustrious career playing quarterback under Coach John McKissick at Summerville High, Jerry Nettles could have attended almost any college in the South. He chose The Citadel. There, he would lead them to some of their finest seasons in history.

dozens of scholarship offers but chose to attend The Citadel. Why The Citadel?

Nettles smiles at the question. "I'd like to say it was because of their excellent academic programs. But in all honesty, my mother thought I would look great in one of those sharp uniforms those cadets wear down there, and I knew she'd be very disappointed if I wound up at Michigan or some place where they don't wear uniforms. Plus I really liked Coach Teague. He had just arrived at The Citadel, and I was the first player he offered a scholarship to."

At 6-1 and a slim 155 pounds, Nettles became a starter for the Bulldogs his sophomore season. Their record that year was mediocre at best, but in '59 The Citadel would go 8-2 on the season, including an incredible 20-14 upset win over a great West

In 1960 The Citadel defeated Tennessee Tech 27-0 in the Tangerine Bowl. Here, at the Winners Banquet, Miss Tangerine Bowl presents the trophy to (L-R): George Garrison, General Mark Clark, Coach Eddie Teague, Harry Rakowski, and Jerry Nettles.

Virginia team. In 1960 they would enjoy an 8-2-1 season, with an impressive 0-0 tie with Florida State along the way.

They would also take a trip to the Tangerine Bowl in '60 where they beat Tennessee Tech 27-0. Nettles threw for two TDs in that contest and was voted the game's MVP Award.

"Our big win over West Virginia remains one of my fondest memories," Nettles says, "but the thing I remember about the Florida State tie is the support we got from our corps of cadets. They kept up such a racket throughout that Florida State said they'd never play another game in Johnson Hagood Stadium. But there were so many times that our corps of cadets became our so-called 12th man."

After taking his degree in engineering in '61, Nettles was hired to stay on as quarterback coach of the Bulldogs, a position he held for the next five years. But then Coach Red Parker came in, and Nettles decided it was time to move on. At that point he put his degree to good use, going to work in the aerospace program for a company in Tennessee.

"But then I married Cecelia Quantz from Timmonsville," he says, "and we both wanted to get back down in this part of the country. So we moved to Florence, and I opened the Pee Dee Sportman's Shop here in '71, and we've been here ever since."

In addition to his sporting goods store, Nettles also operates a football camp on a 35-acre tract he owns in the country. It's called Pee Dee Football Camp and specializes in training high school quarterbacks.

"The starting quarterbacks in the Shrine Bowl for the past five years were trained here," he says, "plus we also had the pleasure of working with Shawn Graves, Wofford's all-time great quarterback. But I love football, and this camp allows me to stay in the game a little. Plus there's the added incentive of knowing I've helped some fine young men to sharpen their talents here in my football camp. Really, everything considered, I have an ideal life."

Nettles is a member of The Citadel Athletic Hall of Fame.

Moments of Glory
*South Carolina's Greatest
Sports Heroes*

1960-1969

Mike Bohonak

A Great Clemson Athlete Later Became a War Hero

Mike Bohonak's story begins in Pittsburgh, where he was born in 1941 and later attended Alderdice High School. Oddly enough, he says, Alderdice at one time had a predominantly upper middle class student body, one that annually fielded the No. 1 chess team in the state while beating nobody in football.

"That's the way it was until the late-fifties," he says. "Then they started busing in kids from my Ukrainian neighborhood over to Alderdice. Our dads worked in the steel mills of Pittsburgh and so we were a bunch of pretty hardnosed kids.

"So almost overnight Alderdice went from having one of the worst football teams in the state to having one of the best."

As a senior in 1959, Bohonak made Everybody's All-Everything teams and was widely recruited as an end by such biggies as Penn State and Notre Dame. But then came Clemson's Don Wade and Charlie Waller. Bohonak was impressed. Wade and Waller seemed like nice guys.

Plus, says Bohonak, Wade and Waller assured him that he could play all three major sports at Tiger Town.

"Actually," he says with a laugh, "it's not quite that simple. You can play three sports, just as the coaches promised, if you're crazy enough to try. But the coaches don't tell you that."

Also, he says, his best friend at Alderdice, Harry Pavilak, had just signed with Clemson as a running back, and that is what definitely decided him to give the Tigers a try.

His freshman year, in 1960, he distinguished himself in all three major sports. But his sophomore year he suffered a career-ending shoulder injury in football and retired to the radio booth for the rest of the season working as a spotter.

"It was a great job and any time a Clemson runner made a nice gain I'd point to Harry Pavilak's name on the chart so the radio announcer could tell who carried the ball. See, I had this idea that I could make an All-American of Harry simply by pointing to his name on the chart. I guess fans out in radio land thought Harry was carrying the ball sixty times per contest."

Bohonak then turned his attention to basketball

Mike Bohonak, another of those amazing athletes from Pittsburgh, Pa. loved so dearly by the Clemson Athletic Dept., was named All ACC in both basketball and baseball. (His football career was cut short by a shoulder injury.)

and baseball. As a forward under Coach Press Maravich, he made Clemson's starting lineup his sophomore season. Along with teammates Donnie Mahaffy, Choppy Patterson, Jim Brennan and Bob Benson (now owner of the Charlotte Heat), the Tigers almost took the ACC tournament, finally losing to Wake Forest in the championship game.

Of his close friend Jim Brennan, he jokes: "Actually, we ran a one-guard offense back then. But with Brennan hogging the ball, we didn't need but one guard. In fact, we didn't need but one player."

Despite his success in basketball, Bohonak, who grew up only two blocks from Forbes Field and the Pirates, says baseball had always been his favorite sport. As a power-hitting outfielder, he also made Coach Bill Wilhelm's starting nine as a sophomore.

In both his junior and senior years he was named to the All-ACC baseball squads, and a pro career seemed to loom just over the horizon.

Bohonak tips a rebound to Randy Mahaffey in Clemson's 66-64 win over Furman in '63.

But it was 1964, the war in Vietnam was escalating, and Bohonak, who had taken four years of ROTC, was obligated to serve two years as an Army officer. Pro baseball would have to wait.

Also in '64 he met and married Noni McCullough, daughter of Coach Mack McCullough, who had been a fixture in the NC State athletic department for over thirty years.

Initially, Bohonak was assigned to the 1st Battalion of the 7th Cavalry. But then he volunteered for airborne training and was reassigned to the 2nd Battalion, an airborne battalion. Then the entire 7th Cavalry was off to Vietnam.

The 7th was the first American Division to be hit by the North Vietnamese in a battle that would become known as the Battle of the Ia Drang Valley. In that engagement Bohonak's old battalion, the 1st, was nearly annihilated, losing every officer in the unit. He would have been among those had he not been reassigned to the 2nd a month earlier.

"Occasionally," he says, "I still run into guys who were not aware of my transfer. They've been thinking for twenty-five years now that I was killed at Ia Drang.

Then they see me, and they're really startled. It always gives me a funny feeling when that happens."

On another occasion he was leading a convoy of trucks loaded with munitions deep into the jungle when they were ambushed by a contingent of South Koreans who mistook them for Vietcong. He survived that encounter, he says, simply by luck.

Today he casually shrugs away these near brushes with death. "I'm just like everybody else. I had my close calls, and I have my war stories. Actually, anybody who served in 'Nam is lucky to be alive."

Despite his easygoing demeanor, the excitement of military life proved attractive to Bohonak, and he pursued it as a career. Later, he transferred to the 82nd Airborne Division and achieved status as a jump master.

"When we were making jumps, I was the guy who stood in the door telling everyone else to be calm and take it easy. In fact, I was probably the most shook up guy in the plane."

In 1986 he retired from the military with the rank of major. Today he and Noni are popular instructors at USC-Lancaster, she in computer science, he in P.E.

★

Gary Daniels

He Owns The Citadel Record Book

Browsing through The Citadel basketball record book, one notes that the name Gary Daniels stands out like a white cat in a goldfish pond.

A native of Canton, Ohio, the 6-4 Daniels was a high school all-star forward in 1959 and turned down dozens of scholarship offers from colleges across the midwest after talking with The Citadel's Norman Sloan. (Sloan, by the way, would guide NC State to a national championship in 1974). He says he found The Citadel's spit-and-polish military environment appealing and thus he decided to cast his lot with the Bulldogs.

"The Citadel, with all it pageantry, makes a real impression on a high school kid. Plus I really did like Charleston. You must remember they have a real ocean and everything down there, all the things we didn't have back in Ohio.

"Also, my family was rather poor, and Coach Sloan offered me a full scholarship, including books. Buying clothes, of course, would not be a problem because everyone wore a uniform. So all those things just sort of meshed with my financial situation and definitely influenced my decision."

Once arrived at The Citadel, however, Daniels had some adjustments to make. Needless to say, he didn't spend a lot of time gazing out over the ocean as he'd dreamed of doing. "They definitely go out of their way to find out what you're made of the first two weeks you're there," he laughed. "And that holds true for athletes as well as everyone else. Maybe more so for the athletes. We certainly didn't enjoy any special status. But the military is a way of life there, and I took a lot of pride in becoming a part of it."

Daniels became a starter for the Bulldogs in 1961, and immediately school records began to fall. He grabbed off 329 rebounds that year, still an all-time single season record at The Citadel. For his career, he averaged 11.9 rebounds per game, still another record.

As for free throws, forget it! He once scored 22 free throws in a single game, scored 209 in a single season (1962), and 466 for his career. These number still represent all-time records at The Citadel.

Gary Daniels, a native of Canton, Ohio, was named All Southern both his junior and senior seasons at The Citadel and still owns most of the Bulldogs' record book.

As for overall scoring, he averaged 23.9 points per game in '62 (an all-time record) and 19.2 for his career (yep, still another all-time record).

He was also named to the All-Southern team both his junior and senior seasons. And little wonder, since he was, based on the statistics, perhaps the finest player ever to trod the hardwood for The Citadel.

The modest Daniels shrugs off such a compliment. "Frankly, the shooting was not as good back then. Therefore, there were more missed shots and thus more rebounds to be had. But I did take a lot of pride in coming up with the ball."

As for the memory that stands out most in his mind, he says: "My mother and I were returning from Ohio recently, and as we were passing through Cabin Creek, West Virginia, Mom pointed out that Cabin Creek is the home of the great Jerry West."

"And thinking of Jerry West brought back so many memories. I had the honor once of playing on the same floor with him. We were playing them up at Morganton one night, and I believe Jerry and I both wound up the evening with 21 points. But we upset West Virginia that night 83-80, breaking their 56-game winning streak. That, I believe, stands out in my mind more than anything else."

Following his graduation from The Citadel in 1963, Daniels became an officer in the U. S. Army, serving 20 years before his retirement in 1983. Then, he says, he spent a year traveling around and enjoying just being alive.

Then Daniels and his wife opened two gardening centers, one in Raleigh and the other in Fayetteville. They make their home in Raeford, N. C.

In 1953 The Citadel upset the great Jerry West and his undefeated West Virginia team 83-80, thereby ending the Mounties' 56-game win streak. Gary Daniels (#11) had 21 points on the evening.

★

Jerry Smith

He Was Furman's Mr. Corbin Number-Two

Jerry Smith, like Frank Selvy before him, was a native of Corbin, Ky. and one of the finest shooters in the country. He enjoys the distinction of having been named All Southern for three consecutive years.

Speak briefly with Jerry Smith and you'd probably walk away remembering him as a modest gentleman, conservatively dressed, soft-spoken, and with just a hint of a twang in his voice that he obviously didn't learn down in good old South Carolina. He may be just a little taller than the average fellow, but still, you'd probably remember him as the very picture of a successful insurance executive.

And you'd be absolutely correct. Today, at the age of fifty-seven, Jerry Smith is the director of underwriting services for the Liberty Life Insurance Co. in Greenville and a success by anyone's standards.

Ah, but what you would not guess is that at one time this same quiet Jerry Smith was one of the most highly sought after basketball players in America, a real hero of the hardwood, who would go on to stardom at Furman University.

But such is indeed the case.

He grew up in Corbin, Ky, also the hometown of Furman's other all-time basketball great, Frank Selvy. "That's right," grins Smith. "They used to call me Mr. Corbin Number-Two."

A 6-3 guard, Smith was named to one of the most exclusive clubs in America his senior year at Corbin High when he was chosen for the Kentucky All-State Basketball Team. Which meant that he could write his own ticket to any college in the country. But he chose Furman.

"Well, of course I'd always looked up to Frank Selvy," he says. "Frank came along about ten years before I did, but he was still Corbin's number-one hero. And I was recruited by Nield Gordon, who was really a great athlete and a great fellow. Plus, I knew that Furman was one of the finest schools in America academically."

To say that Smith took the Hurricanes by storm is no exaggeration. He became their starting guard in 1960. Smith, along with teammates Gerald Gardner, Dan Pike, Don Frye, John Lemmond, and Gerald Glur, led Furman to impressive wins over the likes of Davidson, Clemson, USC and Florida State. (Glur still remains Furman's all-time rebound leader, averaging 394 per year.)

Smith completed his sophomore season averaging 22.6 points per game and was named to both the All-State and All-Southern teams.

It was pretty much the same story the next season, with the Hurricanes adding a great West Virginia team to their list of victims. Smith averaged a phenomenal 27 points per contest that season and was again named to the All-Southern team.

And so it went. In 1963, his senior season, the Hurricanes knocked off, among others, USC, Clemson, Davidson, Wake Forest, and West Virginia. And again Smith led his team in scoring with a 20.2 per game average, a performance he found somewhat disappointing.

"By my senior season our opponents had learned that we could score against anybody. So they all started running the box-and-one defense on us, essentially freezing the ball. That of course cut down on the scoring average for the whole team."

Still, Smith was named to the All-Southern Team for the third consecutive year. He was also named to the AP Second All-American Team.

During his career at Furman, he compiled some

Here Smith, a 6-3 guard, shows how to go in for a layup as the Hurricanes defeated Clemson 89-63 in 1963.

truly impressive records: leading in scoring for three years, amassing a total of 1,885 points, an average of 23 points per game. Only Frank Selvy ('51-'53) and Darrell Floyd ('53-'56) had ever scored more, and they led the nation in that category.

Nor was Smith a stranger to the free throw line. His 609 total free throws remains second only to Frank Selvy's 694.

His free throw accuracy percentage of 82.2% (609 of 742 attempts) still remains the best in the Furman Record Book.

Smith explains: "I shot a lot from outside, but I also liked to drive the basket. It was driving the basket so much that resulted in my getting fouled so much. Luckily, I made a good many of the free throws."

Looking back, Smith says that the games he still remembers most are Furman's wins over Davidson and West Virginia. "Lefty Drisell was producing some great teams up at Davidson at that time, and of course West Virginia was one of the top teams in the country. To beat those guys really felt great."

Smith was the second player drafted by the Detroit Pistons his senior season. Unfortunately, he was also a high draft pick of Uncle Sam who wanted him for the next three years.

Following his discharge, he says, he decided to forego professional basketball in favor of getting started in business. And it's been insurance ever since.

He and his wife, the former Connie Copeland, make their home in Greenville.

★
Jim Brennan

He Experienced The Best of Clemson Basketball

Jim Brennan would become a starting guard for Clemson in 1961, his sophomore season, then go on to become one of the Tigers' most outstanding players ever.

How did he find his way from the tough steel mills of McKeesport, Pa. down to the pastoral Blue Ridge setting of Clemson University?

"Neenie Campbell," he says simply. "Neenie was my high school coach, and he thought Frank Howard was the greatest man who ever lived. It was like Neenie ran sort of a one-man underground railroad, shipping yankees down to Clemson. It was Neenie, you know, who sent down Ray Mathews, Clemson's great All-American wingback from McKeesport.

"You see," Brennan continues, "back in those days there were no high school sports books or tabloids. There was no networking of who the best high school athletes were. The coaches had only the newspapers and word of mouth to know who the stars were and who to go after."

But in '61 young Brennan turned out to be just what the Tigers were looking for. With Choppy Patterson holding down the other guard position, and Mike Bohonak and Gary Burnisky at forward, and all-time rebounding great Donnie Mahaffey at center, Clemson would field some of its best teams in history.

Brennan still recalls his sophomore season in 1962 and Clemson's trip to the ACC tournament, traditionally a dismal occasion for the Tigers. That week, in the first game of the eliminations, Clemson surprised the experts by knocking off a powerful NC State team 67-46.

Ah, but just wait until tomorrow night, everyone said, when the Tigers would be fed to the Duke Blue Devils, one of the top teams in America. If the experts were surprised at Clemson's victory over State, they were absolutely floored when the Tigers went out and upset mighty Duke 77-72.

Jim Brennan led all scorers that night with 34 points, despite being double-team throughout the second half.

The Tigers' hopes of a national championship

In 1962 Jim Brennan, Clemson's hot shooting guard, led the Tigers all the way to the championship game in the ACC Tournament where they finally fell 77-66 to Wake Forest. Still, after 36 years, the '62 Tigers remain the only Clemson team to make it to the ACC championship.

were dashed the next night as they fell to Wake Forest, but as Brennan points out, "1962 still remains the only time in history that Clemson has made it to the ACC championship game. We old-timers are still proud to have been there."

Brennan would lead Clemson in scoring all three years that he started for them, averaging 17.3 points per contest during that period (still fourth best in the Clemson record book), for a total of 1,317 points. He also led the team in free throw shooting for three years, making a total of 354 of 423 attempts, an .832 average.

He was coached by Press Maravich his first two

Brennan dribbles past a Blue Devil defender as Clemson upset Duke 77-72 in the '62 ACC Tournament. Brennan led all scorers in this game with 34 points.

seasons, and he still remembers Maravich's son, Pete, who would go on to national prominence as Pistol Pete, and how he would hang around the gym in the afternoons, working out with the Clemson varsity.

"Pete was just a kid, maybe ten years old at the time, a real skinny little kid. But even then that kid could dribble and shoot that ball like you wouldn't believe. I mean the Harlem Globetrotters would have envied that kid."

Maravich departed Clemson before Brennan's senior year and in came Coach Bobby Roberts. Still, Brennan didn't miss a beat. He made the All-ACC team that season and was drafted by the Philadelphia Warriors.

"But Coach Roberts offered me a job as assistant coach," he says, "and that was a job I simply couldn't refuse."

He says that coaches were still experiencing recruiting problems even at that late date. "There was still no networking of high school athletes. We'd read the daily newspapers and hope that high school coaches or interested alumni would call us. For the most part we recruited right here in South Carolina, because that's the place we knew about the high school athletes. I had some contacts up in Pennsylvania, so I recruited up there a good bit."

Five years later, in 1970, Brennan decided to go into private business. He and his wife Diane moved to Charlotte where he organized a group, called Jim Brennan and Associates, that serves as sales reps for several manufacturers of women clothing.

Today Jim and Diane still make their home in Charlotte. They have four daughters, all of them Clemson graduates.

He is a member of the Clemson Athletic Hall of Fame.

★

Jim Sutherland

Clemson's Ex-Hardwood Star Became
A Doctor and World Traveler

Talk about a guy who's done it all! Just take a quick gander at Dr. Jim Sutherland, former athlete par excellence at Clemson University and now a globe-trotting pediatric cardiologist from Emory University Hospital in Atlanta.

A friendly, outgoing sort with an easy sense of humor, a man who obviously doesn't take himself too serious despite his great accomplishments, Sutherland was asked if his Emory medical colleagues were aware of his illustrious athletic background. He laughs and jokes, "Oh, I never let them forget it. Not for a minute."

Remarkably enough, Sutherland was born and raised right there in the shadow of Clemson University, where his father was the state agricultural agent. As a youngster, he says, back in the late-fifties, the local YMCA offered the closest thing Clemson had to Little League athletics. So the YMCA was where young Jim got his start in basketball. A teammate was little Pete Maravich, whose father was then the head coach of the Clemson Tigers.

Sutherland attended Daniel High School, where he was coached by Don Carver, an outstanding Clemson player himself during the early-fifties. A 6-5 guard, he was named All-State his senior year and could have written his own ticket to play for any college in the South. So why Clemson, which is far better known for their exploits on the gridiron than the hardwood?

"Well, consider the advantages," he says. "On the one hand, I was offered all the services and facilities of a great institution. On the other, I knew everybody in town. Plus, when I got hungry, which was often, I could always drop by the house to get some of Mom's good home cooking. Very few college students can make that statement."

He entered Clemson in the fall of 1963. The next year, as a sophomore, he broke into the Tigers' starting lineup. His teammates were Joe Ayoob, Ken Gardner, and the Mahaffey brothers, Randy and Richie. For the next three years they would serve the Tigers well.

His most memorable experience, he says, came

A Pre Med major, Sutherland graduated Phi Beta Kappa in '67 with a 3.87 GPR, was named ACC Student Athlete of the Year, and was elected President of the Senior Class.

that year at the expense of Duke University. "When I was at Clemson, Duke had their usual super teams and were always ranked in the top five nationally. We generally played them a good game, but up at Cameron Stadium they'd always end up beating us by a few points.

"But my senior year we beat them 71-68 in a cliffhanger right there at Clemson. They were a great team, and to beat them before our home crowd is something I've always remembered."

Sutherland, by the way, led all scorers that night with 33 points, one of his finest performances ever. In fact, he led the Tigers in scoring that season with a very respectable 18.8 points per game average.

More impressive, however, was his free-throw accuracy. His senior year he hit an incredible .897 percent, which was fourth best in the nation. Today, some thirty years later, this figure remains the third-best in the history of ACC basketball. And his .850 free-throw percentage still remains number-one in the Clemson Record Book.

We might also point out that since 1953, the year the ACC was formed, only sixteen Clemson players have been named to the All-ACC basketball team. Sutherland made it twice, both his junior and senior years as a Tiger.

As a Pre-Med major at Clemson, as one might imagine, Sutherland spent little time hanging around the pool halls or beer parlors of Tiger City. "That's true," he says, "but I really didn't find it that hard. Oddly enough, I've always enjoyed studying and learning new things."

On top of everything else, his senior year he was named Brigade Commander of Clemson's ROTC program, and President of the Senior Class. He also graduated Phi Beta Kappa with a phenomenal 3.87 GPA. Not quite as good as his free-throw percentage, but still good enough to earn him ACC Student Athlete of the Year.

But his story doesn't end there. Then it was on to Charleston and enrollment at the Medical University. After two years at that hallowed institution, he transferred to Emory, where he completed medical school and served a grueling internship, and finally became *Doctor* Jim Sutherland, a specialist in pediatric cardiology.

He served ten years as a medical officer in the Army in Europe and elsewhere around the world. Then, having returned to civilian life, he decided to do what many of us have only dreamed of doing: he and a friend filled their backpacks with survival gear and took a little hike. Not just down the road a piece to the local state park, but around the world.

Indeed, Sutherland says he became a confirmed world traveler. In fact, just mention any Third World

In 1967 he hit on .897 percent of his free throws, best in the ACC and fourth best in the nation. Here he goes in for a layup in Clemson's 73-57 win over USC that same year.

developing nation, and Sutherland most likely has been there. Or perhaps it would be more accurate to say that he has served there, since for many years he and teams of doctors have traveled to these remote areas. "We pay every penny out of our own pockets," he says.

He and his wife, the former Mary King of Batesburg, and their daughter make their home in Atlanta. He is a member of the Clemson Athletic Hall of Fame.

★
J. R. Wilburn

This Gamecock Reciever Still Owns A Place in the Pittsburgh Steelers' Record Book

Mention great receivers for the Pittsburgh Steelers and we think of the Swanns and the Stallworths and we remember all their great Super Bowl games and all the hype and hoopla that went along with them. But hold it, sports fans! There's still another name out there, one almost forgotten today, that retains a prominent place in the Pittsburgh Steelers' Record Book.

We are speaking of J. R. Wilburn, a University of South Carolina graduate who toiled in relative obscurity for the Steelers back in their pre-powerhouse days.

"I had the misfortune of poor timing many times in my career," he shrugs. "At USC, from 1963-65, I suffered through some tough years with the Game-cocks. Sure enough, we didn't see daylight ahead until it was time for me to graduate.

"Then I again suffered through some long seasons, from 1966-70, with the Steelers. Just before I left to play for the Chargers in '71 we started getting guys like Terry Bradshaw and Joe Greene. But I was on my way by then."

Wilburn recalls that he began his football career as a 160-pound end at Cradock High School in his hometown of Portsmouth, Virginia. "I think I was the only guy on the team who didn't make All-State our senior year," he laughs. "In fact, the only reason I got a scholarship to USC was due to the friendship that existed between my high school coach and USC's Coach Marvin Bass."

J. R. Wilburn, one of Carolina's all-time greatest receivers, gets rolled out of bounds after catching a Mike Fair pass in this '65 Big Thursday shootout. He was named All ACC that year, and also South Carolina Athlete of the Year. After thirty years, he still holds reception records for the Pittsburgh Steelers.

Still, despite his poor timing, Wilburn had the pleasure of snagging passes from two outstanding USC quarterbacks, Mike Fair and Dan Reeves.

"Mike Fair remains one of my favorite people," he says. "He was smart as a whip and could throw the hound out of that football.

"As for Dan Reeves, he was without doubt the most intense competitor I've ever seen. He always used his ability to the utmost and had a lot of football savvy. He was simply what they call a winner."

Wilburn relates a story to illustrate Reeves' competitive spirit. "He and I used to frequent a joint down in Five Points that had, among all its other educational paraphernalia, the kind of pinball machines that you feed nickels to. Well, Dan knew the odds were overwhelmingly against his winning any money, but he would stand there and drop every cent he had in that darned thing, just to prove that a machine couldn't beat him.

"The guy who owned the place came over one night—I guess he felt sorry for us—and said, 'Son, you'd better stay away from anything that stands on four legs, backs itself into a corner and takes on all comers.' That was good advice, but of course we didn't listen."

In 1965, his senior season at USC, Wilburn was elected team captain. He caught 38 passes that year for a total of 562 yards. He caught ten passes in the Wake Forest game (then an all-time single-game record) and seven in the Tennessee game. His most memorable play came against Clemson in '65 when he caught a 50-yard bomb from Mike Fair for the last-minute touchdown that beat the Tigers 17-16.

He was named to the All-ACC team, then capped his collegiate career by catching ten passes in the Blue-Gray All-Star Game. He was also named South Carolina Athlete of the Year.

Wilburn laughs when he recalls the banquet held in his honor for the Athlete of the Year Award. "Well, I had just said thanks to a packed house and was about to step down from the stage when somebody swung me around by the arm, right there in front of about a thousand people, and says in this gruff voice, 'Why you little son-of-gun, if I'd knowed you would be that good, I'd a brought you down to Clemson and spared you having to play for them old Gamecocks.'

"Yep, it was Coach Frank Howard. And I must say I still regard that as a compliment coming from a legend like him."

Drafted by Pittsburgh in the eleventh round, Wilburn played for the Steelers for five seasons. His best year came in 1967 when he caught a total of fifty-one passes.

Against Dallas on October 22 of that year he had twelve receptions for 158 yards. Both figures still represent all-time single-game reception records for the Steelers.

Following a year in San Diego with the Chargers, he decided to retire following a severe injury to his left knee. Today, looking back, he says that pro football cannot compare in excitement with the college game.

"I remember more than anything else the Carolina-Clemson games," he says. "After those games the fans would hit the field, and it would be pure bedlam. We didn't have anything like that in the pros. Pro ball is strictly business. We had good fans in Pittsburgh, but nothing like those at Carolina."

Since quitting the NFL, Wilburn has pursued a career as an account executive with the Reynolds Metal Co. (Reynolds Aluminum) in Richmond. He and his wife Leslie and their two children make their home in Midlothian, Virginia.

★
Don Whitehead

One of the Most Highly Sought After Players in the South Chose Erskine Over All the Biggies

In 1963 Don Whitehead, a high school All American, surprised the basketball world when he chose to attend tiny Erskine College. Later he would become the starting forward for the NBA Houston Mavericks.

Back in his heyday Don Whitehead could swish jump shots with the best in the business, whether it was high school, college or the pros. He starred at Brookland-Cayce High School in Columbia during the early-sixties, where he was named All-City, All-State, and All-American. In 1963, his senior year, he led all players in scoring in the North-South All-Star Game, and thus this 6-4 forward became one of the most highly sought after basketball players in the South. The University of South Carolina especially wanted him.

But then he surprised everyone by choosing to attend little Erskine College in Due West, South Carolina. "I really liked USC," he says, "but I just wanted to go off to college, to try my wings, to get away from home. I visited a number of schools, but I was especially impressed with Erskine and Coach Red Myers. They just had such a great tradition. They were always in the running for the NAIA championship back in those days and just had a fine program. Plus their academic programs were also excellent. As for Coach Myers, he'd been recruiting me since I was fifteen years old, and I also remembered that."

Whitehead says that he has never regretted his decision. "By choosing Erskine I did the right thing. There I started as a freshman. On the other hand, I had a teammate at B-C who was really a great player and accepted a scholarship to a major college and never even got to play enough to earn a letter. He simply got lost in the shuffle and sat on the bench for four years. He might have been an All-American at another college, but we'll never know."

As for USC, Whitehead recalls being recruited by assistant coach, Dwane Morrison, who would later become head coach of the Gamecocks. "Coach Morrison frequently visited me at B-C, and I would go to the old Field House and practice with the USC guys at night, guys like Scotty Ward and Art Whisnant. They were guys I really looked up to.

"Later, I spent summers practicing against Jack Thompson, Skip Harlicka and Al Salvadori. So really, when I got to play against them later it was just like a summer practice session—no big deal."

In fact, one of Whitehead's most memorable games did come against USC in 1965. He hit for 31 points on the evening and led Erskine to a near upset of the highly favored Gamecocks before they finally fell 57-55. Then in '67 he scored 20 of Erskine's 21 first half points against USC and finished the game with a total of 36. (In three games against the Gamecocks Whitehead scored a total of 90 points, not a bad average.)

During his senior season, in 1967, this jump-shooting specialist averaged 22.3 points per game, and scored 94 of 106 free throws. For his career with Erskine he scored 1,359 points (despite missing 27 games with injuries).

Following his graduation he was drafted in the

In 1965 Whitehead scored 31 points as Erskine finally fell to mighty USC by a score of 57-55.

14th round by the Chicago Bulls and assigned to their franchise in Trenton, N. J. in the Eastern Basketball League. Then the next season his contract was picked up by the ABA Houston Mavericks. There he became their starting forward.

But then came the torn ligaments in his left knee. "And that, for all practical purposes, was the end of my career. I underwent a lot of rehabilitation and refused to give up. But really that was it, and deep down inside I knew it."

Since that time his basketball activities have been confined to coaching and refereeing in Columbia area youth leagues.

He also manages his own business, the Don Whitehead Insurance Company, and has been kept busy helping raise five children: Kirk, Chryssie, Benjamin, Jordan and Julia. They make their home in Columbia.

★
Bill Belk

His Athletic Ability And Cordial Disposition
Have Taken Him To The Top

Bill Belk is a bear of a man whose athletic ability, positive attitude and friendly disposition have kept him in the forefront of whatever society he's found himself in throughout most of his life.

A man of humble origins, his rise to the top can be traced back to 1962 when he went out for football at Barr Street High School in Lancaster. A junior at the time, he already stood 6-3 and weighed 200 pounds, a natural at end for the Golden Tigers, then coached by Sandy Gilliam, who would go on to an illustrious college coaching career at Maryland State College (now Maryland Eastern Shore).

Belk remembers that 1963 was a big year for Barr Street. With teammates like Benny Blocker, who went on to stardom at Ohio State and later with the New Orleans Saints, plus the late Jimmy Duncan, a long time starter for the Baltimore Colts, the Golden Tigers were a force to be reckoned with.

"We played C. A. Johnson in Columbia for the State Championship in '63," Belk says. "I won't say it was the best high school game ever played in South Carolina, but it would have to rank right up there with the best.

"Our offense that year could score on anybody, and our defense was almost as good. But that night, for some reason, our defense just wasn't clicking, and we wound up getting beat 35-33. Interestingly enough, in addition to all the other guys on the field that night who would go on to play pro ball, we also played against Art Shell."

Named to the All-State Team his senior year, Belk received numerous scholarship offers but elected to follow Coach Gilliam to Maryland State. There he again became a member of an all-star cast.

"Oh, yeah," Belk laughs. "Coach Gilliam had recruited some great players at MSC. In addition to Jimmy Duncan and Art Shell, it seems like just about everybody on the team wound up in pro ball."

By then Belk had beefed up to 235 pounds and became a starter at end his sophomore year. "Back in those days we played both ways. But of course we didn't think anything about it because that's just the way the game was played. Today you'd probably wind up with a lawsuit on your hands if you told a guy he'd have to play both ways, but back then that's just the way it was."

Following an outstanding collegiate career, Belk was named All-American and became a high draft pick of the San Francisco 49ers. How many million was he paid to sign?

"Are you kidding? According to a recent article I read, the average NFL salary in 1994 was about $400,000. But back in '68 the average salary was like '$21,000. Playing in the NFL back then paid better than pumping gas, but it was nothing to get real excited about. The other day my son Alex and I were talking about this very thing, and he said, 'Dad, wouldn't it be great if you were twenty years younger?'

"I said, 'Sure, then you and I could be the same age.'"

Belk broke into the 49er' starting lineup at defensive end his rookie season in '68. He recalls that their starting backfield that year consisted of John Brodie, Gary Lewis, and Ken Willard. He says that the best running back he ever faced was the Chicago Bears' Gayle Sayers.

"There's an old story that back in '65 when Sayers first started for the Bears he was going wild, running back punts, kickoffs, and everything else and apparently scoring at will. So Jack Christian, coach of the 49ers, told the press that when the 49ers played the Bears that next Sunday they were going to intentionally punt and kickoff to Sayers and that they were going to kill him. In fact, they did kick to Sayers and he finished the afternoon with six touchdowns. After the game Coach Christian just shrugged at his news conference and said, 'Well, I told you he was going to get killed. Just look at the poor guy. He ran himself to death out there.'"

Belk became a mainstay with the 49ers for the next eight years, and then he was traded in 1976. At that time he decided to give Canadian football a shot and signed with the Toronto Argonauts. How different is Canadian football from the NFL?

A collegiate All-American, Bill Belk went on to stardom with the San Francisco '49ers. Today he is an executive with Springs Industries.

"Well, up there you have only three downs to make ten yards, so they put the ball in the air on just about every play. Plus the field is so much wider up there. You feel like you can run on forever, sort of like playing in a big cow pasture."

He retired from pro ball in 1977 and returned home to Lancaster. He is married to the former Linda Jones of Lancaster and they have one son, Alex. Belk is a former member of the Lancaster County Board of Education and says that much of his free time is devoted to working with young people.

Also, after eighteen years of service, he is currently Manufacturing Manager for Springs Industries. He and his family make their home in Columbia.

★

Mike Fair

One of the Gamecocks' Finest Quarterbacks Ever Became A Leader In State Government

No discussion of great Gamecock quarterbacks would be complete without an in-depth look at Mike Fair, one of the finest ever to wear the garnet and black. During his career at USC (1965-67), an era not known for a great deal of passing, Fair completed 199 passes for 2,486 total yards, a stat that still ranks number-seven in the USC Record Book.

But Fair, unfortunately, had the bad luck to be playing during one of the most dismal periods in the history of Gamecock football, and thus he has never received the recognition he truly deserves.

Today, looking back, he blames his team's poor record (11-19-0) on several factors: "In the first place, we played out of our league far too often back then. We held our own pretty well in the ACC, and in fact we were co-champions in 1965. But we just took on too many SEC schools, and they simply outmanned us. It's hard for exhausted troops to compete against fresh troops.

"Plus you have to consider the injury factor. In 1966, for example, both I and several other key players had to play hurt almost all season. An injury really slows you down."

The Gamecocks also changed head coaches in '66, an event which didn't do them any good. "Yes, and all those things combined to keep us off balance during that entire period."

A Greenville native, Fair distinguished himself at Parker High School, where he was chosen Back of the Year in the Big 16 (AAA) football in 1963. He was also named to the All-State Team and then led the Sandlappers to victory in the '63 Shrine Bowl.

He was heavily recruited by such schools as Clemson, Duke, Georgia, Alabama, and Furman. "But in the end it was Carolina's Coach Marvin Bass who persuaded me to become a Gamecock."

Fair enjoys the distinction of having played under both Marvin Bass and Paul Dietzel during his career. Asked to compare the two, he says: "They were total opposites. Coach Bass was a big, nice guy and very personable. If he had a fault, I guess he was too easy going. On any team there are always a few guys who require stern leadership. Coach Bass was

Not only was Mike Fair one of USC's finest quarterbacks ever, he was also named to the All ACC baseball team. Later he would play for the San Diego Chargers

famous for giving those guys three dozen last chances.

"As for Dietzel, he went to the other extreme. He was pretty aloof and a stern disciplinarian. But I admired both of them."

Fair also enjoys reminiscing about his teammates: "Gosh, everybody remembers the late Rudy Holloman. He was a great runner, one of those little waterbug types, and he could really snag a pass. He was faster than Benny Galloway, but he didn't have those juking moves or the power that Galloway had.

"Then there was J. R. Wilburn. He was a senior my sophomore year. He was an incredible receiver and made me look good many times. He later had an outstanding career with the Steelers. But I guess I remember him most for catching passes no matter where I threw them."

Indeed, Fair completed 38 passes to Wilburn in

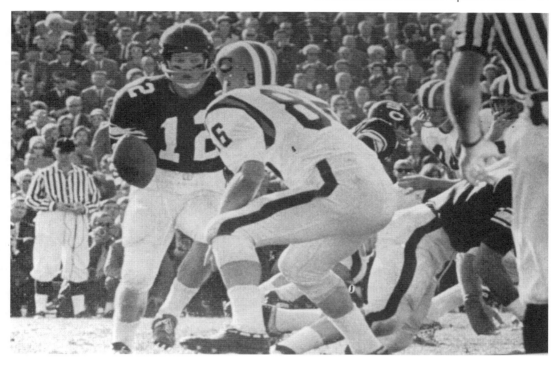

In 1965 Fair led the Gamecocks to an upset win over the Clemson Tigers (17-16) when he completed a 50-yard TD pass to J. R. Wilburn in the closing moments of the game.

1965, including seven against Tennessee and nine against Wake Forest. He also completed a 50-yard TD bomb to Wilburn in Carolina's 17-16 win over Clemson that year.

"Freddy Zeigler was another one with great hands," adds Fair. "I think he's still second only to Sterling Sharpe in most reception records at Carolina."

Fair recalls that Tommy Suggs stepped in as starting quarterback in '68: "With the possible exceptions of Todd Ellis and Steve Taneyhill, Suggs had the best arm of any quarterback ever to play for Carolina. It's incredible that such a little guy—he was only about 5-8 and 155 pounds—could zing that ball from one end of the field to the other the way Suggs did. Where all that power came from I don't know. But he was really phenomenal."

In his spare time, so to speak, Fair hit .352 as a Gamecock center fielder his senior year and was named to the All-ACC Baseball Team.

Then it was on to San Diego where he played backup quarterback to John Hadl of the Chargers for the next two years. His roommate was Clemson's Harry Olszewski. "Harry was a great guy, and I spent two years just learning to spell his name," laughs Fair. "But really I was just a marginal pro player. I was grateful for the opportunity, but I was not quite good enough to make pro football my career."

In 1970 he returned to Greenville, where he coached for several years. Then he joined the Jordan and McCallum Insurance Company. Well known and popular with the people of Greenville, he was elected to the Greenville County Council for three terms before being elected to the S. C. House of Representatives in 1984. He was elected to the S. C. State Senate in a special election in September of 1995.

A religious man, Fair comments: "Very few people ever have a chance to take a public stand, so I feel that the Lord has truly blessed me."

He left the University in 1968 without taking a degree. But by attending evening classes over a long period of time, he graduated some twenty years later, in 1988.

But that's typical of Mike Fair. He doesn't give up easily.

★
Buddy Gore

He Remains one of the Finest Runners In The History of Clemson Football

For three exciting years Buddy Gore was called the workhorse of the Clemson Tigers. During that time (1966-68) he carried the ball 600 times in 27 games, gaining a total of 3,273 all-purpose yards (that's two tough miles), an average of 109.1 yards per contest.

Incredibly enough, despite the fact that freshmen were ineligible for varsity competition during his playing days, Buddy Gore still holds numerous rushing records for the Tigers.

Twice he led the ACC in rushing ('67 and '68), and was named to the All-ACC Team both seasons. Indeed, in '67 he was named ACC Player of the Year. Yet at 6-1 and 190 pounds, Gore is not exactly a giant of a man. How did he do it? What accounts for his speed, quickness and stamina?

In 1968 Buddy Gore was named ACC Player of the Year, and for good reason. He gained 3,273 all-purpose yards for Clemson, an average of 109.1 yards per game.

An articulate individual, Gore ponders the question. "Well," he finally says, "I think that genetics has a lot to do with it. Plus there's what some call the X-factor, sort of the unknowns, you might say. It's like so many unknown factors—coaches, teammates, and the time even—converged to work to my best advantage. Change any one of those X-factors and I might never have accomplished much of anything."

He quickly adds: "Plus we had some great linemen when I was at Clemson. And after playing together over a period of time, it's like a certain empathy began to develop. For example, Wayne Mass was our pulling guard, and I'd be flying around end with Wayne leading the way, and I could just tell, maybe the way he'd incline his head a little to the left or right, which way he was going to block that defensive back, so that I'd know which way to cut. I don't know, there are so many intangibles in playing football, so many things that are difficult to put into words."

The son of an optometrist, Gore was born in Conway, S. C. in 1946. He enjoyed an idyllic childhood, he says, playing Little League Baseball, Mite football, and spending his summers with his parents at their vacation home in Myrtle Beach.

At Conway High he played football under Coach Buddy Sasser, himself an outstanding quarterback for

UNC. His senior year he played in both the North-South All-Star Game and the Shrine Bowl.

Heavily recruited, he says he knew that he didn't wish to leave South Carolina to play college football. "My family almost never traveled. My father had a busy practice in Conway, and we had our house at the beach where we went for vacations. In fact, I'd never seen the Blue Ridge Mountains in my entire life until I visited Clemson in 1965."

But why, of all the colleges that were scrambling to sign him to a scholarship, did he choose Clemson? "I remember sitting with Coach Howard and he said, 'Buddy, I know you visited The Citadel, and while you were there you saw all them little bitty blue buses running 'round with The Citadel painted on the side. Well, they travel to all their away games in them little bitty blue buses. Now Hattisburg, Mississippi is a long way to ride on a little bitty blue bus. You get to see a lot of country that way, true. But you also get to see an awful lot of the inside of that little bitty blue bus. But you think about Clemson, now. Clemson flies to all their away games in a great big ol' airplane.'

"I was only seventeen" Gore laughs, "but I got the point."

Gore breaks away from these NC State defenders for a TD in Clemson's 24-19 win in '67. He led the ACC in rushing yardage in both '67 and '68.

Gore frequently alludes to Frank Howard during the conversation, and it is obvious that he feels an abiding admiration for his former coach. "Coach Howard taught us so many things. He taught us to always tell it like it is, to admit our mistakes and try not to blame them on someone else. The important thing is not the mistake, Coach said, but what we did to correct that mistake."

Gore chuckles as he recalls Howard's so-called "cheer-blocking": "At practice Coach Howard would point to his linemen and say, 'Now when the ball's snapped, I want you ri-cheer, and you ri-cheer, and you ri-cheer.'"

He is also lavish in his praise of his former teammates, fellows like Jimmy "The Needle" Addison, Ray Yauger, Wayne Mass, Harry Olszewski, and the Ducworth brothers, Ronnie and George: "Man, those Ducworth boys were something else," he says,

shaking his head, "and they took it personally if you tried to turn the corner on them. They'd really stick you."

It is senseless to try to list all of Gore's great days at Clemson. Enough to say that by his senior year he had broken the records of such Tiger immortals as Ray Mathews, Joel Wells, and Fred Cone.

He took his degree in Biology in 1969, then served two years as an officer in the Army Medical Corps. Since that time he has made his home in Myrtle Beach, where he is owner of Buddy Gore and Associates, Insurance and Investments.

His three main hobbies now, he says, are his wife Pam and their two sons Buddy and Justin. They are active in the First Presbyterian Church of Myrtle Beach.

He is a member of the Clemson Athletic Hall of Fame.

★
The Ducworth Brothers

A Clemson Football Dynasty

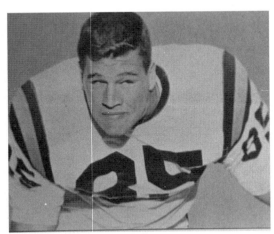

Ronnie Ducworth, a native of Anderson, S.C., was the first of four brothers who would leave their mark on Clemson Football.

Of all the families in this great land of ours there is not one that has furnished more great football players to Clemson University than has the Ducworths of Anderson, S. C.

First there was Ronnie Ducworth ('66-'68). Then came George Ducworth ('67-'69). Then Tommy Ducworth ('73). And finally C. H. Ducworth ('74). They are all brothers, and they all served Clemson well.

Indeed, for many years no Clemson lineup was complete without a Ducworth somewhere in the crowd. In fact, following the Tigers' shootout with Carolina in 1974, one disgruntled Gamecock fan was heard to grumble, "Wonder why Clemson don't go on and graduate that Ducworth boy? He's been up here for about ten years now."

Ronnie, like his younger brothers, was raised on his father's dairy in Anderson. "For as far back as I can remember," he says, "we all worked at the dairy both before and after school every day. And that's hard work. There's one thing about cows. Whether it's Christmas or the Fourth of July or whatever, those cows have to be milked every day. Cows never take a holiday."

By the time he'd entered high school Ronnie felt

he'd learned enough about dairying to teach Sealtest a thing or two about cows. And he probably had.

He attended T. L. Hannah in Anderson, also the old alma mater of such former Tiger standouts as Bobby Gage and Don King. By his senior season he stood 6-2, weighed 215 and was considered one of the premier defensive ends in the state.

But then came trouble. "I broke my ankle in the second game of the season and couldn't play anymore. So all those coaches who'd been scouting me my junior year just sort of didn't come around anymore. Except for Clemson's freshman coach Goat McMillan. He said Clemson still wanted me."

Which was fine with Ronnie Ducworth. He says that attending Clemson had been his dream since he was six years old.

After a successful freshman season in '65, he joined the varsity as a defensive end in '66, playing behind Joey Branton. He got a chance to show what he could do in Clemson's first game of the season against a highly ranked NC State team.

"Joey went down with an injury early in the second quarter. I jumped up to go in, but Coach Howard grabbed me by the arm and held me there on the sideline. I could tell he was hoping Joey would get up, and he wouldn't have to put me in. Frankly, I was hoping the same thing myself. My heart was about to jump out of my chest."

But Joey didn't get up. And soon, having recovered from his first-game jitters, Ducworth served notice on the Pack that trying to run his end would not be good judgement. After the game he was named defensive player of the day in recognition of his sterling performance.

There are still many games that stand out in Ronnie's mind. He still smiles when he recalls the several occasions when he laid the wood to Kenny Stabler in Clemson's narrow 13-10 loss to Alabama in '67. But the play he remembers most, he says, the one he most wishes he could re-play, came late in the fourth quarter of the Carolina-Clemson contest of 1968.

"Carolina ran one of those razzle-dazzle plays where quarterback Tommy Suggs handed off to their

Here Ronnie nails a Duke receiver in 1968. As a defensive end, he was named to the All ACC Team in both '67 and '68.

end on what appeared to be an end-around play. But then their end held up and passed the ball back across field to Tommy Suggs. Well, I was standing there, right beside Tommy Suggs, when he caught the ball. I could easily have intercepted it had I only reached out. But for some reason, call it mental blackout or whatever, I just stood there and watched him catch it. I have re-played that particular play a million times in my mind over the past 25 years."

At this point, good natured Ronnie Ducworth smiles at his recollections: "Of course, during my re-plays, I always intercept the ball, run 60 yards for a touchdown, and walk away the great hero of the afternoon. It's too bad we don't get second chances in real life."

In addition to the Ducworth brothers, this was the era when Clemson fielded such all-time Tiger greats as Buddy Gore, Charlie Waters, and Hugh Mauldin. Few were surprised when Clemson won the ACC championship in both '66 and '67.

Another thrill came Ronnie's way his senior season in '68 when his younger brother, George, became Clemson's other defensive end, thus giving the Ducworths total control at the corners of Clemson's defensive line.

As far as can be determined, this marks the only time in history that two brothers have made the Tigers' starting eleven. And there were two more brothers yet to come.

Ronnie was named to the All-ACC team in both '67 and '68. He took his degree in dairy management in '69, then returned to Anderson to manage Ducworth Dairy for several years. Then it was back to Clemson University once again where he accepted a position in the experimental division of the LeMaster Dairy Center. "Our purpose here," he says, "is to produce more efficient milk cows through experimentations in breeding and growth hormones."

He is married to the former Debra Stancil of Anderson, and they have two sons and a daughter. His favorite hobby, he says, is coaching YMCA athletics.

George graduated from the USC School of Law and is the longtime solicitor of Anderson County. Tommy is farming in Paris, Tennessee, and C. H. is teaching physical education in the Anderson Public Schools.

★
The Eckstein Brothers

These Unlikely Gridiron Heroes Still Own the Record Book At Presbyterian College

The Eckstein brothers, Dan and Dave, seem an unlikely pair to achieve athletic excellence. But appearances can be deceiving, as in this case, and today they are remembered as two of the finest football players ever to enroll at Presbyterian College.

Dan Eckstein came along first. As a senior at Atlanta's Sylvan High School he was famous for his blinding speed, having been clocked at 9.6 in the 100-yard dash. He led his team to a perfect 10-0 record that year.

Still, when it came time for the college recruiters to come calling, Dan was ignored. "The kid's just too small to play college football," they insisted.

But PC's head football coach, Cally Gault, had other ideas—and visions. Today he remembers: "I looked at Dan Eckstein and Dan was small—about 5-10 and 170 pounds. But I also saw future greatness in that young man. Signing him to a scholarship was the best thing I ever did."

During his four years at PC Dan was required to play both ways, averaging 50 minutes of playing time per contest. Still, despite such exhausting work, he broke every school rushing and receiving record and in 1968 was named to the AP Small College All-American Team, as well as the NAIA All-American Team.

Also in '68 he was named the South Carolina Collegiate Player of the Year, then topped it all off by playing in the Coaches All-American Bowl along with such famous teammates as O. J. Simpson, Ted Kwalick, Ron Sellers and Bill Stanfill.

Indeed, Dan was beginning to make Cally Gault look smarter and smarter!

It should be pointed out that Dan was also a leader off the field. He recalls that he was a member of the Fellowship of Christian Athletes and spent his summers working in youth camps.

He was excited when he was drafted by the Green Bay Packers, and remembers his first scrimmage and catching a long pass from Packer quarterback Bart Starr. Back in the huddle, Starr said, "Nice catch, Dan."

"I just stood there with my mouth hanging open," Dan laughs. "All I could think was—Gosh, the great Bart Starr! He knows my name! He called me Dan!"

But Dan was the last player to be cut by Green Bay in 1969, leading him to write his highly acclaimed book,

In '68, Dan Eckstein was the South Carolina Collegiate Player of the Year.

The 41st Packer. He then spent a year playing Canadian football and another year with the Miami Dolphins.

But he was never happy playing pro football. "Football should be played for fun, the way it's played in the small colleges. For example, back at PC, just before the Bronze Derby game in '68, Newberry College announced that they had this huge turkey which would go to the winner. As we were lining up for the kickoff, we heard the crowd roar and we looked up and there, dressed in a chef's tall white hat and a long apron, was our line coach, the late Billy Tillman. He was running up and down the Newberry sideline stalking that turkey with a long fork.

"I mean we were just moments away from kickoff in our biggest game of the season and there was coach Tillman in a chef's costume chasing a turkey. Well, that episode just sort of put everything in perspective for me. It was like Coach Tillman was telling us that football is just a game to be played and enjoyed. When it gets to be more than that, then it's not a game."

Once Dan departed, then little brother Dave Eckstein arrived on the PC campus. It was a simple matter to tell them apart.

"My diminutive stature was matched only by my slowness of foot," Dave laughs. "At least Dan was fast, but I ran the 100-yard dash in about 13 seconds. I mean,

David Eckstein (#40) talks it over with Coach Cally Gault and his '71 teammates. Like older brother Dan, Dave in '72 would be named Little All American and also receive the South Carolina Collegiate Athlete of the Year Award.

there were old ladies at PC who could beat me in the sprints."

Dave remembers his first humiliating day of practice at PC and a coach telling him, "Son, you're small and you're slow. But don't worry. You can still serve as team manager and keep your scholarship."

Which was all the motivation Dave needed. "That really got my goat, and I swore to myself then and there that I would make that team or die trying."

To everyone's surprise, Dave did indeed make the team.

Cally Gault remembers: "Dave had two things going for him, things that cannot be taught—grit and determination. He was probably the toughest boy I ever coached.

As a senior in '72, Dave ran for 1,036 yards, the first PC player ever to break the 1,000-yard mark. He also succeeded in breaking Dan's career rushing record on his way to being named Conference Player of the Year. He was also named to the NAIA All-American Team. And,

like Dan, he was named the South Carolina Collegiate Player of the Year.

Not too bad for a little slow guy.

Following the '72 season PC retired jersey number-40, and they also established a memorial award named for Dan and Dave's father, Oscar Eckstein, a former Salvation Army officer. Every year that award is presented to the player who demonstrates the most courage on and off the field.

Today Dan is a clinical psychologist in Scottsdale, Arizona. He is noted for having published five books on clinical psychology.

Dave, on the other hand, lives with his wife Gale and their three children in Marietta, Georgia. He is an executive with U.S. Sprint ("No pun intended," Dave laughs).

So what do their stories prove? Simply this: that the size of the fight in the man is often more important than the size of the man in the fight.

★

Harold Chandler

Meet A Real Life Jack Armstrong

Quarterback Harold Chandler (#18) surrounded by his Wofford teammates in 1970.

Back when we were kids, many of us followed the athletic exploits of Jack Armstrong, the All-American boy. But now that we aren't kids anymore, we've learned that there aren't too many Jack Armstrongs out there. Not in real life.

But hold on. There is this one guy, a guy named Harold Chandler, just one of eight kids in his family, who excelled in everything, an ace in both the classroom and the athletic field.

A product of Belton, S.C., he recalls that Belton and Honea Path high schools were combined his senior year, which led to tensions on the football team.

"Honea Path had always been our big rivals. Then suddenly we were thrown together and expected to play as one team," he says. "Initially, since we didn't know one another, we tended to regard one another with some suspicion, which led to a great deal of tension. Still, we finished the season with an 11-1 record."

But such a situation has its positive aspects too. "I honestly believe that having to make that transition at such an early age, of having to adjust to new people and a new situation, has helped me tremendously in my professional life."

At 6-1 and 190 pounds, Chandler played quarter-back in the 1966 North-South game his senior year and received numerous scholarship offers. But he chose Wofford over them all. "I don't know why. I just liked the idea of attending a small liberal arts college. Plus I liked Wofford's balance between athletics and academics."

He chalked up some playing time as a freshman in '67, but then he was forced to sit out the next year because of a shoulder injury. It wasn't until 1969, his junior year, that he truly hit his stride.

"Coach Jim Brakefield installed the wishbone formation that year, with the triple-option as our bread-and-butter play. For the quarterback, this is an extremely complex offense. To make matters worse, we played the first two games of '69 in driving rainstorms. I didn't execute well in either game and we lost both of them."

But from there on out, once Chandler had gotten the hang of being a wishbone quarterback, the Terriers were unstoppable. In the backfield with him in '69 were such standouts as Bobby Jordan, who scored five touchdowns against Carson-Newman that year (still a Wofford scoring record), as well as the late Cliff Boyd, whom Chandler describes as "a truly great guy and a devastating fullback."

In addition, there was wide receiver Skip Corn ("the best all around athlete on the team"), and All-American guard Sterling Allen.

As for Chandler, he aptly demonstrated his talents when he threw for 309 yards versus Catawba College that year (still a Wofford single-game passing record).

Following those first two losses of the season, Wofford then reeled off nine consecutive wins, including an incredible 49-7 victory over Furman.

In 1970 the Terriers picked up where they'd left off in '69, recording 11 straight wins before losing to Texas A&I in the Division II national championship game.

That 20-game win streak, under the direction of Harold Chandler, remains another all-time Wofford record.

Chandler served as team captain in 1970, was

Chandler on a rollout versus Catawba College in 1967. He threw for 309 yards in that contest, still an all-time Terrier record.

voted the MVP award, and was selected for the All-State team. His 1,610 yards passing that year broke an all-time Wofford season passing record, one that still stands in the Terrier record book. For his career he completed .561 of his passes, still another all-time Wofford record.

All of which is fine, you say, but what about off the football field? Was he a zero when not wearing cleats?

Well, not exactly.

Besides all his gridiron honors, he served as Battalion Commander of Wofford's ROTC program, and in his spare time he was a member of the Blue Key Society and the Sigma Alpha Epsilon social fraternity.

As for his classroom work, he was no slouch there, either, serving as valedictorian of the class of 1971 and graduating Phi Beta Kappa. In fact, he was nominated for a Rhodes Scholarship.

He was offered graduate scholarships to numerous universities as well as a free-agent contract from the Cincinnati Bengals.

"But at that point in my life," he says, "I felt my future lay in the business world. So I kissed football good-bye and accepted a scholarship to USC where I earned my MBA in 1972."

With a track record such as he had, with a reputation for making the most of very opportunity that passed his way, Chandler could have written his own ticket as far as professional careers were concerned. He chose banking.

Today, after serving in various offices in various banks, surviving numerous mergers and consolidations, Chandler is President of NationsBank for Maryland, the District of Columbia, and Northern Virginia. Quite a responsibility.

He is married to the former Delores Wilson, also of Belton, and they have two daughters, Jennifer and Stephanie.

★
Warren Muir

The Gamecocks' Greatest Fullback Ever

Warren Muir was a big kid, he says, but really possessed little natural ability as a football player. He had to work extra hard to develop what talent he did have, but then he was highly motivated.

You see, he was a poor boy who dreamed that someday athletics would be his ticket to freedom from a life of drudgery in the steel mills of Fitchburg, Massachusetts. His efforts paid off finally, and in 1964, his senior year at Fitchburg, running from his fullback position, he led the state in scoring. Sure enough, scholarship offers poured in.

Muir considered all the angles before making his decision. The war in Vietnam was heating up, and thus he decided if he did have to go to war, he'd prefer to go as an officer. So, when George Terry, Paul Dietzel's offensive coordinator at West Point, came calling, Muir was ready to listen.

He enrolled at Army in '65 and enjoyed an outstanding freshman season. But then came news that Dietzel had resigned in order to accept the head coaching job at the University of South Carolina. Muir says he loved West Point but that he was convinced that Paul Dietzel was the best football coach in America and the man for whom he wished to play.

Warren Muir, called the greatest fullback ever to play for the Gamecocks, was named All-ACC for three consecutive years, and All-American in 1969.

Thus he made the move. After a redshirt season in '66, he broke into the Carolina lineup in '67. Broke in with a bang, in fact.

In his first game as a Gamecock, versus Iowa State, Muir started the second half. Over the next thirty minutes he gained 74 yards and scored two touchdowns to lead USC to a 34-3 win.

Then, two weeks later, versus a powerful Duke team, it was Muir who scored in the final moments to give USC a 21-17 upset win.

A list of his teammates reads like an encyclopedia of Gamecock greats. Guys like Mike Fair, Tommy Suggs, Fred Zeigler, Pat Watson, Rudy Holloman, Benny Galloway, Tyler Hellams, Billy DuPre, Jim Mitchell, and Dickie Harris.

Following his sophomore year, despite Carolina's mediocre 5-5 season, Muir was named to both the All-ACC team and the All-American team. Indeed, he was named All-ACC for three consecutive years, one

of the few Gamecocks ever to be so honored.

The game he now remembers most, he says, was the Carolina-Clemson shootout of 1969. This was Frank Howard's last game as head coach at Clemson, and Muir knew it would prove to be a highly emotional contest for the Tigers. Indeed, the game-cocks suspected that Clemson would do anything to win it, short of dropping an A-Bomb on Williams-Brice Stadium. But in the end, not only did the Gamecocks prevail 27-13, they also remained undefeated in the ACC and won the conference championship.

During his career with Carolina, Muir rushed for 2,234 yards (still ninth in the USC Record Book), which is a long way to run even if you don't have a couple of linebackers hanging around your neck. He was again named All-American in '69 and was a starter in the Coaches All-American Bowl.

Indeed, Muir has often been called the greatest fullback ever to wear the garnet and black, and he is

In 1967 sophomore Warren Muir started the second half for the Gamecocks versus Iowa State. Over the next 30 minutes he would rush for 74 yards and score two TDs as he led USC to a 34-3 win.

still remembered as a true clutch player. No matter how desperate the situation, the 'Cocks had only to give the ball to Muir, and more often than not he'd somehow grind out that needed yardage. But Warren Muir is a well rounded, quality individual, and he made it a point to excel in the classroom as well as on the gridiron. And thus he graduated from USC in 1970 with a degree in a tough civil engineering course.

Also that same year he met his future wife, Jeanne Miller, an accomplished singer who was crowned Miss Aiken of 1970 (she was runner-up in the Miss South Carolina contest that same year).

Today Warren and Jeanne Muir have two children and make their home in Aiken, where he has worked for many years in the construction business as a planning engineer with Gillam and Associates. And Aiken, sports fans, is a long way from the steel mills of Fitchburg, Mass.

★

John Roche

He Is Still A USC Basketball Legend

His name is John Roche, and his numerous outstanding performances on the hardwood at USC have become a matter of legend. Indeed, there are those who would argue that Roche remains the greatest complete basketball player ever for the University of South Carolina. And for good reason.

He was a product of LaSalle High School in New York City, another in a long line of brash Irish kids so dear to the heart of Coach Frank McGuire. "Nice kids but tough competitors" was the euphemistic way McGuire usually descried them, which really meant that you'd better have your jockey cup in place if you got on the court with 'em.

In addition to Roche, McGuire imported to USC such memorable Irishmen as Bobby Cremins, Mike Dunleavy, Kevin Joyce, Tom Owens, Mike Doyle, Brian Winters, Jackie Gilloon, and many others. So many, in fact, that fans joked that Carolina should change their nickname to the Fighting Irish.

A hot-shooting 6-3 guard, Roche was named to the All-City team his junior year at LaSalle in 1965. Which was quite an honor, considering the level of competition. "I think it was then," recalls Roche, now a Denver attorney, "that it first occurred to me that I might be good enough to play college basketball."

He was again named to the All-City team his senior year, and college scholarships rolled in by the hundreds. He could literally have taken his choice of any college in America. Oddly enough, he chose to enroll at USC, traditionally a football college.

"Well, there are several reasons why I chose Carolina," he says. "My high school coach, Dan Buckley, had played for Coach McGuire at St. Johns College, and he thought that Frank McGuire was the greatest coach in America—and he probably was. Plus Bobby Cremins and I had grown up together in the same New York neighborhood, and were childhood friends you might say. Bobby had enrolled at Carolina the year before, and he thought it was a wonderful place and urged me to come on down. Believe me, the advise of an old friend is worth more than all the scientific evidence in the world."

Roche entered USC in the fall of '67, and lived in The Roost, rooming with another all-time Gamecock great, Tom Owens. He then spent the next four years, he says, "going to class and playing basketball. And, like a lot of undergraduates, I also spent a lot of time just fooling around."

(For those who've ever been away from home, the term "fooling around" doesn't require a lot of explanation.)

In 1970 aided and abetted by such Carolina greats as Cremins, Owens, and Tom Riker, and John Ribock, Roche and the Gamecocks enjoyed a sensational 25-3 season. In the ACC Tournament that year they beat both Clemson (34-33) and Wake Forest (79-63) before losing the big one in a double overtime to NC State (42-39).

As indicated by the above scores with Clemson and NC State, opponents quickly learned in '69 that the only way to stay in the game with the high-scoring Gamecocks was to freeze the ball. Indeed, frustrated fans complained that these contests resembled kids playing keep-away more than college basketball. Still, Roche is philosophical about such schemes.

"It was pretty frustrating for us, yes. But freezing the ball was legal back then," he says. "It was a defensive tactic that worked, so I can't complain about it. Besides, we froze the ball on a couple of occasions ourselves."

At the end of the '69 season Roche was voted the ACC Player of the Year Award and was also a consensus All-American. Did such accolades go to this young sophomore's head?

"Nah," laughs Roche. "I made it a point never to believe anything I read in the newspapers, especially in the sports section."

The next season, 1971, was also a memorable one for Roche. For that was the year that the long-suffering Gamecocks finally won the ACC crown. That win came on Owens' shot at the buzzer, giving USC a 52-51 victory over a great UNC team. That was also the year that Roche set an all-time USC record when he hit an incredible forty-one consecutive free throws. Again he was named ACC Player of the Year, and again he was named to Everybody's All-American team.

Roche and his 1968-69 teammates, the first to play in Carolina Coliseum, pose with Coach Frank McGuire. (clockwise from left): John Roche, Tom Owens, Bobby Cremins, John Ribock, Billy Walsh, and Coach McGuire.

After his senior season, in 1971, he became USC's only three-time All-American basketball player. His career total of 1,910 points and his average of 22.5 points per game, remain all-time records at USC. (Had the 3-pointer been part of the game back then, there's no telling how many points the long-shooting Roche might have accumulated!) He also made 548 free throws during his career, another all-time USC record.

In recognition of his greatness, the school retired his jersey, number 11, in 1972. Only three other players have been so honored. He was the top draft pick of the New York Nets in '72. Eleven years later, in 1983, after an outstanding professional career with the Nets, Los Angeles Lakers, and the Denver Nug-gets, he decided to retire and pursue another profession. He initially thought of coaching, he says, but he'd seen so many good coaches come and go that he refused numerous coaching offers and instead entered law school at Whittier College in California.

Today he is attorney John Roche, specializing in commercial litigation with the firm of Graham, Davis and Stubbs in Denver. And just how stimulating is his new profession? "Oh, I can't honestly say that the legal court is as exciting as the basketball court," he chuckles. "But we lawyers do have our moments from time to time. Besides, when I go home at night I don't have to lie awake worrying about how I'm going to keep a million fans happy the next day."

★
Freddy Zeigler

This Walk-On Became One of the Finest Receivers
Ever for the Gamecocks

Sterling Sharpe notwithstanding, there are many who claim that the greatest receiver ever to wear the garnet and black of the University of South Carolina was a small, unassuming, nearsighted country boy from Reevesville, SC named Freddy Zeigler.

Again, this is to take nothing away from Todd Ellis or Sterling Sharpe, who doubtlessly won more games and furnished more thrills than any other passing duo in the history of USC football. But still it's interesting to make some comparisons.

For example, Sharpe, in four years of varsity competition, made 165 catches for 2,497 yards, an average of 41 catches for 624 yards per season.

Freddy Zeigler, a product of Reevesville, SC, is still remembered as perhaps the finest receiver ever to play for the Gamecocks. In 1968, versus Virginia, Zeigler caught 12 Tommy Suggs passes, three of them for touchdowns, to get his name permanently etched in the USC Record Book.

Zeigler, on the other hand, in only three years of varsity competition, made 146 catches for 1,876 yards, an average of 48 catches for 625 yards per season.

Oddly enough, despite his excellence as a receiver, Zeigler says that baseball was actually his favorite sport in high school. "As for football," he grins, "the thing I always liked most about football was the cold shower after the game."

He had always been hampered by severe vision problems and was considered just so-so as a high school football player. Thus upon his graduation in 1965 he received not a single scholarship offer, and matriculated at USC just like any other freshman. He went out for football, he says, just on a whim, just because he was bored sitting around his dorm room. His freshman year he did nothing to distinguish himself from a dozen other young receivers. Then his sophomore season he gave it another try. This time he broke his arm in pre-season drills and had to sit out the season.

So far his football career at Carolina had obviously been nothing to write home about. But filled with determination, he gave football another shot in '67. This time this small lad from Reevesville (he stood 5-10 and weighed 170) amazed his friends and delighted his parents by being named to the varsity squad.

Not only did Coach Paul Dietzel put him on scholarship, he also outfitted him with special contact lens. "I could actually see the football for the first time," laughs Zeigler. Mike Fair was the USC quarterback in '67, and he completed 35 passes to Zeigler for 370 yards during the season. Not a bad start.

But it was in '68 and '69 that Zeigler, now teamed with Tommy Suggs, would begin to demonstrate the miracle catches that would win him a place in both the USC Record Book and in the hearts of the Gamecock faithful everywhere.

Perhaps the highlight of his career came on November 2, 1968, a bright afternoon in Charlottesville, against the Virginia Cavaliers. Amazingly, he snagged 12 passes that day, three of them for touchdowns, and finished the game with 199 yards in receptions. All three figures still remain all-time USC records. That same year Zeigler caught nine passes against Georgia and eight against Virginia Tech. In fact, many fans swear that if Zeigler ever got a finger on the ball, he'd come down with it. And he was Tommy Suggs' favorite target.

He explains: "Back then our basic pass play was the rollout, and after a while Suggs and I just developed a sort of empathy for one another. Or at least he could always read my mind. I'd either curl, break out, or go up, depending on how I was being played. In other words, I'd go where they weren't. And that was our passing game. Simple but effective."

Zeigler says that getting open isn't difficult--if the receiver is given time. "That's where our great offensive line came into play. They could hold out the defense and give Suggs time to look down field. And Suggs had a knack for finding me. He could throw on the dead run, and that ball was always right on the money."

Indeed, it would be twenty years before the Suggs-to-Zeigler passing attack would be surpassed by Ellis and Sharpe with their pass-oriented run-and-shoot offense. But in '68-'69, with fine runners in their backfield like Warren Muir, Benny Galloway, Rudy Holloman, and Zeigler's roommate, Dickie Harris, passing was considered only a minor part of the Gamecocks' offense.

He says his most memorable play came against the highly ranked Volunteers of Tennessee in 1969.

"They'd done a great job of defending our receivers all afternoon," he says, "so we went back in the huddle and Suggs knelt down on the grass and diagrammed a new play for us. Right there in the huddle. He took his finger and outlined a play down on the grass. He was going to fake a deep pass, then hit Rudy Holloman coming out of the backfield with a little swing pass.

"Well, the Vols were totally faked out. Holloman caught that ball and streaked 60 yards for a touchdown. But it's always amused me to think of making up a play in the huddle that way, like kids playing ball in the back yard."

His most memorable game, he says, came in the 1969 Peach Bowl against West Virginia. "That game was pure misery. It had been pouring rain for a week, and the field was about two inches deep in water. Actually, it was more like a mud wrestling contest than a football game. I think everybody was happy when that one ended."

As for his personal activities, Zeigler says his hobby is reading. "I always liked to read. Back in college, when I wasn't studying or at practice, I liked to just lie around with a good book. That's why I majored in English."

He graduated in 1970, then received his law degree from USC in 1973. Since that time he has been in private practice in Columbia. He is modest to a fault and expressed skepticism that his career with the Gamecocks deserved discussion. Still, just looking at the statistics, Freddy Zeigler must be considered one of the finest receivers ever to play for Carolina.

★

Billy DuPre

USC'S First Great Kicking Specialist

"How ya doing, Billy?" the kids at USC used to ask Billy DuPre. "Oh, I can't kick," was his stock response. In fact, nothing could have been further from the truth. For little Billy DuPre at that time was the finest kicking specialist in the history of Gamecock football.

He was also among the first of those super soccer-style kickers in the Palmetto State. Indeed, prior to his arrival on the scene in '68, USC (like most other colleges) generally chose as their kicker the guy with the biggest right leg on the team, someone who kicked the ball straight-on.

Ah, but then came Billy DuPre and nothing in the kicking department would ever be quite the same again. Standing 5-5 and weighing all of 140 pounds, DuPre remembers how it all began: "When I was a junior at A.C. Flora in Columbia, we started a soccer team. But we had to play mostly private schools because soccer was unknown in the public schools. And since nobody, including our coach, had any experience in soccer, I had to teach myself how to kick the ball."

DuPre's soccer coach, luckily, was also his backfield coach in football. "I'd suffered a severe concussion in football my junior year and wasn't supposed to play anymore," he recalls. "But my coach thought it would be a great idea to see if I could kick a football the way I did a soccer ball."

DuPre was a phenomenal success his senior year at Flora, and became a statewide celebrity after kicking a 50-yard field goal in a game against Columbia High. Yet he takes no credit for having invented the idea of booting the ball soccer-style.

"In fact," he says, "it was the Gogalak brothers, Pete and Charlie, who must be considered the fathers of kicking the ball soccer-style. They came to this country as refugees from one of those East bloc countries and brought their soccer expertise with them. Everybody in America used to watch them play pro football on TV and kick those amazing field goals from 40 yards out soccer-style. So it was really the

Billy DuPre, the granddaddy of soccer-style kickers at USC, credits the great Pete Gogalak with starting a new style of kicking in America. Here he boots a last-minute field goal versus VPI in '69 that gave Carolina a 16-14 win that sent them on their way to the Peach Bowl.

Gogalaks who got the rest of us started."

USC fans were delighted when they read that DuPre, known as Mr. Automatic, had decided to kick for the Gamecocks. Then, after catching their first glimpse of him, they stood in stunned silence. Was this diminutive little fellow with the horned-rimmed glasses really the gridiron hero they'd been hearing about for the past two years? He looked more like the team bookkeeper.

It was said that when Carolina hosted UNC in '68, a crowd of Tarheel fans watched as the USC bus rolled to a stop at the stadium. Standing in the doorway of the bus were DuPre and Tommy Suggs, USC's All-ACC quarterback, who stood 5-8 and weighed 155. One Tar Heel fan turned to another and said, "Well, here's Carolina's midget team. Where's the varsity?"

For the next three years DuPre consistently booted kickoffs into his opponents' end zone, a distance of some 75 yards, and fans wondered where the 140-pounder found such power. DuPre still shrugs at the question. "I really don't have the answer to that. It's something that just came naturally to me. I guess I just hit the ball right."

DuPre remembers how excited he became when he read that Pete Gogalak had been drafted by the military and was stationed at Ft. Jackson in Columbia. "I thought maybe Gogalak could give me some valuable pointers. So I went out and talked with him. He was really a great guy and took me out for a kicking session. But I had taught myself all the wrong things and had been doing the wrong things for so long that it wasn't possible for Pete to straighten me out. It was like Arnold Palmer trying to work with a guy who's been hitting the ball with the wrong end of the club all his life."

During that era of Carolina football (1968-70),

coaches still had not caught on to what a valuable offensive weapon the field goal really was. Thus DuPre was called on in only the most desperate situations.

One particular desperate situation, and DuPre's most memorable kick, came on October 18, 1969. Carolina, trailing VPI 16-14, was facing fourth and long at the Gobblers' 30-yard line. There were exactly nine seconds remaining on the clock. Hardly a situation for the faint of heart.

The Gamecocks called time out. A forlorn Paul Dietzel turned and looked at DuPre standing nearby on the sideline. "OK, son," he said with little optimism in his voice, "go in and do the best you can."

DuPre set down the can of Gatorade he'd been sipping from, jogged out onto the field, then calmly booted a 47-yarder squarely through the uprights to give the Gamecocks an amazing 17-16 upset win.

Asked afterwards how he felt, the low-keyed DuPre replied, "I feel great. Not because of my field goal, but because we won. I never worry about my individual performance. My only concern is for the team, whether we win or lose."

In 1969, thanks largely to the heroics of DuPre, USC won the ACC championship and its first bowl invitation in 24 years.

After graduating in 1971, knowing that pro ball was not for him, DuPre joined the S.C. Department of Health and Environmental Control, where he still works today.

He and his wife Marsha make their home in Ninety-Six, near Lake Greenwood, where DuPre spends much of his spare time reeling in those big bass.

"The nice thing about fishing," he grins, "is it's so private. Out here if I miss one nobody knows about it but me."

★

Tyler Hellams

Ten Seconds That Will Last a Lifetime

Ten seconds out of an entire lifetime doesn't seem very long. But many of us can recall some 10-second interval in our lives when some event so momentous occurred that those ten seconds seemed an eternity, and we remember those ten seconds for the rest of our lives. Maybe it was your first parachute jump, or perhaps it was the time you got strangled on a piece of steak, or maybe it was the time (fill in the blank with you own example).

Such is the case with Tyler Hellams, one of the greatest defensive backs ever to play for the Carolina Gamecocks.

Following his senior season at Greenwood High School, he was voted Back of the Year in South Carolina and was a starter on the '66 Shrine Bowl Team. Hellams remembers that Coach Paul Dietzel had just arrived at Carolina and that he recruited that Shrine Bowl team like Sherman marching through Georgia, or Wade Hampton chasing those Yankee carpetbaggers out of South Carolina (choose your own analogy).

Hellams observes: "It really impresses a high school kid for the NCAA Coach of the Year to visit his home and tell him what a great player he is." But it worked, and in '67 Hellams became a member of Carolina's freshman team.

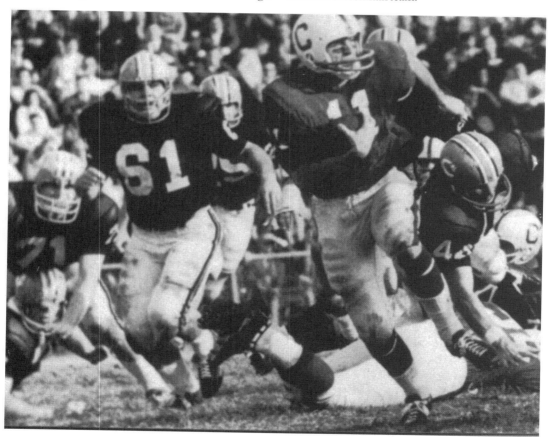

Tyler Hellams starts his 73-yards run-back for a touchdown versus Clemson in 1968 that won him instant immortality. The Gamecocks held on then to win 7-3.

The next year, in '68, Hellams established himself as a defensive back and return man to be reckoned with. But the 'Cocks lost five of their first six games that year, and were sporting a poor 4-6 record going into the Clemson game.

Then came that memorable day, November 23, 1968, and young Tyler Hellams' date with destiny in Death Valley.

Early in that contest Clemson took a 3-0 lead thanks to a Jimmy Barnette field goal. And that score began to look bigger and bigger to the Clemson faithful as time progressed. Indeed, the peerless Tommy Suggs marched the Gamecocks down inside the Tiger 20-yard line on six occasions, but each time they came away without a score. By the end of the third quarter, based on the progress of the game so far, that 3-0 Clemson lead was beginning to look almost insurmountable.

At that point the Tigers' Sammy Cain went back to punt. Waiting downfield to receive, standing at his own 20, stood Tyler Hellams.

"I remember waiting for the punt, but I wasn't really thinking anything in particular, except to catch the ball and then try to run it back as far as possible, which is what I always thought.

"But Cain's punt was a low line drive, and their coverage overran it, which was a big break for me. I caught the ball and looked upfield. There were two big Clemson linemen right in my face, but Al Usher and Jimmy Pope nailed them, and I popped through. In fact, the only purple jersey I saw between me and the goal line at that point was Sammy Cain. He closed in, but I put a little move on him and he went down. At that point there was nothing but daylight ahead. All I had to do was outrun all those purple jerseys chasing me.

"I remember I was running as fast as I could. But suddenly it was like my feet were made of lead and like the whole world went into slow motion, like in a bad dream where you're trying to run away but can't. But then, somehow, I made it across the goal line, and it was really a great feeling, one that I'll never forget."

Thanks to Hellams' last minute heroics, the Gamecocks upset the Tigers 7-3. He was asked if anything he's done since can match those electrifying ten seconds when he almost single handedly beat the Clemson Tigers.

"Well, I try to see things in their proper perspective. That game was important to me, yes, but I've never let it dominate my life. Thoughts of my family and job are far more important to me today than something that happened thirty years ago."

After a brief fling with the Kansas City Chiefs, Hellams returned to graduate school at USC where he earned his MBA in banking in 1973.

Today he is Vice President of Nations Bank in Columbia, where he and his family make their home.

★
Tommy Suggs

This Little Guy Was One Of America's Greatest Quarterbacks

Tommy Suggs, one of USC's greatest quarterbacks.

Back in 1966 *Parade Magazine* named Tommy Suggs the best high school quarterback in America, and college scholarships began to pour in. All of which was pretty amazing, considering that Suggs looked more like the team manager than the quarterback, plus he hailed from Lamar, S.C., a tiny farming community in Florence County that was hardly fa-

mous for producing great football players.

But if you think that's pretty amazing, just hold on. There's more. Now we learn that the 5-8 Suggs played guard on his high school basketball team, and that Davidson's Coach Lefty Driesell practically offered him the college library if he'd agree to play basketball for the Wildcats, then one of the top teams in the country. For a while he was interested in Driesell's offer, and now admits that he began spending hours in his backyard hanging from tree limbs in hopes of adding a few more inches to his height.

But everyone who saw him play agrees that Tommy Suggs was truly phenomenal. And despite his size, he could absolutely rifle a football. Fans still wonder how he did it, where he found the leverage needed to throw the way he did. He explains: "My strength comes not from my shoulder and arm, as with most quarterbacks, but from my elbow and wrist. I threw from the elbow down, flicking the ball with my elbow and wrist."

Following an outstanding performance in the '66 Shrine Bowl game, Suggs spoke with USC football coach Paul Dietzel and forgot all about Lefty Driesell and the college library.

"It was Coach Dietzel's first year at Carolina," Suggs explains, "and there was a tremendous amount of excitement in the air. He recruited just about everybody on the Shrine Bowl team from both states, and I just really wanted to remain part of that team."

He became a starter for the Gamecocks in '68, and incredible things began to happen. There was that game with UNC, for example, which found the Gamecocks trailing 28-3 with only ten minutes remaining. During those ten minutes Suggs ran and passed the Tarheels silly, and USC finally came away with an amazing 32-28 comeback win.

That same year, Suggs broke a longtime school record when he tossed five touchdown passes in Carolina's 49-28 win over a strong Virginia team. Then he threw for four more the next week against Wake Forest. And this, remember, was back when USC was famous not for their passing but for their terrific running backs.

Tommy Suggs remembers the Clemson Game of 1970: "I threw three interceptions in the first half and was thus credited with making three tackles, which is pretty unusual for a quarterback."

"I also remember the Clemson game my senior year," Suggs laughs. "In the first half I managed to throw three interceptions. And thus I was credited with making three tackles, which is pretty unusual for a quarterback. But then I threw for three touchdowns in the second half, and we won the game."

Despite such outstanding performances, Carolina won only fifteen games during Suggs' three years at the helm. His explanation: "We won convincingly in the ACC, but we also played a number of independents and schools from the SEC. The ACC required a score of 800 on the SAT for admission, but the SEC required score of only 700. So they were obviously getting athletes who couldn't qualify for the ACC. I remember one year we played Georgia and almost their entire defensive team was from South Carolina. That's the big reason we got out of the ACC."

Despite the fact that Todd Ellis and Steve Taneyhill demolished most USC passing records, Suggs' name still appears prominently in the Record Book. He still remains number-three in both career completions (355) and in career passing yardage (4,916). He was twice named National Back of the Week by *Sports Illustrated*, and was also named to the All-State Team for three consecutive years.

Most of all, fans still remember Tommy Suggs as a winner, a cool-headed player who had that rare ability to turn disaster into a big gainer. Suggs shrugs off the compliment: "It's what I call vision. Jeff Grantz had it, and so did Todd Ellis and Steve Taneyhill, and I suppose to a certain extent, so did I. But it's like some people have the ability to see the entire field and everybody on it at all times. It's great vision, and it's something that can't be taught."

Suggs, who has been a constant source of listening pleasure as the color-man on Gamecock Radio since 1973, is today President of Rooney and McArthur Insurance, Inc. in Columbia. He is active in civic affairs and has twice served as President of the Columbia Chamber of Commerce, and is on the Board of Directors for the Richland Memorial Hospital Cancer Treatment Center. He is also a member of the Board of Visitors for USC.

He was inducted into the South Carolina Athletic Hall of Fame in 1984 and served as President of that body in 1989.

He is married to the former Jane Patterson of Greenville, and they have a daughter, Betsy, and a son, Dan. They make their home in Columbia.

Moments of Glory
South Carolina's Greatest
Sports Heroes

1970-1974

★

Donnie Shell

From Whitmire High To the Charlotte Panthers

Donnie Shell was an outstanding all-around athlete at Whitmire High School, playing under Coach William Johnson, and led the Wolverines to state championships in all three major sports in 1969, his senior year. He himself was named to the All-State Team in both football and baseball.

But at 5-10 and 170 pounds, young Donnie simply wasn't quite big enough, or good enough, to make it as a college linebacker. Thus no Big Time recruiters ever came calling.

"Well, finally, I did get two scholarship offers," he laughs. "One in basketball to Belmont Abby, and one in football to South Carolina State. I was pretty small at that time, but I liked Coach Oree Banks and decided to give State and football a try."

By the following fall, when he reported for pre-season drills, he had gained another twenty pounds. More importantly, Banks had decided to shift him from linebacker to safety. So at last Shell had found a home, one where his speed, quickness and aggressive play more than compensated for his lack of size, and, sure enough, he became a starter for the Bulldogs his freshman year.

By the time he'd finished his collegiate career (1973) he'd been twice named to the Mid-Eastern Athletic All-Conference Team and to the Kodak All-American team.

Then came the pro draft of '74. Shell says he sat by the phone for days, but no calls came. Again the experts had decided that he was not quite big enough or good enough to make it in pro ball.

Undaunted, unwilling to take the experts' word for it, he decided to try out with the Pittsburgh Steelers as a free agent. To make a long story short, he definitely made the team. But did he ever entertain any doubts that he could play with the big guys?

"Nope," he says simply. "I never felt any anxiety on that point whatsoever. I knew I could make it if they'd give me the chance. But what did cause me concern was wondering if I could make the adjustment from the system I was accustomed to at State to the system employed by the Steelers. But Coach Willie Jeffries had come in at State my senior year and installed a 4-3 defense, which was very similar to what

the Steelers were using. So really the adjustment wasn't that tough."

Shell recalls with a smile that practice sessions in pro ball were not as physically demanding as they had been at State. "I was very surprised and delighted to find that practices in pro ball are not as tough physically as in college ball. They were much more mental, and we'd spend most of our sessions learning our opponent's offense and what we should do in various situations. There was rarely any contact drills. We were supposed to already know the fundamentals. That really came as a pleasant surprise to me, for I was still pretty small for a professional defensive back."

With Coach Chuck Noll at the helm and Terry Bradshaw at quarterback, Shell relished the knowledge that he broke in with one of the finest football teams ever assembled and that he soon would become an essential cog in that machine at strong safety.

Indeed, between 1974 and 1987, Shell would establish himself as one of the greatest players ever in the NFL, and he has the records to prove it.

Among his many distinctions, he is still proud that as Captain of the defensive unit, he helped lead the Steelers to an amazing four Super Bowl wins, an NFL record.

Shell was named All-Pro for five consecutive seasons, and he still holds the NFL record for career interceptions with fifty. He holds another NFL record with twenty-two fumble recoveries. He also started an incredible 202 games for Pittsburgh, and all-time Steelers record.

And in 1991, four years following his retirement, he was named to the All-Time Super Bowl team. Soon thereafter he was inducted into the South Carolina Athletic Hall of Fame.

All of which isn't too bad for a skinny little guy out of Witmire, S. C., and the recipient of only one football scholarship.

He earned his masters degree in counseling during the off-seasons, and today is back in pro football as Director of Player Relations with the Charlotte Panthers.

He is married to the former Paulette Richardson of Darlington, and they have three children--April, dawn, and Lamont.

★
Carter Davis

He Remains Wofford's All-Time Passing Leader

Carter Davis turned down scholarship offers from colleges throughout the SEC to play at Wofford College, a decision that he today calls the best thing that ever happened to him.

Carter Davis is remembered today as one of the finest quarterbacks ever to wear the black and gold of Wofford College.

Still, had his personality and ambition been just a little different, he could be touring the country at this very moment as "The Morristown Mauler," prancing around those professional wrestling ring-like all those other masked buffoons we see on TV. But that was not his style.

At 6-2 and 200 pounds, he went undefeated in 38 wrestling bouts his senior year at Morristown (Tenn.) High School in 1970, winning the state championship in the bargain. He was also named to the AP All-American High School Wrestling Team that year, and college scholarships poured in.

But Davis had other plans. Yes, despite his reputation as a tough guy on the wrestling mat, he was also the star quarterback on his high school football team. Obviously he was no prima donna, too delicate to be touched by those ruffians from opposing institutions. To the contrary, he thrived on ruffians, and he wanted more than anything to quarterback a college football team.

"I really loved wrestling, the one-on-one competition," he recalls. "Football, you know, is a team sport, and the credit or blame, depending on whether you won or lost, is spread around among about forty guys. But in wrestling, you're out there totally alone. I honestly don't think you can find a better character builder for young men than wrestling.

Davis' father, a longtime football coach, was athletic director for the city of Morristown when young Carter was coming along, and he offered his son some good advice.

"I was offered scholarships to most of the colleges in the SEC my senior year. But my dad had seen so many promising young athletes get lost in the shuffle at those big schools. He strongly urged that I attend a small college where I'd get a chance to play."

For several good reasons he chose to attend wofford: "They had gone 10-0 in 1970 and were considered one of the top small college teams in the nation. But what really impressed me were the phone calls I started getting from Wofford alumni all over the country. Not a single one of those callers ever mentioned football to me. Instead, they talked about Wofford's excellent academic programs and how Wofford graduates are considered prime catches for businesses and industries all over America."

Wofford's celebrated Harold Chandler graduated after leading the Terriers to an undefeated season in 1970, and into his shoes stepped freshman Carter Davis. The Terriers didn't miss a beat.

"We also got a new head coach in '71, Jack Peterson, who installed the veer offense. So I really didn't get as many opportunities to pass as I would have liked. Still,

Davis still holds the career passing yardage record at Wofford with 3,838 yards as well as career TD tosses with 35. Here he scrambles for good yardage against Gardner-Webb in '73.

we went 6-4 on the season with upset wins over both Furman and Davidson, so I'm not complaining."

Davis' most outstanding season came in '73, his junior year. "Coach Peterson and I had a talk just before our opening game that year, and he asked me if I had any suggestions that would make the offense move better. I told him I thought it would help if he'd start letting me call my own plays in the huddle instead of him calling them from the sideline. He said OK, and so that's what we started doing."

And why would that be an advantage?

"Well, the quarterback gets so much feedback from his teammates in the huddle. One player might tell me that he's getting beat to death over there, and we should run it the other way for a while. Or another might say that the guy across from him is a creampuff, and we should run his way for a while. Or a receiver might tell me to watch him across the middle, that he's wide open out there. The coach doesn't hear all those comments, but the quarterback does and he should be able to react immediately to them."

Based on the statistics, Davis' suggestion paid off as the Terriers averaged 20 first down and 29 points per game that year (both figures still remain all-time Wofford records).

As for Davis himself, he set all-time Terrier records when he threw for 1,916 yards in '73, including 15 touchdown tosses.

Also, despite the awesome performance of the great Shawn Graves for the Terriers (1989-92), Davis still holds the all-time record for career passing yardage with a total of 3,838 yards, and career touchdown passes with 35.

Nor was he any slouch off the field. He served as President of the Pi Kappa Phi fraternity and was active in the Fellowship of Christian Athletes. He took his degree in economics in 1975 and was immediately recruited by Deering-Milligan for their prestigious management training program.

Today, some 18 years later, he manages the Milligan plant in LaGrange, GA., where he and his wife Angelia make their home.

★
Casey Manning

Race Was Never An Issue

Surely everyone this side of Hong Kong must know by now that the first black basketball player recruited by the University of South Carolina was an aspiring young man from Dillion, S.C. named Casey Manning.

Today he is a successful lawyer and judge. When asked if being the first black at USC caused him any anxiety, he replies:

"No, absolutely not. You must remember that I was born and raised in Dillion and attended Dillion High School, which had been segregated up until the time I came along there. So being the first black to do this or that was not a situation I was unaccustomed to. In fact, I really thought of going to Carolina as a great adventure, something I eagerly anticipated."

Manning was coached in high school by Mark Fryer, a well known USC football player. Did that give the 'Cocks a leg up when it came recruiting him, a high school All-American with more than one-hundred scholarship offers?

"No, Coach Fryer really had nothing to do with it. In fact, Davidson College was my first choice. Mainly because I liked Coach Lefty Driesell so much. But in the end, being a South Carolinian, I decided that I'd best stay in-state. Plus I liked Coaches Frank McGuire and Bill Loving."

Mannning quickly became part of an all-star cast during his career with the Gamecocks (1971-73), joining such luminaries as John Roche, Tom Owens, John Ribock, Tom Riker, Alex English, Kevin Joyce, Mike Dunleavy, Nate Davis, Bobby Carver and Brian Winters.

"As for my teammates, they were really a great bunch of guys," he says. Then he pauses and grins: "Pushy Yankees from New York maybe, but still a great bunch of guys.

Which raises another great social issue of our era: not only was Manning the first black on a Gamecock basketball team, but he also enjoys the distinction of being probably the first black and only Baptist ever recruited by Frank McGuire, who was famous for recruiting out of the Irish neighborhoods of New York.

Manning, a man of keen wit who enjoys a good

Casey Manning, trailed by Tom Riker, goes in for a layup as the Gamecocks pound Virginia 92-70 in 1971.

laugh, responds: "Would you believe I was the only guy on the team who didn't cross himself when he went to the free throw line? Somebody once suggested we should change our name to The Fighting Irish, but then we discovered that another outfit had beaten us to the punch on that one."

Manning enjoyed an outstanding career with the Gamecocks and says that a couple of events are still italicized in his mind: "Believe it or not, I had to go all the way to Salt Lake City to ever lead the team in

Casey Manning and his teammates of 1971-72. Front Row (L-R): Brian Winters, Danny Traylor, Tom Riker, Kevin Joyce, Rick Aydlett. Back Row (L-R): Jimmy Powell, Rick Mousa, Ed Peterson, Bill Grimes, Bob Carver, and Casey Manning. This team went 24-6 on the year.

scoring. But I did it in games with both Utah and Providence in the Utah Classic of '72.

"And of course I still remember the big night in '71 when we up-ended UNC 52-51 to win the ACC championship. We're still the only Carolina team ever to win the ACC crown. And to do it the way we did, on a last second shot from Tom Owens, is still a very sweet memory."

During Manning's varsity career, by the way, USC won 69 of 87 games, an excellent record.

He graduated in '73 with a double major in history and political science, then worked for a year as an agent with the State Law Enforcement Division. In '77 he received his law degree from USC, then opened a practice in Dillion, where he remained for several years.

In 1983 he returned to Columbia and became a prosecutor for the attorney general's office, a position he held for five years. Then again he went into private practice, this time in Lexington with the firm of Walker, Morgan and Manning.

Extremely active in civic affairs, Manning says that his wife, LaVerne, and their three children remain his top priority. They make their home in Columbia.

As for the future, Manning says: "I'm very content where I am; as a judge I can serve far more people of this great state."

★

Vince Perone

Like His Father Before Him, Vince Perone, Jr. Was An All-Southern Performer at Furman

Congenial and modest to a fault, he was one of the finest defensive aces ever to wear the purple and white of Furman University. His name is Vincent Perone, JUNIOR. The astute reader will note that the latter part of his name is emphasized in capitals letters. That's to distinguish him from his father, Vincent Perone, SENIOR, who was an All-Southern guard for the Paladins in 1953.

Vince, Jr. was born in Greenville (where his father owned a popular restaurant) and later attended Wade Hampton High School. His senior year he played in the North-South All-Star game, but at 5-7 and 170 pounds he was just too small to make it in college football. Everyone said so. Everyone believed so.

Everyone that is except for Vince. So, following his own instincts, in 1970 he became a walk-on at USC. He impressed the coaches from the very beginning, and following the first game of the season he was named a starter for the Biddies on both offense and defense. Elated, he felt his future with Carolina was assured. But at the end of the season, oddly enough, Coach Paul Dietzel informed Vince that his athletic budget would not permit him to offer a scholarship,

"So then I did what I should have done in the first place," Vince says. "I transferred to Furman. My father played and coached there, and I sort grew up around campus. Plus I loved Greenville. Looking back, it was the best decision I ever made."

After sitting out the '71 season Vince became a starting defensive back for the Paladins under Coach Bob King in '72. Though the Paladins suffered through a miserable 2-9 season, Vince proved his worth, and set an all-time Furman record in the bargain by intercepting ten enemy aerials. (Note: this remains an all-time Furman defensive record.)

Then came '73 and the appearance of a new head coach on campus, the ubiquitous Art Baker. The Paladins went 7-4 that year, and the Associated Press voted them the most improved team in America.

"I think it was largely a matter of attitude," Vince speculates. "We actually had better talent the year before, but Coach Baker was such a positive influence on the players. He had us believing we were winners, and pretty soon we started to play like winners. Plus he

A member of the Furman Athletic Hall of Fame, Vince Perone, Jr., is still remembered as one of the finest return men in the history of Paladin football.

was a great recruiter and brought in some really fabulous freshmen--like David Whitehurst, for example, who was probably the best quarterback in American."

Vince pauses and ponders the situation for a moment. "Plus he assembled an excellent coaching staff in Dick Sheridan and Jimmy Sattefield. He just built us a winning foundation all around, a tradition that continues to this day."

Vince was voted Furman's outstanding defensive back in both '73 and '74, which is quite an honor considering the Paladins led the nation in pass defense both years. In '74 the Paladins held opponents to an incredibly low 69.1 passing yards per game, still an all time defensive record.

But how could 5-7 Vince Perone intercept or bat down all those passes to tall receivers? "I've gotten asked that question a lot over the years," Perone laughs. "But I never considered my height a disadvantage. Even if the receiver was 6-3, the ball had to be perfectly thrown, or I had as good a chance of coming up with it as he did.

"Plus Coach Baker had us so well prepared by game day, and I knew our opponent's plays so well, that I could see a play developing, and I knew exactly where the primary and secondary receivers would be, and I just made it a point to get there before the ball did."

Lest we leave you with the impression that Vince was good for nothing but batting down enemy passes all day, let us hasten to point out that he was also an ace return man for the Paladins. Indeed, he returned sixty-six kickoffs for Furman during his career, still an all-time record.

Incredibly, he still shares the record (with John Popson) for the longest kickoff return for a touchdown at Furman (103 yards versus Wofford in '73).

He served as team captain in '74 and was also voted the team MVP Award. In passing (no pun intended), we should also underscore the fact that Vince, like his father before him, was named to the All-Southern Team for three consecutive years.

He took his degree in business administration in 1975, which is indeed a tribute to his academic ability, for as he himself says, "At Furman they don't give the athletes any breaks. We had to dig for it just like everybody else."

Upon graduation, Vince became an equal partner with his father and uncle in the restaurant business. Today they have expanded to three restaurants in the Greenville area, restaurants known simply as VINCE'S.

He is married to the former Jill Turner, and they make their home in Greenville. So, like father, like son. But where will it all end? "I think we just reached the end," Vince grins. "Jill and I raised three of the cutest little cheerleaders you've ever seen with not a single football player in the whole bunch."

He is a member of the Furman Athletic Hall of Fame.

★
Ricky Satterfield

At Wofford and In Business His Determination Has Always Taken Him To The Top

At Wofford College in Spartanburg, they reckon time in terms of their great Shawn Graves, who has broken just about every conceivable offensive record in the books. But believe it or not, football was being played at Wofford for some ninety-nine years before Graves ever put in an appearance there.

Back in the old days, between 1972-75 BG (Before Graves), the offensive pacesetter for the Terriers was a stocky young man out of Woodruff High School names Ricky Satterfield.

Not only was Ricky a star running back in high school, he also excelled in the high hurdles, an event that generally attracts only the tall and slim. Satterfield is built much like a fire hydrant. So why the high hurdles?

"Well," Satterfield shrugs, "nobody else wanted to run the hurdles, so Coach Willie Varner informed me that I had just volunteered to do it. It took a lot of practice, but after a while I became fairly good at it."

Which is just one example of the determination that characterizes Satterfield's life. His senior year he was named to the All-State football team and selected for the Shrine Bowl.

He then accepted a scholarship to Wofford, where he enrolled in the fall of 1972. Standing 5-8 and weighting 180 pounds, he was running as the deepback in the I-formation and became a starter for the Terriers after the fourth game of his freshman season. He would start the next forty games before his career ended.

As everyone knows by now, Wofford is a fine liberal arts college that does not suffer fools gladly, a place where football players have to excel in the classroom if they have any hope of remaining football players. Was it tough for Satterfield?

"YES!" he says emphatically, and he isn't smiling when he says it. "And for several reasons. Wofford is a tough school, and my ambition in college was to become a dentist, which placed me in one of their more demanding academic disciplines.

"I had double science courses and labs every semester. And, coming from a small high school, I

Satterfield rushed for an incredible 3,686 yards for the Terriers between 1972-75. The only collegiate player from South Carolina ever to surpass this record was USC's Heisman Trophy winner, George Rogers.

wasn't as well prepared as some of the others, It was tough, but I made the Dean's List five of my eight semesters there."

Which left him how much time for tom-foolery? "Absolutely none," he insists. "I was up by seven every morning, then attended classes and labs until time for football practice at three, then I would eat dinner from six until seven, then back to my room to study until about one. I never got more than six hours sleep."

By his senior year Satterfield held more offensive records at Wofford than Elvis Presley ever thought about. In fact, in one game, versus Guilford College in 1973, Satterfield already had 214 yards rushing before

Ricky Satterfield, a native of Woodruff, SC., and friends gather at a recent banquet at Wofford College. He did not appear nearly this cordial when wearing a football uniform.

half-time (an all-time Wofford record). We can only imagine the yardage he'd have accumulated had he been allowed to play the second half, but he wasn't.

Most impressive is the fact that he amassed a total of 3,686 yards rushing during his career with the Terriers (that's two long miles, which is a long way to run when you've got two linebackers squeezing your windpipe!). At the time that figure represented a rushing record never before approached by any player from any college in South Carolina. It was finally broken in 1980 by USC's great Heisman Trophy winner, George Rogers.

Following his graduation in 1976, he passed up invitations to both the Atlanta Falcons' training camp and to dental school in favor of accepting a research position with Milliken Co.

Today he is Division Coordinator on the President's Staff at Milliken, and lives in LaGrange, Georgia.

He is still remembered at Wofford as a scholar and athlete who always gave 100% in every situation, a young man whose determination has taken him a long way.

★
Jeff Grantz

In 1992 He Was Selected USC's All-Time
Greatest Quarterback-- and for Good Reason

Carolina has fielded many great quarterbacks over the years, but those who had the pleasure of watching Jeff Grantz in action will agree that he was one of the best, a cool-headed, make-things-happen sort of guy, one who had that rare knack for turning an obvious disaster into victory. In a word, he was a winner.

Indeed, the greatest mistake an opposing defense could make was to cover his receivers on a pass play. For if there was anything Grantz could do better than pass, it was run the ball. USC fans can recall numerous occasions when finding his receivers covered, Grantz would simple turn upfield and make like red Grange, leaving tacklers in his wake.

In 1973, for example, his first year as a starter for the Gamecocks, he rushed for 260 yards versus Ohio University, a new single game rushing record for USC, one that broke Steve Wadiak's long standing record of 256 yards rushing versus Clemson in 1951. (Note: Grantz's single game rushing record was broken by Brandon Bennett in 1991.)

Born in 1954, Grantz grew up in Bel Air, Maryland, in a rural area just north of Baltimore. His father served as head coach and athletic director for thirty-three years at a nearby high school, so Jeff grew up in an athletic family.

"Oddly enough," he says, "the first game I started for Bel Air High was against my father's team. It put me in an unusual situation, because I wanted Bel Air to win, but I hated to see my father's team lose."

He was an outstanding all-around athlete at Bel Air, and his senior year he was named to the All-State Team as well as being named the Baltimore Area's Athlete of the Year.

To say that he was highly recruited would be an understatement. He could have played for any college in

In 1992 Jeff Grantz was voted Carolina's all-around greatest quarterback ever. His most memorable game, he says, was the '75 contest against Clemson. Carolina won 56-20.

America, and he knew it. But in the end he narrowed his choices to Michigan State, UNC and USC.

"In fact," he says, "I'd really planned to sign with UNC. But then I came down and visited with USC, and really liked the school. I was also impressed with both Coach Dietzel and the baseball coach, Bobby Richardson. They assured me that I could play both sports at USC, and that's the big reason I came here."

In addition to becoming a great quarterback for the Gamecocks, Grantz also became a mainstay at shortstop on some of the finest baseball teams the University has ever produced. During his junior year, in 1975, Carolina made it all the way to the College World Series before finally losing the national championship to the University of Texas.

Meanwhile, back at William-Brice Stadium, the Gamecocks went 7-4 his senior year, losing by only a few points to some truly tough competition.

The Gamecocks also suffered an upset that year at the hands of Appalachian State. Asked how he recovered from such a loss, Grantz replied:

"Maintaining my morale was never a problem. To me, it never mattered what we'd done the week before. That was ancient history as far as I was concerned. Saturday was a new game, and I always did the very best I could."

He was elected captain of the '75 Gamecocks, and his most memorable game came that year when USC blasted Clemson 56-20.

"Everything just came together that day," he says. "We scored every time we got our hands on the ball, eight touchdowns."

In '75 Grantz passed for 1,815 yards and 16 touchdowns (a TD record surpassed only by Todd Ellis and Steve Taneyhill). For his career, he passed for a total of 3,440 yards (a figure surpassed only by Todd Ellis, Tommy Suggs, and Steve Taneyhill). This despite the fact that he was operating out of a run-oriented offense.

He played his first two seasons under Paul Dietzel and his final two under Jim Carlen. Asked to compare the two, Grantz says:

"Coach Dietzel was a great organizer. He never left anything to chance. He just had a tremendous eye for detail. Coach Carlen, on the other hand, was more of a hands-on type coach. He was always right down on the field with us, talking to us and offering coaching tips. Coach Dietzel would rarely do that. But I thought they were both great coaches, and I enjoyed playing for both."

Grantz won the team MVP Award in '75, and played in both the East-West Shrine Bowl and the Hula Bowl. He was also named a second-team All-American by the Associated Press.

He was drafted by the Miami Dolphins, but they were already loaded with quarterbacks, so they shifted him to a receiver position.

"I had no objections to becoming a receiver, but I simply found pro ball to be a grind. I didn't enjoy it at all. So I left camp and returned to USC."

He then served two years as a graduate assistant under coach Jim Carlen. But, he says, he lacked the patience to successfully follow in his father's footsteps in the coaching profession.

He did find, to his great surprise, that he was an excellent salesman, and that selling was a job he thoroughly enjoyed. To that end, he became a sales representative for Budweiser in Columbia in 1979. It is a position he maintains today, and he says he's delighted with his career choice.

(It might ne noted that former Clemson quarterback great, Rodney Williams, is a colleague of Grantz's at Budweiser.)

He and his wife, Jill, have two children, Derrick and Kathy, and make their home in Columbia.

Brian Ruff

He Was The first Citadel Player to Have His Jersey Retired

Brian Ruff says, "I was an extremely average high school linebacker and certainly not widely recruited. I would say I wound up at The Citadel just by luck more than anything else." In fact, looking back, he recalls that he wasn't sure he wanted to attend The Citadel despite their offer of a full scholarship.

But, as fate would have it, he accepted Coach Bobby Ross' offer and one of those proverbial matches made in Heaven soon developed.

By 1975 he was recognized as one of college football's finest linebackers. He was named to the All-Southern Conference Team three times, and, more

impressive, he was named Southern Conference Player of the Year both his junior and senior seasons. Also in '76 he was named the outstanding collegiate player in South Carolina. That same season he received the highest honor accorded a college football player when he was named to the Associated Press All-American Team.

He played in both the Hula and Japan Bowls, appeared on the Bob Hope television show, and became the first Citadel player in history to have his jersey retired.

Oddly enough, he says, his proudest achievement doesn't concern football. "I was promoted to Company Commander my senior year. That meant more to me

Bryan Ruff was named to the AP All-American team in '73 and became the first player in the history of The Citadel athletics to have his jersey retired.

than anything in football. To make good grades and become an officer in the Corps of Cadets took a lot of effort."

In 1972 after suffering a knee injury during his senior season in high school, in Mountainside, N.J., Ruff discovered that major colleges had lost interest in him. But Bobby Ross, just named head coach at The Citadel, was still interested.

"Coach Ross was hired at The Citadel late in the year," Ruff says, "and nobody had recruited anybody down there. He had no in-coming freshmen. I think he just wanted to get some recruits in. Luckily, I was one of them."

Ruff says he didn't make a good impression on his first visit to The Citadel. "I'd lost about thirty pounds to compete in wrestling, and I remember getting off the plane at the airport that morning. Coach Charlie Rizzo met me, and I could tell from the look in his eyes that he thought Coach Ross had lost his mind. He was probably thinking, "How can we be bringing in this gaunt little beanpole to play college linebacker?"

Ruff credits two people--Coach Ross and senior defensive lineman Tony Cicoria--with convincing him that The Citadel was the place to be.

"Coach Ross made a tremendous impression on my parents--and me. He is truly a great guy who cares about other people. That's the big reason I wanted to play for him."

Cicoria, a letterman from 1971-73, is now a surgeon in New York, but he gave Ruff some sound advice. "I asked him if he missed the partying that goes on at other schools," Ruff grins. He told me 'Yes I really do. But remember, four years from now when all the partying has ended, what are you going to be doing? You've got four years to learn some skills you'll need in the real world.' And I'll tell you, Cicoria was a tough guy, and I really looked up to him. After our conversation, I decided to get serious."

Ruff lettered from 1973-76, took a fling at pro football, then married his high school sweetheart and returned to Charleston. Today he is still there pursuing a successful career in the insurance business.

He's past president of the Charleston Citadel Club and currently on the board of the Charles Webb Center for Crippled Children. "I have a healthy child of my own," he explains, "and I want to do whatever I can to help those less fortunate."

Today he tells anyone who will listen that he credits The Citadel with preparing him to become a productive citizen.

"The Citadel instills the self-discipline that prepares you for what's happening in the real world. Life isn't easy. You get knocked down a lot, and you can either stay down or have the guts to get up and come back again. The Citadel teaches you to come back."

★
Tommy Southard

A Furman Walk-On Makes It All The Way To The Pros

Talk to Tommy Southard five minutes and you feel that you've known him all your life. He has a great sense of humor, an easy laugh, and a tendency to totally downplay his many accomplishments on the collegiate and professional gridiron. In other words, he's a fellow who doesn't take himself particularly serious and goes out of his way to make sure that no one else does.

After spending five minutes convincing him that this interview was not just a practical joke dreamed up by his cousin, we learned that he attended Atlanta's Druid Hills High School, where he was considered an outstanding running back. What postseason honors did he receive his senior season?

He jokingly replies, "I know it'd make a much better story if I said that I made the AP High School All-American Team back in '74, but it's been so long now that I really can't remember whether I made anybody's all-anything or not. I think I made the All-City Team, and I'm really not positive about that."

Despite the fact that he stood 5-10 and weighed only 155 pounds, he was heavily recruited by Georgia Tech, Tennessee, Auburn and Furman.

"The problem was they all wanted me as a walk-on. Then, if I made the team, they'd put me on scholarship. Which was risky business. So I decided that I had a better chance of making Furman's team as a walk-on than any of the others. And that's how I wound up in Greenville."

At the beginning of his freshman year Southard found himself listed as a fifth-string running back with the Paladins. Discouraged, he had about decided to become a walk-off when he got what he calls a lucky break.

"A few of the coaches and I were just tossing the ball around before practice one afternoon, and I got lucky and made a couple of nice catches of some bad passes. So they asked me if I'd like to switch to a flanker position. That's when I finally got a chance to play."

It was indeed a smart move on Furman's part, especially when it's remembered that the Paladins had a sophomore quarterback that year named David Whitehurst, who would go on to become a star quarterback with the Green Bay Packers and one of the finest passers in the NFL.

Tommy Southard, long hair and all, remains one of Furman's leading receivers ever, catching 103 passes for 1,443 yards. He would later play for both the St. Louis Cardinals and the Houston

Almost immediately Whiteburst and Southard hit it off, and Southard would become Furman's leading receiver for the next three years. In 1976, his junior year , he led the Southern Conference in receptions with 39 catches and 510 yards. For his career Southard remains Furman's second all-time leading receiver with 103 catches for 1,443 yards.

He remembers Furman's season opener in '76 when they upset a highly regarded NC Sate team 12-7. Then later in the season they beat a good East Carolina team 10-7, knocking the Pirates out of a bowl bid.

As for Southard himself, his best game came his senior year when he caught 8 passes for 147 yards in Furman's 28-21 win over VMI.

He was named All-Southern in both '76 and '77. By then, it seems safe to say , he was no longer considered just a walk-on.

He received his degree in political science in '78 and

was preparing to return home to enter his family's business, SBS Associates in Norcross, Georgia, when he received a surprise telephone call one afternoon.

"It was some guy inviting me to come try out as a free agent with the St. Louis Cardinals. I really thought it was one of my teammates playing a practical joke on me. It took him five minutes to convince me that he was legitimate."

To make a long story short, he made the Cardinals' team that year. "Jim Hart was playing quarterback and he threw a pass that would absolutely melt in your hands. I'd finally gotten my weight up to about 175 pounds, but I still avoided those 300 pounds linemen like the plague. But in the fourth game of the season they got me, and I wound up on the injured reserve list for the rest of the year."

Later he was informed that he had been traded to Houston. "Burn Phillips called me and invited me to camp with the Oilers, and I reported and made the team. But be darned if the same thing didn't happen again-- I was hit and injured in the fourth game of the season and had to return home. But this time I told Bum not to give my telephone number to anybody. I was through with pro football."

Today the gregarious Tommy Southard makes an ideal President for a company like SBS (Southard-Brown-Southard), a firm that serves as sales representatives for various hardware manufacturers.

As for his personal life, In 1983 he married his high school sweetheart, Candy Gober, and they now have two children and make their home in Roswell, Ga.

At the conclusion of this interview, as we were already packing up our pencil and note pad, Southard gave us a pained look and groaned, "Say, you aren't going to run that old photo of me that Furman still sends out to everyone, are you? The one taken back in '74 when my hair was growing down to my waist?"

We assured him we were.

"Well, listen, "he suggested, "couldn't you take your air brush and erase some of that hair? Maybe give me a nice neat flattop?"

We assured him we would not think of it. We want the world to remember him just as he really was.

★
David Whitehurst

This Furman Quarterback Went On To Become An
All-Time Great With The Green Bay Packers

Between 1974-77 David Whitehurst would start 42 consecutive games for Furman Universtiy, an all-time Paladin record. He turned down a contract with the Atlanta Braves to play college football.

The date still stands out in his mind. It was September 5, 1974, and the temperature down on the field hovered around the 95-degree mark, a sweltering afternoon better suited for hitting the pool than for playing football.

But inside Sirrine Stadium in Greenville things were getting even hotter for the Furman Paladins. It was now half-time and Furman trailed Presbyterian College by a score of 7-0. As though that were not bad enough, Furman's starting quarterback had just been carried off the field on a stretcher. He would be out for the season.

The Paladins' locker room was somber as Coach Art Baker looked at the young freshman quarterback seated quietly on the back row. "When we go back out for the second half," Baker said, "David Whitehurst will start at quarterback."

Whitehurst still remembers that his stomach was in a knot the first time he stepped under center to take his first snap in a real college football game. But he guided the team like a veteran, and led them on a 60-yard march for a touchdown on their first possession of the second half, running the last 5 yards himself for the tying score. Later he would complete a 60-yard TD pass for the winning score.

Today he recalls that PC contest as probably the most important game of his career.

"It's great to have an opportunity to play early in your career and do well," he says. "That first game with PC gave me the confidence I needed to think of myself as a college quarterback. Plus it gave the coaches confidence in me. Who knows, If I'd had a miserable day against PC, I might never have played again."

Whitehurst then went on to start the next 42 games for Furman, still an all-time record for consecutive starts.

He had been an all-state baseball and football player at Walker High School in DeKalb County, Georgia, and refused a contract with the Atlanta Braves to attend Furman. Why?"

"Well, I had visited Furman, and I thought Art Baker was a good man and Furman a great school. But mostly I was impressed with Coach Dick Sheridan. You talk with Sheridan two minutes, and you know there's something special about him. Call it charisma, honesty, or whatever, he just makes tremendous impression. And he always kept his promise."

Whitehurst was selected by The Green Bay Packers in the eighth round of the 1977 professional draft.

Again, as at Furman, opportunity knocked early. In the fifth game of his rookie season, the Packers' starting quarterback, Lynn Dickey, was sidelined with a broken leg. Coach Bart Starr turned to Whitehurst. "Okay, son, this is your big chance."

David Whitehurst would go on to become the starting quarterback for the Green Bay Packers for the next seven years.

Again, as he had done against PC years earlier, Whitehurst led his team on a sixty-yard march that ended in a touchdown. For the next seven years then he was the man under center for the Packers. In 1984 he was traded to Kansas City, where he played for only one season.

"I'd promised myself all along that I'd never become a journeyman athlete," he says. "My wife Beth and I had just had our first child, and I decided we needed a truly stable home life. Playing pro ball was great, and I met many interesting people, but I knew when it was time to hang it up and go home."

Whitehurst returned to Atlanta and opened David Whitehusrt Home Builders, Inc., a residential construction company.

Today, looking back, he says he wouldn't change much in his life. "I would advise any young athlete to choose a school like Furman where he'll get a chance to play, and to look for great role models like Art Baker, Dick Sheridan and Jimmy Satterfield, people who really care about you and will give you a chance. No, in all honesty, there aren't too many things I'd do differently if I had my life to live all over again."

Conclusion

Well, there you have it, Sports Fans, interviews with 105 of the finest athletes ever affiliated with the great state of South Carolina. Now the questions arise--"why stop here", and "why wasn't so-and-so included in this little survey, when everybody knows he was greater than that little so-and-so you included?"

The answer to the first question is this: I had to stop somewhere. Besides, most of us know already whatever happened to most of the great athletes who came after 1975. So why beat a dead horse?

The answer to the second question is this: there were indeed other great athletes I wanted to interview but just couldn't track them down. And I still don't know where they are. And there were others whom I did track down but was unable to connect. George Rogers is a good example of this latter group. He's been associated with the USC Athletic Department for many years now, and I phoned him for an appointment on numerous occasions. But I could never catch him at home or in his office. So I left messages on his answering machines. But my calls were never returned. So we'll just have to comfort ourselves with the knowledge that George is alive and well and working for the University.

And, too, it's comforting to know that there are still a bevy of great athletes out there just waiting to be interviewed for another little volume such as this one.

In conclusion, let me say that I thoroughly enjoyed talking with all the fellows whose stories are contained herein, and, despite the fact that our meetings were brief, I consider it an honor to have been associated with them in some small way.

My best to them all!

Index